WHO I AM
MY LIFE IN SHORT STORIES
MEMOIRS TO MY FAMILY AND FRIENDS

EDWIN D. ROBINSON, SR.

Copyright © 2025 Edwin D. Robinson, Sr.

All rights reserved.

No part of this publication may be reproduced, distributed, or transmitted in any form or by any means, including photocopying, recording, or other electronic or mechanical methods, without the prior written permission of the publisher, except as permitted by U.S. copyright law.

For permission requests, contact:

edwin.drew.robinson@gmail.com.

For privacy reasons, some names, locations, and dates may have been changed.

Published and Designed by ACES Publishing Group

First Edition 2025

Printed in the United States of America

ABOUT THE AUTHOR

Born Edwin Drew Robinson, Sr., in Wheeling, West Virginia, to William James and Mary Barbara (West) Robinson-Cobb. A product of the Columbus, Ohio, Public School System, Ed graduated from Marion-Franklin High School.

During his military and federal careers, he attended and graduated from the Army's Department of Logistics Management College, the Military School of Music, the Department of Defense Equal Opportunity Management Institution (DEOMI), and various leadership schools. Ed continued his education by receiving his dual Bachelor of Science in Human Resource Management and Public Administration from Franklin University, and he is a United States Navy and Army veteran. In the Navy, he served as a Yeoman Third Class Petty Officer before reenlisting in the Army Reserves, where he performed as a Saxophone Player. He later re-enlisted as a Finance Specialist before joining the Virginia Army Band. During his musical stint, he performed for four sitting presidents: Ford, Reagan, Carter, and Bush. Sr. Ed served as Chief Gunner in Field Artillery while deployed to combat during the Gulf War. He received the Army's Bronze Star and various Accommodations and Achievement Awards.

Early in his career, he married Allison Della (Armstrong) of Columbus, OH, and they soon became proud parents of four children and four grandchildren. They enjoyed forty years of marriage. Ed remarried to Pamela Sue (Stuck/Dixon), and they share a blended family of 6 adult children and 10 grandchildren. He has published several poems and articles under his name and received awards for his writing prowess. He cultivated his leadership, writing, and motivational skills by attending several military leadership and teaching schools and becoming a long-standing member of Toast Masters.

Ed co-founded and was the keynote speaker of "The Friends of the Tuskegee Airmen" Association. His influences consist of writers and poets, such as Paul Lawrence Dunbar, Langston Hughes, Edgar Allen Poe, Maya Angelou, James Baldwin, Robert Schuller, Norman Vincent Peale, Walt Whitman, and Alex Haley, to name a few. After his return from combat, he continued to rewrite and finalize his poetic memoirs and stories of his life. His verses are a testament to his survival during wartime and a pictorial of the ordinary experiences and events shared with his comrades during combat in Southwest Asia.

Ed continued to serve with the Ohio Army National Guard Band as a Saxophone Player. Once promoted to Sergeant First Class, he was assigned as the first Senior Non-Commissioned Equal Opportunity (EO) Advisor. After training, he applied to the Warrant Officer's Corp. as a Supply Systems Technician. Ed's other duties as assigned were Equal Opportunity Officer, Equal Employment Opportunity Counselor, and Mentorship Program Manager. Ed retired in 2009 after 34 years of honorable service as a Chief Warrant Officer Two under the United States' First African American Commander-in-Chief, President Barack Obama. He then accepted a Civilian Federal position with the Department of Logistics Agency in Customer Assistant Supply and retired in 2012.

Today, Ed and Pam are active members at Tri-Village Christian Church in Pataskala, Ohio, performing in the Worship Band. They are Lifetime Members of VFW at Paul S. Lawrence Memorial Post #9857, Columbus, OH. Ed has volunteered for over 15 years and is a board member of Nehemiah House of Refuge, a non-profit organization providing resources for men. Although a licensed minister in Ohio, Ed says he prefers to be where God has called and placed him.

DEDICATION

I dedicate this book first to my Savior and Lord, whose love, mercy, and forgiveness have carried me through every season of my life. His grace covered all my indiscretions and guided me toward becoming the man I am today.

To my parents, who gave me life and laid the foundation on which I stand.

To my siblings, who looked to me for guidance, strength, and support, and whose love has remained a constant anchor.

To Allison, who was a devoted mother to our biological children — Ilyas and Ayrika — and to Corey and Shawn, whom God blessed us with along the way.

To my faithful helpmate, Pamela Sue, my loving wife, supporter, and partner in every meaningful step of my journey.

To all my past and present in-laws, who have continued to embrace me as family through every chapter of my life.

And to the newest additions to our lives — the ones Pam and I cherish as part of our Splendid Blended Family — thank you for your open hearts and the love you have shown.

To my educators, who shaped my thinking, nurtured my gifts, and encouraged my growth as a man, musician, and servant leader.

To my friends in the military—brothers and sisters in uniform—whose camaraderie, loyalty, and shared sacrifices helped forge my character and strengthen my resolve. Each of you played a role in my journey, and I carry those experiences with honor and gratitude.

And finally, to those unsolicited prayers my whole life has been blessed with, I thank God for your and his blessings. I know for a fact that I was put here for more than this.

Each of you, in your own way, has accepted me for "Who I Am", and this book is a testimony to that love.

With much love and gratitude,

TABLE OF CONTENTS

STATIONS IN LIFE 17
SOLDIER IN THE ARMY OF THE LORD 18
"WHO I AM" 21
ALLIE CAT 28
CHILD 30
BRYDEN ROAD 32
A CONVERSATION WITH MY FATHER 39
DYSFUNCTIONAL 41
I CALLED HIM DAD 46
MOTHER 59
BE-BOP 62
I LOOK LIKE ROCK 66
"EDWIN, NOT EDDIE" 70
NEVER GETTING MARRIED AGAIN 74
OUR CHRISTMAS CHILD 79
PAMELA SUE 84
A SPLENDID BLENDED FAMILY 91
RETURNING THE RING 94
RIGHT WHERE I AM 96
SEX TALK WITH MY SON 101
MY SIBLINGS 105
THEY CALL ME MR. ROBINSON 110
TUNNEY'S WELCOME HOME 114
WHERE I BELONGED 117

A SOLDIER'S CHRISTMAS	122
DEATH VALLEY	125
THE DOWNBEAT	128
DUTY NOT REWARD	132
MIA	137
MILITARY INJUSTICES	141
PAYING IT FORWARD	155
POTUS #38	160
POTUS #44	164
PRIVATE WAYNE HAGWOOD	166
RELIEVED	169
DAMN UNDERTOW	172
MY FRIEND JOE	175
NO FEAR	179
NOT ONE TO BE BULLIED	184
SERGEANT'S TIME	191
BLACK LIVES MATTER	195
BROWN PEOPLE CARRY GUNS	199
CHERRY VALLEY	203
DON'T CALL ME BOY	210
DWB	216
I WROTE A LETTER	220
ROCKING THE BOAT	225
THE HNIC	228
DR. KING	242
CHOCOLATE-COVERED ANTS	246

HE LOOKED LIKE A SHARK	250
HOW I GREETED THE POPE	253
HOW SWEET IT IS	257
I GET THE BROWN ONES	262
IT DOESN'T SMELL RIGHT	264
MY SEVENTIETH	266
PISSED	272
STRIKES, NOT STRIPES	276
THE DARNDEST THING	280
THE WHISTLER	283
TWISTED	286
WOODY	288
YOU'RE NOT MICHAEL JACKSON	290
DEAR EDWIN	295
GETTING PAID	298
HOUSTON, WE HAVE A PROBLEM	302
I AM	307
I OWE A FEW WRITERS	309
LOOKING FOR FAULT	313
MY CYCLE CHASE	319
MY EGO WALL	321
MY FIRST DATE	324
MY FIRST HANGOVER	328
MY FIRST SAX	331
MY FIRST GRANDSON	335
FROM FOSTER TO ADOPTION	338

MY LITTLE RED BUGGY 343
NINE STITCHES..346
OH, HAPPY DAY 349
PEOPLE I'VE MET 353
PLACES I'VE PERFORMED..356
SAVE THE WIN 358
SIGNIFICANT LIFE EXPERIENCES 364
TALK ABOUT SEX 367
THE GHOST WITHIN 371
YOU GET USED TO IT...374

....381
SEEDS OF THE ROBINSON CLAN 381

FOREWORD

Edwin Robinson is a multifaceted man of his generation who might easily be called a Renaissance Man. This book reflects this gentle patriot's life journey as he becomes the remarkable person he is today. Ed's artistic storytelling has shades of a modern Mark Twain as he uses actual events in his life, laced with some hyperbole and antidote against the backdrop of a journey through the tapestry of social, economic, and political circumstances of his times as he matriculated through his environment. Indeed, this Baby Boomer born and raised in the Heartland of America paints a picture using the landscape of his life with his unique style, revealing the hidden truths of the universe through the lens of his Christian values.

I have known Ed since childhood. Amazingly, I have witnessed his evolution from a curious, mischievous boy into a driven, committed, hardworking Husband, Father, Son, and Brother. He possesses an insightful gift to see the essence of a situation and poignantly introduces sensitivity where it is most needed. When my sister Cheryl died after a long, arduous battle with Ovarian Cancer in 1980, I was devastated and bewildered because of our close relationship. Ed attended the funeral and presented me with a poem he had personally authored to comfort me. Ironically, I had not seen him for many years before he showed up and gave me what was a genuine healing salve in poetic form. In fact, in his humble and creative manner, the presentation of his gift was written using calligraphy on white paper with burnt edges, mounted on cardboard, and placed inside a white envelope. I remember thanking Ed for a thoughtful gift and sympathetic remembrance, but I didn't open and read his remarkable masterpiece until weeks later, in my grief over the death of my sister and best friend.

Edwin Robinson's "Who I Am" is a gift that is compassionately and honestly prepared using humor to you, the reader, a healing salve for these turbulent times. I encourage you to laugh, cry, and relate to his stories of his life experiences, and allow yourself to reflect and remember your moments of triumph through real life. I hope you enjoy this manuscript and share these stories with friends, family, and strangers.

Sincerely,

Bishop Robert O. E. Keyes, B.A., M.R.E., D.D.
Pastor and Founder of Refuge Temple Church of Christ

FAMILY EXPERIENCES

STATIONS IN LIFE

SOLDIER IN THE ARMY OF THE LORD

I guess God had plans for me all along, before, during, and after my military service, because there were so many avenues I thought I had planned and was headed in my career. But at every turn, when I thought I could see my future, there seemed to be either a block or someone denying me entrance to that pathway. But, as I grew in faith, I was reminded that despite the adverse actions of man, which seemed to be adverse events, they only turned out to be met with positive reactions that I did not see, yet because of my faith, I was graced with favor. As you will see throughout my stories, some tried to hinder my will. But let me share this one that sealed the deal for me: knowing that God has had my back and that all I have to do is trust in him and that he will direct my path (Proverbs 3:5-6), not my plans. The following proves that we cannot plan our lives without God. I don't know where this statement originated, but it is true. I have often shared it: "If you want to make God laugh, tell him your plans." And that is the truth! In my example, I was given a contract before reenlisting in the Army Band that Boot Camp and the School of Music were not a requirement because I was a qualified 02L (Saxophone Player), having been a member of the 338th Army Reserve Band for over eight years. However, once I was in the active-duty band in Virginia, the band director had plans for me. He had planned for a few band members for promotions. However, knowing I was next in line, had the most promotional points, and would be promoted once the Promotional List was published, I would make the list before them, and he felt he needed to roadblock my promotion. He informed me that I had to attend school before I could be promoted.

I was unaware until after participating in the school that a fellow band member from Virginia contacted me to inform me that the band commander had set me up. The commander had reached out to a close friend at the school who was an instructor or someone with some influence. The instructor approached me and informed me that although I had graduated, all the saxophone slots back at my band at Fort Lee were full, and if I wanted to re-enlist, my only options were: 11B (Infantry) or 13B (Cannoneer). I wanted to be promoted, so I selected 13B, was sent to Fort Sill, OK, for cross-training, and afterward, I was sent to Germany. I ended up going into combat. I didn't let that stop me; I made lemonade from that bitter lemon. While deployed, I took my saxophone and provided music for my soldiers and others. I even played in the foxhole when it was permitted. I was the only music we had during our church services in the desert. When asked to lead Easter Sunday Mass by our Chaplain, I played "To God Be the Glory". It  was his plan that I was there with our soldiers so far away from home, knowing they would need to hear his word in song. And when we gathered for Christmas, I played Donnie Hathaway's "This Christmas". Soldiers from all the units camped with us, with various backgrounds surrounding me, singing in one voice (some in harmony), and if they didn't know the lyrics, they hummed them. I recall how joyous it sounded when we all chimed in on the last stanza, *"Shake a hand, shake a hand, wish your brother Merry Christmas, all over the land"*. At that moment, God's love was real, and brotherly love was felt among all men. Although I was no longer in the Army Band, God continued to

use my talent, which brought joy during what could have been a sad period of celebration, especially for those who would have dwelt on being so far away from loved ones. I thought nothing of it then, but I know now that I had played a crucial role in bolstering our morale while we were in combat so far away from home. That was not my plan but God's.

When Facebook became available, I heard that the band commander had joined. This person thought he knew what was best for me and sought to plan it. He retired as a CW2, which I had been promoted to then. Once I found his page, I thanked him for encouraging me to switch my MOS (Military Occupational Skill), which enhanced my resume of upward mobility to the senior enlisted status, which later assisted in my qualifying for the Warrant Officer Corps. I elaborated on how I had been blessed over the years, shared my various awards after leaving the band, and my decorations for my service during the Gulf War. I further acknowledged that had it not been for his foresight in seeing that Field Artillery would be a good fit for me, I may not have been as successful as a Combat Soldier, which also qualified me to be a member of the Veterans of Foreign Wars, which also opened many doors for me. He knew what that meant, as he had not served in combat. I left the message, "…with God's Blessings" and a verse from Genesis (50:20), which states, "As for you, you planned evil against me, but God planned it for good. I signed off with, once an army soldier, but always a *"Soldier in the Army of the Lord"*.

"WHO I AM"

I am a member of the Robinson Clan. Hello, first-time readers, listeners, family, and good friends. Don't go anywhere yet. I want to tell you about a man who has experienced a good life in America, even as a black man. And for those who don't know or refuse to accept it, the truth is America has not always been great for people of color, especially black folks like me. In case you didn't know who I was, I just wanted to get that out. I want to share with you how I overcame the many adversities I had that my white counterparts never had to worry about or think about living in America. To name a few, they have never struggled to obtain a higher and better education, been denied better job offers, lacked invitations to be involved in social or group events as equals, or faced the stigma that continues towards blacks in America, especially black men. I had to deal with that first as a kid. However, because of my strong fortitude, will, and desire to prove my worth and abilities, I fought and took advantage of the minimal opportunities available. I overcame the obstacles with less struggle than some and maybe with more than I desired. But that is not all. If you will allow me, as you read on, I will share my thoughts with you. I have experienced many significant events in my life. It wasn't long after I became a family man that I realized I would have to fight for the same things that came easily for whites, if I wanted them for my family, like a decent place to live. So, I did. And I shared those events that soon became repeated stories of my life. Many have since told me that I had a knack for telling a great story. I soon noticed that many enjoyed listening to my exploits or the humorous situations I found myself in.

At one time or another, someone would tell me, "You know, you should write about that." So, I did. I started jotting them down, one by one, and realized I had much to tell and share. Maybe too much, but I'll leave that observation to you. My name is Edwin Drew Robinson, Sr. My friends call me Ed. I've been called Smokey, Rob, Robbie, or Rock at various stages in my life and career. You know, people love creating a shortcut to your name. I'm the son of William James and Mary Barbara (West) Robinson. My father was a mechanic, and his father, my grandfather, was a coal miner in West Virginia. I am the eldest of seven children, five boys and two girls, and later, I was the oldest of ten, with the addition of two stepbrothers and a stepsister, children of our stepmother, Nathelene Morris. I was born in Wheeling, West Virginia. I am the product of the Columbus, Ohio, Public Schools System and one of the "kids" who was told, "You're good for nothing," or "You're never going to amount to anything good." So, I latched onto all that I found good and positive to pour into my soul and life because I was the offspring of Carlton James Robinson, which meant something to me. I believe my father was proud of that fact, too, but when it came to receiving any personal support in my dreams and endeavors, he fell short of my aspirations, and most of them were crushed by him. I thought that until, as life had it, despite my father's lack of fatherly nurturing of my ambitions, I turned that ship around. I had never been a troubled child or caused any real grief that I can recall. Sure, I was a teenager and had a few teenager moments, like a car accident, because I was racing and said I wasn't. I was never picked up off the street and arrested for a crime. 2016 changed that for me when I forgot I still had my weapon holstered on my person. I took my mother to Washington, D.C., to visit the National Museum of African American History and Culture. I approached the guards to inform them I was carrying and wanted to ask if I could return it to my car.

Moments later, a Black Officer, who made it clear he was in charge, needed to assure his white superior that he showed no favoritism to his people and ordered my needless arrest (story is covered in "The HNIC"). I left home because I knew if I stayed, I'd grow up to be "a worthless nothing", an expression my father often labeled me. I would have probably ended up doing what he had planned for my life, his life. As I will undoubtedly mention throughout this book, our father could be one evil SOB and could utter the evilest statements. One that I most clearly remember was when, as a child, he whispered to me, "I should have *killed you* when you were a baby". Did that hurt? Hell yes, it hurt and stayed with me. Do you think it kept me down? It should have. It stung for years whenever I thought about it, and once, I made it my motivator. But I no longer think much of it or need it. There were times that I felt I couldn't love my father, yet I did, and I forced myself to tell him that I loved him, more times than any of his wives or children would have. So, writing to expose my truths became cathartic for me. For me, that can only be God. But leaving home was one of the best decisions I had made. I made a few more later. I enlisted in the Navy in 1974, after graduating from high school. I watched my birth mother wave goodbye to her son from Columbus Airport as my plane lifted into the sky, my first time flying. I was headed into the blue skies of my future, which was awaiting me in *"The Prairie State"* of Illinois. Before I arrived at the Great Lakes "Boot Camp", still in flight, my mind wandered, and I imagined who I would become and what my foundation would be as a man. There were so many things. One of those was that I hoped to return home after accomplishing incredible feats. With optimism about this venture, I was about to embark on it. I motivated myself to believe that all I endeavored would have significant outcomes because I received that at home. Odd, but Les Brown, now a Motivational Speaker, was who I thought of. He was a well-known disc jockey on WVKO, a local Radio Station in Columbus.

Mr. Brown visited our Junior High School, George C. Beery, and shared the story about "The Street Sweeper" with my classmates and me. It was Martin Luther King's speech that Mr. Brown borrowed, and he shared it with us. It is prudent that I share it with you here. Dr. King said, "… my friends, even if it falls your lot to be a street sweeper, go on out and sweep streets like Michelangelo painted pictures; sweep streets like Handel and Beethoven composed music; sweep streets like Shakespeare wrote poetry...sweep streets so well that all the hosts of heaven and earth will have to pause and say, "Here lived a great street sweeper who swept his job well. If you can't be a pine on the top of a hill, be a scrub in the valley, but be the best little scrub on the side of the hill; be a bush if you can't be a tree. If you can't be on a highway, be on a trail. If you can't be the sun, be a star; it isn't by size that you win or fail; be the best of whatever you are. And when you do this, you've mastered the length of life." Mr. Brown told us we could be anything we wanted to be, and the phrase "Be Black and Proud" was taken from James Brown's famed 1968 hit title, "Say it Loud, I'm Black and I'm Proud." That story changed the trajectory of my life, among other stories and readings I later ingested and absorbed into my very being. I was going to become someone; I wanted to make a difference and prove that I would become someone of worth. After Boot Camp, I volunteered as a saxophone player aboard my ship, the USS NIMITZ, and honed my skills to the best of my ability. I earned a position in the Legal Department and practiced improving my typing skills there. I was typing at 70-75 wpm by the time I was discharged. Not obligated to continue my military career, I returned to the armed forces in the Army. By then, I had set my goal on a decent retirement. I joined the 392nd Army Band and was soon promoted to Sergeant (E-5). I re-enlisted again for another promotion as I transferred into Field Artillery.

The army sent me to Fort Sill, Oklahoma, where I became a Gunner. As a Chief Gunner, my new skills carried me straight into the arms of combat in what is now known as the Persian Gulf War (Operation Desert Shield/Storm) from December 19, 1990, to May 1991. I returned from Germany to Fort Hood, Texas, with my family: wife and two children. I was honorably discharged on March 10, 1995, as a Staff Sergeant (E-6). By then, I had visited countries such as Africa, Cuba, England, Germany, Italy, Puerto Rico, Scotland, and Spain. Back home, I enlisted in the Ohio National Guard 122nd Army Band as a Saxophonist and continued for 5 years. In 2000, I was promoted to Sergeant First Class (E-7) and felt I had arrived, much like a Chief Petty Officer in the Navy or a Gunny in the Marines. They're considered "Cream of the Crob", experienced leaders and highly respected. It was said that a Chief Petty Officer almost had to kill someone before they could be brought up on charges, given an Article 15, or "Let Go". I wanted to join that club. By now, I was aware that God was ordering my steps. He was not done with me. I enrolled in the Warrant Officer Corps and rose to the highest rank recorded in our family's military history (That I know of). At the time, our grandfather's brother, Uncle Joe, retired after 30 years in the Navy as a Senior Master Chief. He died in 1974, months after I completed Boot Camp. My father and I attended his services at Arlington Cemetery in Washington, D.C. After I attended several required officer courses, I graduated from the Warrant Officer Candidate School in 2002, Franklin University in 2003, and the Department of Equal Opportunity Management Institute in 2005. I felt I was finally accomplishing significant personal goals and making a tangible difference. As far as I knew or was ever told, I was the first in our family to become a commissioned officer in the military and the first male to receive a four-year college degree. It may not be a significant feat for some, especially my white counterparts. These things are a norm in their society, not ours.

I wasn't impressed that it could be a reality for me. As I will probably reiterate, my father never encouraged me or my siblings to seek higher education after high school. His thing was just plain old hard work. Music and the arts weren't for him, and they didn't pay the bills. Yet, I did very well with my music in the military and church. Now in my seventies, I still feel I have much love to live for, realize, accomplish, show, tell, and share with my children and theirs. And yes, I probably have become an overachiever. Maybe that manifested from a thirst and yearning for the attention of a father's love I never received. Wow, yes, I heard myself. It's a shame, but I know of male friends who suffered from the same lack of fatherly nurturing. I pray that it is not you. If so, there is a father who loves and cares for all his sons, and you are one of his. And so, I welcome you to read as much as you can of my stories, as hopefully you will enjoy learning and knowing more about *"Who I Am"* and my significant life experiences. Like an open book, I have laid my life out, revealing some of my darkest hours that will make you wonder, "How I Got Over". Some of you may find that I am not much different from you. Especially as a black man in this country. Too much? Sometimes, the truth can be a big-ass-horse-pill to swallow. Some of my humorous experiences might help the medicine go down. Others may lead you to take a break or a breather before you go on. I shed a few therapeutic tears along this journal's journey. And if you should find one or two of my stories putting you in a place of disagreement or discomfort, that's okay; it's alright. I've forgiven myself many times for the things I shouldn't have done and learned to forgive those who attempted to hurt me. I wasn't perfect all my life, and neither were you. I will recall and say things as Ms. Jane Pitman did (Google it) with clarity. I've come this far, and as you will find out, many attempted to discourage me in my endeavors, but their quest were defeated, and "I'm still standing". We know what is said about *opinions.*

And *my truth is not yours!* If you found yourself there, I would ask this: *"Blame it on my head and not my heart".* And I leave this with you.... *As water reflects the face, so one's life reflects the heart.* (Proverbs 27:19). This is *"Who I Am."*

ALLIE CAT

She was in the 7th grade, and I was a senior at George C. Beery, Jr. High School. Another friend of mine, Joe Freeman, and I headed to our class late again, and it happened to be a crowd of classmates that had gathered now around a couple of girls going at it. It was Allison Della Armstrong, a short but spunky and feisty young girl in the fight with one of the biggest 7th-grade girls I, or, for that matter, most of the Beery students knew, and no one usually went against her. As Joe and I stood side by side, we could quickly remind a well-read person of the bond and friendship of the characters in the storybook, "Of Mice and Men." I, being George, and Joe, who stood several feet over me, was Lenny. The same could have been said about Allison Armstrong and Lydia Gains. That girl towered over Allison, yet Allison did not let Lydia get the best of her during their struggle to dominate the other; Allison was getting the best of her opponent. It was David (Allison) taking on Goliath (Lydia). Allison seemed fearless in strength and was "Buffy, the Slayer" that day. Joe and I, after watching for a few minutes as most teenagers did to see who was winning and who was getting their ass handed to them, intervened to break it up. Joe took hold of Lydia, and I took hold of Allison from behind, who was still swinging haymakers as I ducked a few. Her feet were still looking to land a couple of blows toward her victim, whom Joe was removing. It seemed that at the exact moment we were pulling the girls apart, school authorities were making their way toward us. The crowd had cleared the stage, and Joe and I were left to explain what had just transpired between the two girls who had not stopped shouting at each other. The story was that Lydia said Allison had broken the then-street rule, saying she had said something about her mother. Allison denied the accusation, replying that she would have said it to her face had she done so, but she was not afraid of her, like most other girls. Allison was never known for backing down from altercations, especially when she felt right. Joe and I were informed that we should return to class as the authorities walked the two girls to the principal's office. I was impressed by the fight with Allison, and I had already known her from previous encounters, although not in a fight. At the time, she played drums in a concert band, and I played saxophone.

I also performed in marching and jazz bands. And as a member of a community band called "Just Us," which consisted of neighborhood school classmates. I first met Allison at her elementary school, Hymandale Elementary. Our band was requested to perform at her school during "Black History Week." It was then that I first noticed Allison. I took a sax solo during our rendition of James Brown's "Papa's Got a Brand-New Bag." She was sitting in front of me, in front of my classmates, in the center. I had an audience and played directly before her as she stared at me with attentive ears. Later, a close friend and a member of our group started dating Allison. It probably lasted a couple of weeks until they broke up. You know how that goes. We were young. Neither would tell the truth about the break-up, especially boys. However, after I heard that they were no longer "an item," I approached the guy and asked him if he had any problem with my asking Allison out. He smirked and said, "I don't care, but she ain't putting out." Of course, we all knew what that meant, but I replied, "Okay, I just wanted to talk to her. We married four years later, had four children (two were adopted), and four grandchildren. Thirty years later, she was forced to fight an even greater opponent than she had ever faced and soon succumbed to her health issues. Yet, anyone who knew her will tell you she lived up to her name, *"Allie Cat"*.

CHILD

Our Uncle Donald was the family photographer, capturing many of our pictures for prosperity. I later picked up that mantle as I decided to catalogue photos of my immediate family for our children, so they knew who they were and who they came from. As technology increased with the introduction of the internet, I found Ancestry.com and became a faithful account owner for about twenty years. However, before that application came along, I did the footwork by going from family member to family member to get pictures of our relatives, mainly those that had passed away, so that I could document and archive them in a folder of my design. I documented the photos with names, dates of birth, and any information I was made privy to. The thing about gathering family information, which I touched on in another story, was the secrets people did not want to share, and I honored them. Like the real father of a child, I would put their names behind the photo before I glued it into my booklet. So, I guess I didn't keep the secret. I did not make it visible to anyone who might have looked through my family tree booklet. I attempted to provide as much information concerning our family as I could before I gave up doing so. I handed the mantle over to my daughter, Ayrika, and other relatives, and I hope they will continue to update it. There was one funny incident when I questioned my mother, Barbara Cobb, about her history, birth, parents, grandparents, and when she and my father, William James, got married. She said, "October 17, 1954." As I looked over the date of their marriage and slowly calculated my age and date of birth, I quickly looked toward my mother and said, "Mom?" Her head had already lowered as if in shame. I did not have the nerve to ask her if I was a mistake, but my siblings, who came after our parents married, were all born after that. I could see how she was not proud of it and what I might have thought about it, so I said, "Hey, I'm good at coming in just five months before being considered illegitimate. At least, I know that I'm not a *"Bastard Child"*.

BRYDEN ROAD

The census probably never listed 1032 Bryden Road as my *"Home of Record"*, as we would say in the military, I would soon find out once I enlisted nineteen years later while being processed into the Naval Boot Camp. I was asked many times, "What is your Home of Record?". I thought they meant the address of the last jail I was in, thinking I had a Police Record. It was the 70s, and the world held some very prejudiced stereotypes about me, a black man, which have not changed much today. Those held beliefs haunted me then and still haunt us today. But I digress (get used to it, because I will do it a lot). They wanted to know where I was from and where I was born. My home of record was where I lived most of my life with my family. So, although 1032 was not my home of record, it was my first and most memorable home address, where I lived with my father's grandparents and his five brothers and two sisters. Yes, it was a "Full House". I was a week older than my father's youngest sister, Donna, my aunt. My mother and grandmother were expecting to give birth and did so just seven days apart in the same hospital. I was born on March 25, and Donna was born on March 31. We grew up as brother and sister, rather than Aunt and Nephew. Something that families did back then. But that tradition has long left our culture, unlike other societies. What a rich experience and memory for a child to have grown up with the patriarch and matriarch of his clan. I have known, touched, and talked with them, and 1032 Bryden became the meeting place for many years until it wasn't. Today, I can speak about who they were to me, tell my children, and share with my grandchildren, and God willing, leave a lasting impression on my great-grandchildren. Further into my book, you may read about a lot of turmoil and grief about me and my family; however, through it all, I can say our families, especially mine, have truly been and are blessed. I mentioned the meeting place, right? That tradition was shared with me through my first wife, Allison. Because, like my grandparents' home, her parents' home at 512 Stambaugh Avenue was their hub, and we all met there as often as we could until we couldn't. It brought back memories from my childhood. I recall those Saturday or Sunday morning breakfasts or brunches that my grandmother, Thelma Ree (Combs), would labor with love to prepare for our grandfather, Carlton James.

He was a coal miner who commuted from West Virginia to Columbus. There was always a big feast waiting for him. Grandma would have regular breakfast fixings like eggs, grits, bacon, toast, biscuits or rolls, jams and jelly (she jarred), and a strong pot of coffee on the stove. Then, she would further cook up Granddaddy's favorites that he liked to eat. There was cornbread, sliced bread, smothered pork chops, fried chicken, cabbage or greens, baked or green beans, and some of her famous canned vegetables or fruits. I favored her canned pickled hot tomatoes. Okay, I'm going off the path here. When I was in Boot Camp, I wrote to her and asked for some jarred hot pickled tomatoes. Don't you know, she sent them? I shared them with my new sailor friends, and by the time the jar was empty, the whole barracks reeked with the smell of the vinegar in which the tomatoes were jarred. And those who were not used to such jarred items paid the price because those peppered tomatoes made you move, if you get the gist. Let us move on or back to the kitchen. To finish, she always had mashed potatoes and homemade gravy. Of course, back then, we didn't have to say it was homemade cause it all was homemade. My grandmother made it all from what we called "Scratch." Ready-made Pie Crust was not available at the local grocery store's freezers. So, her peach cobblers were usually the topper of the meals, with a cup of ice-cold milk or a steaming cup of "Joe" (coffee) that stayed ready for seconds on the stove for the day. That was when I first fell in love with the peach cobbler, and it must be homemade to meet my approval. I can't help but think that my sister Sheila, my junior, may have picked up on how Grandma prepared some of her fixings because everyone I know, besides myself, has at one time or another said, "That girl can cook! "And I'd have to fight if I heard someone say differently. She continues our grandmother's way of cooking her fix-ins with love for the craft. While on this subject, I'd be remiss if I didn't tell you about my baby sister, Angie. She ended up as Sheila, one hell-of-a-chief, preparing exotic cuisines, as her big Sheila did. They were both business-minded and started their separate catering services. And all my brothers cook well. I haven't met a Robinson (in my family), who can't cook. We cooked to survive. Some years later, in Cadiz, Ohio, when Sheila would get up and make breakfast for us, after we had picked some wild blueberries, Sheila would clean them, and we'd eat 'em up in a bowl of cold milk sprinkled with sugar.

I'd go out and catch a couple of Bluegill fish in the pond close by, and she'd clean them, batter them, and then fry 'em up with some cut fried green tomatoes and her famous biscuits from scratch. Man, load one up with butter and some of our mother's mom, Grandma Gregory's jarred apple butter; it was on! So yeah, Sheila could always lay out a spread just like Grandma laid out on her kitchen table for granddaddy. Sheila's peach cobbler always puts me in a moment at our grandmother's kitchen table, eating a large square of her peach cobbler topped with, yes, "Homemade" ice-cream, our grandfather would churn for us. I think Sheila has a piece of our grandmother's foot hidden away in her kitchen because, I swear, she is putting her or her grandmother's foot in her cooking. "It's a Black thing". As in most families back then, no one got to eat until the head of the family was served first. Granddaddy would arrive home, freshened up from the coal dust and the long drive. He then would come down the stairs adjacent to the kitchen and, once he noticed me, would say something like, "What do you say, Dootie-Bootie?" Then he would let out his resounding, deep, and rich laughter as he sat down at the kitchen table just before kissing grandma, complimenting her, and jokingly saying something like, "Everything smells good enough to eat." He'd then laugh out again with excitement. We'd all sit down and wait for my great-grandmother, Mama Ada, my grandfather's mother, to say the blessings over the food. Mama Ada was part Native Indian and was once a schoolteacher after graduating from Spelman College in Atlanta, Georgia. To this day, I love Horehound candy, which she would give me after making me swear not to tell anyone because it was her medicine. She could go on when it came to providing the prayers. The things I remember from living on Bryden Road. I remember the haircuts my brothers and I never wanted from our grandfather, because he used what I recall looked like "Sheep Shears" and not a day went by that those shears did not pull my hair, ouch! And grandma's fetish for needing to clean our ears with bobby pins. And she always seemed to have one of those damn things in her hair. Man, I always wished that she couldn't find one. It never happened. There were the model cars, most of my uncles took pride in assembling and staging on the fireplace mantle in their bedroom, where I stayed. I remember how Uncle Jimmy took his time and care in spit-shining his dress shoes, and I believe that, from watching him, I learned the art, and it came in handy once I enlisted in the Armed Forces.

I can still see my Uncle Tony joking with Mama Combs (my grandmother's mother), trying to take her cane, and she is chasing him, whirling her cane above her head. Hey, I thought she needed it for walking. And I remember Mama Combs hushing me as Mama Ada did, and she'd tell me how vital it was that I told no one as she pretended to secretly share a sip of her favorite beverage, Vernors Ginger Ale, with me. She would suspiciously look around as if someone might have been watching, then whisper to me, "Now, this is Mama Combs's medicine, you can have just a little sip, but don't tell anyone. I believed it was medicine because it tickled my nose. Vernors Ginger Ale was much stronger than it is today, just like Coke is not like the original Coke, back when one of its secret ingredients was an addictive substance obtained from the leaves of the coca plant, forming cocaine. In all honesty, Mama Combs could not wait to watch me sip her Vernor's to watch the reaction to the effervescent bubbles of her so-called "Medicine" that *fizzled my nizzle,* and I looked forward to that sip of Mama Combs' medicine as well. Yes, I was getting a lot of medicine at 1032. It was like my granddaughter Jerniah, once she was about 2 years old. And I had conditioned my grandkids with my medicine, Werther's Hard Caramel Candy. She reminded me of how I used to look for Mama Ada or Combs to get that fix, that tingling in my nose. Jerniah, whom we called "Niah," was like that. During her stays with us because her parents were deployed, she would track me down daily to give me a big old wet kiss on my cheek and the tightest of hugs. I quickly caught on to her ulterior motive. She was all about the Werther's I always seemed to have. I would stash them away somewhere, so I knew what she wanted, not Papa Egwin (she couldn't pronounce Edwin). She wanted a fix. Okay, let's take a sharp turn here to return to 1032. Once we had moved out of 1032, I recall our families would meet at 1032 regularly. My father later told me it was called a *"Mule Train".* It was a tradition when family members would travel to and from one family, spend a little time at each home before everyone ended up at the hub, where they were all rounded up at one central location. In this case, it would have been 1032 Bryden Road. I have many fond memories with my uncles and aunts at Bryden Rd. One last memory, and I'll share another story with you, but not as long as this one. I recall when I was sitting and riding as I held onto the handlebars of my uncle's bike. I sat over the front wheel, trying to balance my body by swinging my legs up, down, and side to side.

It all depended on how my uncle would steer the bike to avoid hitting bumps in the road. We were moving fast, and I tried my best not to show my fear of falling, and I easily could have. My aunt Donna was on the handlebars of one of her other brothers, possibly Uncle Jimmy, but I don't remember who. However, I believe (my truth) that we were touring through what was then called Franklin Park, which was occupied mainly by black folks, fishing, outings, or just there to clean or wax their cars. It had become dark, and later I believe grandmother had called the police and fire department in fear that something terrible had happened to her children and grandson, me. I remember us ending up at the Hendersons, who were close family friends. Donna and I were friends with their daughter, Sheryl. I was young, so I don't remember being punished for being out in the streets after the streetlights had come on. We all knew what that meant. However, I'm sure my uncles, who were in charge, caught it. I had asked them about that night. No one remembered it. It was only my truth. Riding a bike as we did is no longer done or legal. It was dangerous. Yet, those are some of my fond memories. So, looking back on where I lived, what I experienced just at 1032 lets me know that today, we are blessed, I am blessed that I can see my offspring, hold them, enjoy and listen to them, especially when they start each sentence with Papa Edwin. I affectionately called my granddaughter, Jerniah, "Niah," who likewise called me Papa Egg-win, which always warmed my heart. She knew how to lay it on to soften me up, saying, "Papa Egwin - with the cutest sad eyes accompanied with a slight tilt of her head - Can I have some of those candies - pointing to my not-so-secret hiding place, anymore, sock drawer - over there?" She would continue giving me the biggest smile you couldn't deny. I cherish those special moments. I'm sure my great-grandparents and grandparents loved those memories of me as a child. I hope that my children and theirs one day will be able to remember, recall, and share their most fond memories of me, Dad, Pops, Papa Edwin, with their children, and when I secretly gave them some of my medicine. I still conjure up a few fond memories that make me laugh and smile when I think of my time at Granddaddy and Grandma's house on 1032 *"Bryden Road"*.

A CONVERSATION WITH MY FATHER

As I mentioned, Bill Robinson was not too serious about lengthy conversations, especially with his children. However, in his defense, Dad had some very enlightening thoughts of concern and advice, and that is when he wanted to share them. And it was short, clear, and to the point. My first love was Lisa Bradley, and I was not ashamed to go home in big, bold red letters and tell the world in an even bigger red heart, "I love Lisa Bradley." Well, our father will be the first to say to you, "I work too damn hard for you to destroy it"! Then he would commence beating our asses with whatever he felt would meet that requirement at that very moment. Sometimes, it was a switch from one of the trees in the field next to our home before being replaced by the two prefabricated homes. Then it could have been an electric extension cord or his belt - my preferred choice of ass-whooping. But that day, the "I love Lisa" was on a new mattress our father had just brought us. Whew! He entered the home, and I knew the ass beating was soon to come, only after he either belittled me as he usually would do, cursed me out while biting his bottom lip, which would raise the little goatee straight up in the air as if it was pointing at you, but neither of these things happened. I thought this was the day he was going to strangle me to death, as he had promised on many occasions when he found fault in me. I thought that once he came into the room and sat down beside me on my freshly decorated mattress, he would say, "I ought to strangle you." He could be mean like that. But he did nothing of that kind that day. Instead, my father was mild-mannered as he looked at me and glanced briefly at what I thought was a great expression of my artwork on the brand-new mattress he had just bought and placed on my bed. He questioned me, "Edwin, who is this girl, Lisa? Who is she to you? I took them as rhetorical because he gave me no time to respond, as he continued to say that he understood how I might have feelings for this girl, but I didn't have to write it on his mattress. He explained how hard he had worked to purchase the mattress.

He further expressed how he could appreciate my fondness for "This girl Lisa," as he put it, but that I didn't have to write it on my brand-new mattress. That was my first time having a civil conversation with my father. He didn't hurt me with what would have been his everyday distasteful words, nor did he physically harm me. He just patted my leg as he rose from the mattress and asked if it would be the next time. I felt the need to write about a girl, so I should write it on paper, not on my mattress. Out of all the ass beatings I received from him as a child, it was one of the most extraordinary times that I can remember; although mostly one-sided, his, I guess it could be counted as *"A Conversation with My father"*.

DYSFUNCTIONAL

I believe that everyone has grown up in a home where there was some degree of dysfunctional behavior. I don't think there has ever been a perfect home. Folks with money, those born with the proverbial "Silver Spoon", have their family issues as well as "The Ozzie and Harriet" and the "Cosby Show", which were TV shows that attempted to show America what a perfect family should look like. However, they had their family issues as well, no matter how small they may have seemed. That being said, yes, I was raised in a dysfunctional home, which was probably worse than some. Yet, there was dysfunction in every home and neighborhood, whether people wanted to accept it or not. My parents divorced when I was very young, and I believe I was ten or eleven years old when they had me and four other younger siblings. Our father remarried, and they had two children with our stepmother, Nathelene (Morris) Threatt, who had three children (Doug, Tina, and Duane) from a previous marriage. At the time, our father was a heavy drinker, and when he drank, he became another person, someone I didn't like to be around. And he took out his frustrations with my mother and then our stepmother, and a lot of times, with us, his children. It's a wonder that we all succeeded in life and careers with all the horrors we dealt with. We dealt with witnessing how abusive he could be as a husband and father. But we survived. We found a haven in school and in church where we could experience a sense of peace. I eventually joined organizations like the Cub Scouts and Boy Scouts because they took me away from our home for a period of peace and freedom. Like other families, we probably let on that all was well on the home front. I'm sure if our friends were experiencing family issues, it would have been embarrassing if their family secrets were told. No one wants to share the hell they're going through at home. Most of the time, I feared it when it was time for our father to return home from work, not knowing what state of mind he would be in. Bi-Polar probably had not yet been a diagnosis back then, but I'd bet my annuity that he was all of that and much more. I didn't know what devils he was fighting, but years later, when he thought he could confide in me as an adult, he shared a few personal things he seemingly had harbored for years and probably, all his life.

He told me his mother, my grandmother, favored his brother, Wesley, because his family and children were light-skinned. Wow! In my sixties, my father laid that little load on me. If that wasn't painful enough for me to take in, he informed me that his father, my grandfather, was once in prison. I was, of course, shocked to hear that, coming from my father. He was the oldest child and son of Carlton James Robinson. He idealized his father, and he loved his mother. I felt my father had no reason to lie about either of them, but needed to release a truth he had harbored all those years. He probably thought that I was mature and able to accept his words. I, too, idealized and loved my grandparents, and even after that, the information didn't change my feelings about them. I understand that those were different times, things were very different, and they changed over time. So, I never felt I was treated indifferently by my cousins or grandparents, even after my father told me these things. I did not hold it against him for telling me his truth. As singer Jamie Foxx sang his song, "Blame It", he coined the phrase, "Blame It on the Alcohol." And I did. I know alcohol can loosen your tongue, having you share your feelings, and tell your deepest thoughts or secrets. No, I never told anyone about the hurtful things his parents may have told him. Nor did I inquire about it with anyone in the family. Because, for the most part, they probably would have lied or said they didn't know or believed me and called my father a liar. Yet, there were times later in his life when he proved he could be. We know that there have been many secrets, truths, and lies that family members have taken to their graves, not just in our families but in more than we know. Remember, I come from an atmosphere of dysfunction, and it didn't just affect my family; father, mother, and so forth, it touched all of our relatives and their families. I wish we all could emulate the philosophy one of our relatives has tried to live by: "Keep It Real." Today, the kids say, "Keep It One Hundred." I guess it's the same. I grew up with most of my uncles and two aunts, and we were like brothers and sisters, if not cousins, because of our ages being so close together. However, as we all grew up and our matriarch and patriarch of the family passed on, our family began to deteriorate. I've noticed it is not just in our family, but also in others. Brothers fight against brothers, and others have stopped communicating with each other.

Let's not forget that Thanksgiving is the most dysfunctional holiday we celebrate. Folks find it hard to visit certain relatives because of differences in beliefs, politics, etc. There are more family feuds than you and I have watched on TV shows like "The Family Feud". Yes, money (the love of it) is usually the basis of many of the issues between us. Families used to have annual family reunions. The demise of communication has, however, destroyed the desire to get together, and they have mostly come to a complete halt. For me, parties and get-togethers stopped, and our children started growing up without knowing their relatives. Sound familiar? When I returned from the military, all screwed up from the war, I hardly wanted to see anyone. Because when I did, they wanted to share who and why they were feuding against this one or that one, or why they weren't talking. Hell, I had just returned from combat into what seemed to be another theater of war. It was too much to handle since I was trying to get my feet back on the ground of family life, away from the military. I soon found myself in counseling for depression for several years until I decided to give it to God and stopped taking the pills the VA Clinic was pushing me to take. And it wasn't just my family that suffered from dysfunctional behaviors, but it was also my ex-wife, Allison's. She was hand-fed medication by her mother from childhood through grade school and likely beyond. She continued to rely on medicines after we married. Of course, I didn't know it until later, especially when her family started falling apart. And that happened once their parents passed. Once the heads that kept the family together are gone, the animals will play or go astray. I'm not pointing fingers to bring shame to our families but if I am "saying this", who in our family "is thinking it?" I have been now for years of a positive mind to want our families to love each other and drop the past hurts or thoughts, or the "he said, she said" and re-build our families. Yes, I come from a dysfunctional home, but like our home, our neighbors were just as dysfunctional, if not worse, but we didn't know "What Goes on Behind Closed Doors". And they probably will never tell you of the horrors they had to endure or suffered in keeping "The family secret." Their father or mother was a drunk, or their father had another family (which happened), or their mother was a drug addict. Some family members have loved ones who have been or are incarcerated, as I do, my oldest son.

When he was sentenced for a crime, my heart broke. To this day, I hurt from remembering his phone call to me while I was at work, telling me that he had been arrested. I want to say here that I remember only one member of my family, and no one else from my or Allison's immediate or distant relatives, coming to our aid or calling to console us during the whole ordeal of our son's trial or sentencing. The one person who showed up and "Kept It Real" with a sign of love and care was James Carlton Robinson, Uncle Jimmy. He sent us a card and note to comfort us, knowing that what we were going through was hard. And a check as a sign of monetary support. It made Allison and me both cry. But the silence from our family concerning our son added to the hell we were going through, making it even worse. It was very telling about who we could count on, and at that moment, it was God. Yes, the list of secrets families keep is long. And I would bet that many of my grade school friends went to bed with fears that came from within their homes. I recall a family where the father shot their mother in front of them and then turned the gun on himself. That's tragic. Yes, I learned many secrets our families kept, but they soon came out. Yet, in all that I endured, I still found that I could love our father for the man he was as a provider and protector. No one can tell you that he was not a hard worker. He was an innovator and resourceful, and sometimes he knew how to have a good time. And on his dying bed, as I prayed for him, I told him that I loved him. And asked if I could pray with him. Although he could not speak, he nodded, and along with my brother, my Uncle Bruce, we prayed. I thanked our father for showing us how to work hard and be resourceful. I told him in so many words that even though he left us no legacy (I'm sure he understood), I assured him that he had nothing to worry about because we, his children, were all successful and doing fine. Some may question my reasoning for writing about these things, but sharing my history, experiences, and truths with my family and children is essential. So yes, I will be the first to say I'm an unwilling product of what haunts us all, that is known in some way or fashion as the term *"Dysfunctional"*.

I CALLED HIM DAD

Bobby or Mr. Bobby, known by most, was born Robert Theopolis Armstrong. He was my father-in-law, and he and I became closer as friends as his Alzheimer's got worse. I think I have loved him since the first day I met him. He had memories of his daughter, Allison, my wife, and the love of his life, "Bee", his wife. Bee was the nickname everyone knew and called her by. That name was also known to her by relatives and close friends. Bee was born Mary Elisabeth Washington, who passed before him. I believed he mourned for her until his last days with us. Yet, he left us with memories of laughter that only he could provide. He always had a funny story about some "monkey" – he'd call a person he was talking about, mainly because he had forgotten or didn't know their name. He would laugh just as hard as you did once he had approached and finished his punch line of the event. Those stories always seemed to come during a conversation that reminded him of a particular experience. And so, I'd like to share some of his humor, antics, and funny things I recall of Mr. Armstrong, my father-in-law, whom I soon called Dad. Dad made you laugh just from hearing him laugh at something that caught his funny bone on the television, and then he would go on to get your attention and recite what he had just seen, which he thought was so funny. His laughter would show all his 32 pearly whites. He had all his teeth when he passed. His grin was pleasantly inviting, and his smile would travel from ear to ear. He was never shy about giving them either. However, when Alzheimer's started to sit in, making itself home with Dad, I could sense his awareness of his unwanted visitor, and his coping method was to respond quickly, "Well, I'm glad you told me". We accepted that it was his way of acknowledging that his memories were starting to contain an inevitable demise. I don't know what laughter Dad left behind with others, family members, and friends, but I can easily recite several humorous things I may never forget about him. He had a natural knack for humor, which was his own, and he was always readily prepared to share it with whoever was present and who he thought was a willing listener, which we all were.

Years before Alzheimer's, one of the first encounters of Dad's humor was when I was still enlisted in the Navy and visiting Allison's oldest sister, Phyllis, and her husband, Willie, an Air Force veteran, at their home in Maryland. I was stationed in Norfolk, Virginia, and had an open invitation to their home on the weekends. To this day, I don't recall if I called first, but if I didn't – still a little young – I apologize to both Willie and Phyllis. They both were gracious hostesses to me, and I wasn't even married into the family yet. So, on one of those weekends I visited, Mr. and Mrs. Armstrong – my future in-laws- were also visiting. During our weekend stay, Phyllis and Willie had to do some errands. Before they left, always wanting to make everyone comfortable in their home, Willie informed me and Mr. Armstrong that we could help ourselves to his imported beer in their basement bar. The house was soon quiet with just me and Mr. Armstrong, who had quietly and quickly disappeared. I was engaged in a TV show in the adjoining kitchen. It wasn't more than an hour before Phyllis and Willie returned. I was still sitting on one of the stools around the kitchen island and could easily look over into the living room, where Phyllis was now standing over her father, who was sitting in front of her. I overheard Phyllis ask her father, "Daddy, did you drink up all of Willie's beer? That was a whole case, 32 bottles!" Mr. Armstrong was now comfortably reared back in Willie's black leather "La-Z-Boy" recliner, engulfed in another one of his favorite pastimes, reading the newspaper. If you hadn't figured it out, his other favorite pastime was drinking beer. Mr. Armstrong was not acquainted with being a connoisseur of fine beers. Yet, he had his favorite, and it was

Stroh's. It was not a great favorite but a reasonably priced beverage that suited his pocket and appetite. This reminds me of an incident that happened years later, when I was part of the family. We made a road trip convoy to Pontiac, Michigan, to visit family. Allison's third sister, Linda, and her husband, Ricky, traveled with us in our car as we followed Mr. and Mrs. Armstrong in theirs. Halfway through our journey, we hit a freeway overpass near a brewery. It was two Stroh's towers that had their logo plastered on them. Suddenly, Mr. Armstrong's car swerved off the road toward the towers and abruptly came back on the road. We burst out laughing, knowing that there was no doubt that Dad had noticed the signs.

Back to Phyllis and Mr. Armstrong's conversation. As Phyllis hovered over her dad after asking him about Willie's beer, he nonchalantly looked over the paper at Phyllis through his bifocals, which had slid down his nose. The paper had been completely opened and stretched across his face. With a straight "Poker Face", he said, "Yeah, why?" Now distraught and probably somewhat embarrassed that her father drank so much of the beer, Phyllis promptly replied, "Cause, Daddy, that was an expensive imported beer!" Mr. Armstrong volleyed back quickly, "Yeah, well, it tasted like cat piss!". Oh, he had many sayings. His famous one to me was, "It was so quiet, you could hear a cat piss on cotton in Russia." It was a short encounter between Phyllis and her father. She left quietly but was upset. Mr. Armstrong returned to the page he had placed a finger on when he stopped reading to reply to Phyllis, and continued reading his sports section of the paper, without the assistance of his glasses, but still on the tip of his nose. "Hey Ervin", (the name he chose to call me), he yelled at me. I was still sitting on the stool by the kitchen island, trying not to notice or pay attention to what had just happened. It was like nothing had happened because he told me, "Cincinnati Reds are playing on channel 10 tonight". I was not much of a football, basketball, or baseball player. I responded, "Oh yeah?" He said, "Yep." The Armstrongs were neighbors and good friends, like family with the Milners, who lived across the street from their home in Columbus. Their kids all practically grew up together. Mrs. Milner was Allison's Godmother. Their son was Eddie Milner, with whom I had attended High School, and the Cincinnati Reds had drafted him to play for them. I imagined that Mr. Armstrong was eager to see him play. We returned to what we were doing. I was watching the TV show in the kitchen, and he returned to reading the sports. Baseball was his favorite sport, and when baseball season began, you couldn't get him to watch anything else. He watched teams play that he didn't even like or support. It was all about the game. At home, if someone was swinging and catching, he was sitting and watching in his favorite rocking chair, a permanent fixture just feet from the front of the living room console television, where he only had to lean forward to change the channel. It was way before remote controls were available. Yet, he would quickly lean forward to find another ball game.

You could find him laughing about a play, a missed catch, an out that the referee miscalled, or a homer that always got him to call out laughing, "Look at the monkey go!". No, his calling the player or a person a monkey had nothing to do with the relationship; many blacks were called by those who grew up racist. He called that name when he didn't know their names, whether white, black, brown, or yellow. It was his way, not name-calling or calling someone out to be harmful. I can't remember when he attempted to hurt anyone's feelings. But when he got mad enough, he could even quiet Mrs. Armstrong with his anger because his voice was seldom raised. Now his go-to name for white folks was "honky", yet when he said it, he still wasn't trying to be derogatory. It was either monkey or honky, if he was white. Yet, I never heard him call a black monkey the N-word. Ask anyone what his greatest love besides that of Mrs. Armstrong was, and they'll tell you it was baseball or beer, not necessarily in that order. Later, after Dad's death, Allison and I found a photograph of him in a baseball uniform lineup photo shoot with the Indianapolis Clowns, of the Negro American League. After inquiring of relatives who were old enough to remember, I discovered that "Bobby" had run away from home at an early age. At the time, he was living with and being raised by his Aunt Jubee. From what we could gather, he was 17 and played baseball for a season with the Clowns before his aunt found him and brought him back home. We never found any documentation to prove our findings. That is why Mr. Armstrong loved baseball and was always found laughing and finding humor in the game's play, as he watched it religiously. I believe he was probably reacting to some of his old antics that the Clowns were known for during any of their games. Players like Hank Aaron, Harlem Globetrotters' "Goose" Tatum, and Satchel Paige were among the many players who played for the Indianapolis Clowns, once known as the Ethiopian Clowns and Cincinnati Clowns. Dad may have met or even played with several of those who were popular and became well-known among the blacks and whites who enjoyed the game of baseball back then. The Clowns were known for their field antics and trick plays, much like the basketball players of the renowned Harlem Globetrotters. We will probably never know, but I'm more inclined to believe that Bobby Armstrong did play for the Indianapolis Clowns, and if he didn't, he was one at heart.

Dad was diagnosed with Alzheimer's, and I believe he had started to show symptoms long before Mrs. Armstrong passed. He was probably being shielded by Mrs. Armstrong's love for her husband. She would quickly ensure that he got his supper and then rush him off to bed after returning from work. I recall many days when we visited before my re-enlisting into the Army, Allison would ask her mother, "Mother, (what the family called her), where's Daddy?" Mrs. Armstrong would reply with statements like, "He's sleeping, he had a hard day today", or something similar. I think she knew that her husband's memory was becoming vague and showing signs of dementia. Several years later, during a military leave, now with children, Allison and I visited Dad. Mrs. Armstrong had passed earlier. She and I didn't see eye to eye. We both struggled to accept each other's roles in her daughter's life and who should have the last word in our marriage. I often went to Mr. Armstrong alone to discuss my dilemma in dealing with his wife, and he always seemed to understand my trials in getting Mrs. Armstrong to respect me as her daughter's husband. He'd calmly leaned back in his favorite rocking chair and given me his advice, always coupled with, "Now, you don't have to, but I would……" and he'd explain a situation he once experienced in dealing with his mother-in-law. He'd say, "Now, Ervin, just give it time and it'll pass." And it did. Mrs. Armstrong and I became good friends, and I was soon comfortable calling her mother. When I was dating her daughter, I was her best friend. I was the only one who would stay behind as Allison and her friends would leave me at her home when we were dating, and I'd play Bingo with her. She introduced me to thrift stores and taught me how to save money by purchasing used or like-new items. I even stood in line with her from 6:00 am on the morning of Columbus's most significant annual Bargain Box Garage Sales, which didn't open until 9:00. It was held at the Ohio Veterans Memorial Center downtown. Mrs. Armstrong approached the door from the living room. She greeted them and immediately invited them in. Ricky said, "Oh, this is going to be good." We sat back in an adjoining study but could see what was happening at the dining room table, where Mrs. Armstrong invited her guest to sit. She offered them coffee and a slice of her famed Seven-Up Cake. It was delicious. They refused, but she left the cake on the table and sat with them. After the niceties, the gloves came off. Ricky and I could hear verse after verse from the Witness, and Mrs. Armstrong's warm smile with her counterblows. Mrs. Armstrong easily could have been a preacher or pastor. She was masterful in her conversations with the young men. One of her favorite sayings was, *"You can catch more flies with honey than with vinegar."*

I doubt if she knew it was made popular by Benjamin Franklin. And it was no wonder the Witnesses rarely stopped by 312 Stambaugh after their encounters with the fly catcher. Only those who Mrs. Armstrong's pleasant demeanor had not indoctrinated her counter-scriptures to their verses, and thought-provoking explanations had made the mistake of doing so. Once they fell victim to her gracious hospitality, they too soon realized there was no arguing or influencing her on their way of faith. She was a fierce competitor. Her will and faith were stronger, and they found themselves in a hurry to bring their conversation to an end, lest they concede to her. Ricky was still laughing as the young men left in a hurry, looked at me, and said, "What did I tell you, Edwin?" I was very impressed and somewhat amused by the show. But it was not a show to Mrs. Armstrong. She was all about the Lord's Business of saving souls. And that was what I had to wait for, what Mr. Armstrong had told me to keep in mind for me to realize and accept - that his wife had a way of growing on folks, and before you knew it, you'd forgotten the little things that you thought were big things. I soon enjoyed my "Mrs. Armstrong Times". She was all about family. Yes, we still had some head-to-head moments, but because of Mr. Armstrong's great listening and insight, he got me to focus on the finer memories, clearing my head as he shared yet another one of his funny stories. Sometimes his actions were just as amusing. "I'm glad you told me" became his saying in his attempt to deal with his little knowledge of his disease; he would respond with it when he had forgotten why or where he was going or doing something, and one of us would remind him. Once, he and I were shopping at a local mall, and I purchased him a sandwich and drink to keep him occupied while I shopped at a nearby merchant. So, I sat him at the closest bench where I could keep an eye on him. I turned away from his preview for a few seconds, and once at the sales counter, I returned my glance in the direction he was seated, and he was gone. He moved like a thief in the night. Suddenly, my heart dropped at the thought that I would have to tell his daughter, my wife, Allison, that I had just lost her father at the mall. I searched for him in the area where we were, but couldn't find him. I looked toward one end of the mall and then the other, and there he was – at the main intersection of the mall amid a crowd of shoppers. I yelled, "Dad! What are you doing there?" He replied, "Well, I was looking for you!" He was good with the comebacks.

I quickly gathered him up and headed home, forgetting my purchase. There were other memorable times that he left with us. When I took him to the Wexner Heritage Day Care Building in the mornings, we called it the Alzheimer's Center. Dad was cared for there from Monday through Friday, and they would have a bus bring him home at the end of the day. He thought he was going to work. The employees there allowed him to run their printer for them. He was skillful because he had worked for over fifty years as a printer. The staff at the center gave him small tasks and authorized him to run the office printer. He looked forward to going to work in the morning. It was shocking during one of those morning rides because I had put in a cassette tape of a Big Band number, and dad sprang right up, like a Jack-In-A-Box, and started popping his fingers and humming along with the song. It was that of Nat King Cole's "Straighten Up and Fly Right". Immediately, Dad started singing the lyrics verbatim. I was startled, never having heard him sing anything but church songs. I asked, "Dad, you know that song?" He said, "Oh Yeah – as he would start most of his replies – I play that for Aunt Jubee every Saturday night on her Juke Box and she pays me to keep it running." He was speaking in the present tense, but his Aunt Jubee had been dead for some 50 years or more. He thought he was 17 years old and still living with his aunt. I did not refer to his statement regarding her present state. He was happy. I was later informed by his sister-in-law, whom everyone called "Pee-Wee", that "Bobby" was paid a nickel to wind the Victrola when it was starting to slow down during their house parties. Dad thought he was still doing that. Pee-Wee was born Barbara Virginia Washington, Mrs. Armstrong's sister. Pee-Wee told me that Dad was like a big brother to her. As we continued toward the center, Dad continued to sing and hum the songs, strong and loud. I threw in tapes of Cab Calloway, Duke Ellington, Glenn Miller, and Count Basie. He knew them all. There were songs like "One O'clock Jump", "Take the A Train", "All of Me", and even the famed George Gershwin's "Porgy and Bess". I smiled, enjoyed his happiness, and couldn't wait to tell Allison of my experience and her dad's recollection of Nat King Cole. I equipped our 1988 Plymouth Voyager Mini-Van console with all of the old tunes I could find in my repertoire from Dad's youth, and we had a ball on the way to the Center from that moment on. The one story of how Dad's condition made us laugh was during his weekly routine of getting dressed for Sunday morning.

He was the church's Superintendent and Head Deacon. Even when he was stricken with his disease, the church continued to honor his position. So, that Saturday evening, Dad was into ironing his suit. Yes, he was ironing his suit, but we knew he didn't know better by then, so we let him do it with the same suit every Saturday. Sunday morning, we would have one of his good suits ready for wear, telling him that it was the suit he had ironed last night, and as usual, he said,

"I'm glad you told me". That Saturday evening, he was ironing his suit, and I started smelling what smelled like cotton candy. And we could not find where the scent was coming from until the following Sunday morning, as I prepared to iron one of my white dress shirts for church. I smelled the cotton candy again before I noticed the brown spot on my shirt from the hot iron. I raised the iron to my nose, and sure enough, cotton candy. I immediately went to the sink, turned the iron upside down, and drained its contents. The sweet tea had gone missing the evening before, and no one knew where it was. Dad had taken my glass of sweet tea, poured it into the iron, and continued ironing his Sunday suit. The brown spot on my shirt at that time wasn't funny, but I now get a lot of laughs from Dad's antics and memorable moments. They all were extensions of who he was – a hilarious person who could laugh and laugh at himself. Dad's death came too soon. He was diagnosed with lung cancer in the middle of his bout with Alzheimer's. He continued to call Allison, Bee (his wife), up until he passed, and still called me Ervin. When Allison first introduced me to her parents, Mr. Armstrong called me Ervin, Mrs. Armstrong called me Edmund, and her grandmother, Ms. Washington, who was full-blooded Indian (don't know from what Native Tribe), called me Marvin. All five children of the Armstrong family called Mrs. Armstrong "Mother". At one time, they were a very close and tight-knit family because of Mrs. Armstrong, until her death. Their home was where we met on many weekends and during most holidays. And we ate. While being initiated into the fold at the dinner table, my son-to-be brother-in-law, who had married into the family, was very familiar with the family's eating traits and had warned me before sitting down at the table that once we pray for our meal, I shouldn't be shy about helping myself with what was before me. Mrs. Armstrong was great at placing a wonderful spread of the family's favorite foods: fried chicken, greens, depending on the season, macaroni & cheese, homemade cornbread, or a whole loaf of store-bought bread.

She would always prepare a large plate of freshly sliced cucumbers, onions, and tomatoes doused with vinegar. There would be corn on the cob, green beans, or cabbage, and the dessert was her famed and our favorite, 7-Up cake. As I was warned, right after Mrs. Armstrong had finished her sermonette of a prayer, I looked up. All I could see were the retracting arms and hands of Allison's two older brothers, Robert II, the oldest, and Arthur, whom we all called "Damon," and the other family members visiting. It seemed everybody was for themselves and knew it. It was like a table race. All but the plates in front of everyone else were empty. The whirlwind that those arms and hands had created caused the spinning of one lonely biscuit on the serving plate that had just seconds ago been whole. I blinked, and it, too, had found a home on someone's dinner plate, on the side of a fully occupied plate. I looked around, and everyone's plates had been filled, and I was without food. Mrs. Armstrong looked at me and my empty plate. She smiled and laughed as she immediately stopped her sons, who both had excellent appetites, and ordered them to share a portion of their food with Edmund. I was grateful for the scraps they reluctantly gave me, especially from Damon and Robert, Allison's two older brothers. They could both eat. Now, eating at the Armstrong table was more than just eating. The food was good, but the conversations were very insightful and honest. There was plenty of laughter, and at times directed at or about one of the relatives sitting at the table. While being initiated into the family fold, my soon-to-be brother-in-law, Richard, whom we called "Ricky", was very familiar with the family's eating habits. He warned me not to be shy about going for the food after the prayer. So, I listened and tried to fit in. Mr. Armstrong was not one to change his ways, nor was Mrs. Armstrong. They were both very strong-minded people. I guess that's where Allison and her sisters got their strength from. Attempting to engage in the conversations by monitoring the faces before I'd laugh along with them, Mr. Armstrong shouted across the large maple wood table adorned with one of "Mother's" dining room tablecloths. He said as he flicked his arm out towards the center of the table, pointing, "Ervin, pass me the salt". I said, "Yes, Sir" – wanting to respect him as I was raised to respect my elders – but it's "Edwin, Mr. Armstrong". His face stern, he replied, "Yeah, okay, *Ervin*, pass me the salt". I suddenly was the object of everyone's laughter, and I shrugged it off, chiming in with them. I didn't know if he knew my name was Edwin, and he was just playing with me like a cat would play with a cricket just before the kill. I was *Ervin* for years after that. Before he passed, we set up a hospital bed where he received hospice care in our living room.

Dad's last night with us. It was raining hard, and I had just come down the stairs into the living room. I could hear Allison again testing his memory, asking him, "Daddy, do you know who I am?" He looked up at her, smiled that big smile he was known for, and with his loving, bluish-gray eyes said, "Yeah, Bee, I know who you are". I know it hurt Allison that he didn't remember her, but she certainly felt his love for her through his dying love for her mother. And no one at that time could say that Allison didn't look much like her mother, and she took some pride in that. Then, she asked him, "Daddy, do you know who this is?" as she grabbed my hand and glanced at me. He looked up at me and, without missing a beat, said, "Oh yeah! That's my old friend, Edwin." We had been "buds" for years. There was a moment of silence. Just seconds later, we heard the sky crack and roar from the storm's lightning and thunder. It was as if it was welcoming him home. The rain stopped abruptly, and he was gone. My heart fell as it did when I thought that I had lost him in the mall, but this time, it was much harder. It choked me so that

I could not speak, as I am now, from the memory of that moment. He left us saddened, but soon the memory of his humor returned to us as we all recalled his humorous stories, antics, larger-than-life smiles, and joyous gut laughter. These memories are why *"I Call Him Dad"*.

MOTHER

She was born Mary Elizabeth Washington Armstrong, whom her children and grandchildren lovingly knew, and eventually, yours truly, as Mother. If you've ever met her, then I don't need to go into who she was, but she was a strong Christian woman and a very supportive mother and mother-in-law. Of course, I knew that didn't come until she and I had some very head-on conversations with each other, which were mostly about my marriage to her youngest child, Allison. As I would visit often to get to know my in-laws, I sensed that they knew I was interested in their daughter, Allison, whom they called Allie. I didn't start calling her Allie until years later. Besides, I thought Allison sounded better in my ear than Allie. Mrs. Armstrong loved Bingo, and it was one of many candies that she would dangle in front of my face if I wanted to see Allison. So, when I would visit sometimes, Allison would at times be headed out to choir practice at the church just across the street with her friend, Needy-Bug. My mother-in-law-to-be would lure me to stay until Allison returned by asking me to play Bingo or run an errand for her. She knew how to use my desire for her daughter. So, I'd be struck, and of course, I never said no. However, we had fun playing Bingo, and she loved to win. It was those times I got to know her, and she got to know me. Mrs. Armstrong worked for many years for two very prominent brothers; one was a doctor and the other a dentist. After the doctor's office closed, Mrs. Armstrong worked for the Rutan Brothers, a Tupperware sales company, as a sales consultant. She sponsored a party at her home and was recruited immediately to become a member of the team she had the party for. She performed so well that she was promoted to form her very own team, which she called Bee's Bee. She loved people. As I said once before, "She never met a stranger". Before long, folks were holding product parties for her not just in Ohio, but also in Michigan, New York, New Jersey,

Maryland, and other states. With Mrs. Armstrong, there were no excuses. She believed in God, she believed in you, and before too long, she had you believing in yourself. She had a way about her that made you excited about you, and no matter what you did or did not do in your past, she trusted you to do the right thing.

She had won many gifts and awards for her sales prowess, including paid trips to Florida and New York. Linda, whom we call Lindy, one of Allison's older sisters, told me, "That brat, Allison, went on all those trips with Mother and Daddy". Lindy went on to tell me how Mother had a grocery store in their basement. And Mr. Armstrong had a garden that Mother would give away vegetables to many in their neighborhood. The basement store was well-known, and it served many neighborhood families. Some may have received a few biblical words. Like mother, like daughter, if you got on their bad side, they'd let you know with the quickness. Yet, you can say what you want about the two, especially Mrs. Armstrong; they were believers, had faith, and could be gracious givers. Mother didn't just feed the word of Jesus, but she fed many with nourishment. Lindy reminded me that Mother talked me into taking her to the Bargain Box, which was held annually at the Veterans' Memorial. I drove, and she asked me to stop to buy some White Castles. She purchased twenty burgers. I thought they were for us, but she never offered, and I didn't ask. However, once we were in the long line at the Vet's Memorial, someone would say, "I smell White Castle's and immediately Mrs. Armstrong would turn and offer one to whoever said it and start a conversation. Soon, someone would open the door about luck or being happy, and Mrs. Armstrong would introduce the Word of Christ to them. When I was discharged from the Navy, married to Allison, I had a hard time getting used to "Mother" being in our (my) business. She seemed to want to control what Allison, or I, did in our family, and I had to put time between the two of us until God got us both on the same page. And he did, not our time, but his time, and before long, I was calling her *"Mother"*.

BE-BOP

Nope, we're not talking about the origin of jazz, but if you spoke to her, she'd probably end up telling you "...with a glass of wine in her hands, "Yep! That's me!". Yes, I'm talking about our mother, who was born Mary Barbara West. Those who grew up with her in Smithfield, Ohio, called her "Barb". Those friends of hers call her Barbara, and someone coined the nickname Be-bop. Our mother, God bless her, I believe, was making amends for her past indiscretions, although she'll swear she had done none of them; she's still laughing. Oh, yeah, if you know or knew her, you'd know she is a "Party Person," and I've witnessed that the party doesn't start until Be-Bop has arrived. And she always appears late in late fashion. As a kid, I knew our mother loved to have fun. She and her friends would go out shopping, and they all loved to have a good time. Sometimes there were even some good times at our home when our parents would tell us to go to bed before our regular bedtime, mainly on the weekends, because their neighborhood friends would be coming over, and they were going to party. Yes, I remember how our father enjoyed music and dancing in his prime. The music would be blasting on the console record player. I guess that's where my love for music was born. I didn't know that most of the music was our mother's, nor did I know any of the players until late in life. I recall hearing Charlie Parker, Eddie Harris, and, of course, all of the Motown sounds. As I shared earlier, when our father kidnapped us one late night from Cherry Valley, Mom was working (as she recently informed me) at a nursing home in Hopedale. Of course, knowing her history, I assumed she was at a club. Don't get me wrong, I love my mother, but she has always had a party in her veins. I doubt that you could find a friend of hers who would tell you differently. She is always ready to go.

At the age of 89, Pam and I held a party at our VFW Post for her, and true to form, she was out on the floor. Our mother can dance. I don't mean she stands and waits for the music to do the work; she's raring to go, knows all the dances, steps, and moves, and would be too happy to show you. From The Mash Potatoes to The Madison, to name a few, and to today's newest Line Dance, "Boots On the Ground", she's no amateur. Our sisters got that (dancing) from our Mom for sure.

Everyone in the family could dance but me when we were children. It wasn't until I had enlisted in the military and came home to a family get-together to do a line dance to Will Smith's "Wild, Wild West", which we performed at a party for my Aunt Donna. Then Aunt Donna shouted out, "Look, Edwin can dance". I had arrived, and it felt good dancing with my sisters, brother, and our mother. We put on a show with Cowboy boots and hats. Anyway, getting back to Be-Bop, her children, I, Sheila, and Mychaeltodd were trying to get a little something together for Mom's Nineteenth birthday. Her birthday is Christmas Eve (our daughter, Ayrika's, is the day after Christmas). Anyway, Mom isn't known for patience, and I guess she thought that none of her grown kids had any plans to celebrate her 90th birthday and throw a party for her, so she scheduled her own and sent us invitations. And I know she told everyone in the neighborhood, her church, called all her cronies, etc., and said to them that she is going to have a great party. They should attend cause if they didn't, I can hear her now, "Girl, we gonna party all night long. If you don't come, you're gonna miss it and wish you were here!" Every bit of 4'7, five feet at the most, and she Be-Bops when she walks, the epitome of swing. Yeah, that's where I got my energy from, cause I can go a long time, then my body says it's time to sleep. My soldiers used to say, "Chief, why do you walk so fast?, I'd tell them, "I'm drafting opportunities and tracking goals to my dreams." I would attempt to slow down, but I was soon back to my pace. My wife, Pam, told me one day, "Yep, you walk just like your mom. Okay, I could have been born with worse traits. Mom's routine is never to miss an opportunity for fun and adventure. You name it, she has probably done it and is planning to at 90 years old. She would take cat naps between her adventures to rest up, and she'd be out again. No one can say that Barbara Cobb is not a hard worker. Like our father, she always seemed to work and sometimes had two jobs. I remember her working full-time at Western Electric and part-time with Schottenstein or in the Bakery at Kroger's Store. Mom excelled in caring for others most of her life, working at various nursing homes, and she drove for Meals on Wheels for years. Now that I think about it, Mom probably got her nickname Be-Bop from her traveling buddies in Eastern Star, a Masonic Order. I would never have enough time to tell you all the stories I've heard from her partners in crime when they traveled to various states and cities for their conventions and parties, which were her primary focus.

But I recall one friend saying, "Yeah, Barbara would be bopping in and out of the clubs and dragging us with her." She retired as a custodian after 15 years at Marion Franklin High School. Mom no longer drives, but whenever she visits, she calls one or two or three of her friends who still do. She'll schedule things for them to do and places to go. Notice I didn't say she asked them what they wanted to do or where they wanted to go. As she would lie halfway asleep, catching her second wind, I asked her, "Mom, who are you going out with?" and she told me, "Whoever shows up first", which let me know that she had called a few people. People tell me I'm blessed to still have my mother with me. She may outlive me. Her mind is sharp from reading 2 to 3 books a week, generally with a glass of red wine in hand, and she has been known to wake at 5 am for her morning walk before the sun rises, and only the Lord knows what's on her diary agenda.

It doesn't matter which comes first, in my telling you which one I love most, because they're both the same, my love for my Mom and *"Be-Bop"*.

I LOOK LIKE ROCK

Carlton James   Edwin Drew   William James

Maybe you can recall the story about the "Ugly Duckling"? I hated that story! When I was a child, all I would hear was how my brothers and sisters resembled our parents. Relatives would go on and on about how they looked like either William, our father, or Barbara, our mother, etc. Yet, that flattering statement never graced my sensitive little ears as to who I may have looked like in the scheme of things, and I was the eldest of seven offspring from our father's loins. Often, I would hear, Oh, Sheila had William's features (she told me that she thought she was the ugly duckling), Michael looked like dad, or Angela, we called 'Angie', looked like Barbara. And there was "Markie," who was born Marc Allen, who was the spitting image of "Robinson" or "Rob," which most people called our father, especially his co-workers. However, that was prevalent in the military, and our father did not serve one day. Looking back, I probably had a bit of a complex about not looking like someone in our family. It would have been nice to hear I looked like a distant relative, but that never happened. Damn, it bothered me for some time until years later, after I had left home and enlisted in the United States Navy. After boot camp, I returned home on furlough and would come home whenever I could, mostly on or near the holidays. And I would attempt to visit all my relatives, especially my father's youngest brother, Franklin Anthony Robinson, Uncle "Tony", who was a few years older than I, so I was closer to him in terms of having someone to hang out with. Although he was married, his wife and my aunt were very welcoming and made me feel comfortable in their home. Her name was Francis, and she went by "Fran".

Aunt Fran was and still is a beautiful woman. She grew up in the south end of Columbus, where I grew up. Her family lived on the same avenue as my Aunt Deloris, just a caddy corner away. Aunt "Dee" was Tony's oldest sister of two. Donna was the youngest girl and the baby. She and I were born in the same hospital just days apart, but I came out first, on the 25th day of March, and then Donna, on the 31st. Yep, I was born before her, but she was still my aunt, and I always honored her position, although we practically grew up like cousins. Donna and Zippy kept my ass in trouble. Zippy was her favorite stuffed monkey. My father and mother lived with my father's parents until I was born, and Dad could find a home for us. My grandmother and my grandfather's parents also lived in the same house. It was a big house on what is now considered a historical site for the Underground Railroad, conducted by Harriet Tubman. So, I had a lot of family members running around me, holding and feeding me, and assisting my mother in raising Donna and me. I don't recall how old I was when we moved into our own home, but I know that throughout my childhood, I didn't look like "no Robinson". As I mentioned earlier, my siblings, my father, my grandfather, most of my relatives, and I all shared the strong facial features and personality of "The Robinson" family look. The one factor that I held dear, though, was that I, along with most of the Robinsons, had a, should I say, very "distinctive nose." For years, I looked like none of them. Well, I had never been told that I did. But I did have the Robinson trademark, the family nose. That was for sure. Soon, I found out that I had grown into Robinson's nose. During one of my furloughs from my ship, the USS NIMITZ, stationed in Norfolk, Virginia, I visited Uncle Tony, catching up on time and what I was doing in the Navy. As usual, he would pull out some of his "Top Shelf" liquor and pour me a glass, and we'd sit and talk. Although not a musician, he was always into music, like most of us. While the music was playing, he grabbed Fran by her hand, and they began to dance. I watched, somewhat embarrassed. I was still a little shy around women. And suddenly, Tony turned to me and said, "Come on, Edwin, you dance with Fran." I was shocked, believing that was what he was going for. But I pulled myself together, stood up, gently put my arm around Fran's waist, and took her hand in the other. It was awkward, but it felt nice. I was so glad the song was short. I thanked Fran.

She smiled and said, "Oh, you're welcome, Edwin; you're a good dancer." I liked how she said my name. Today, my wife reminds me of how it sounded to me that day when Fran said it. I sat down and took another sip of whatever I was drinking. We continued to talk about what I was up to. As we spoke, Uncle Tony abruptly interrupted the conversation by saying, "Boy, you know who you look like?" Of course, I was still having issues with it and was interested in who he might have thought I looked like because by then, I had been told that I looked like many folks, but none of the Robinson descent. So, of course, I was hoping he was talking about someone in the family. He said, *"You look like Rock!"* Rock was my grandfather's nickname. His fellow West Virginia Coal Miners nicknamed him. Wow! I looked like Carlton James Robinson. As you can imagine, I was elated. From that day forth, as I matured into a grown man, I took his and my father's likeness more and more. Many started to say that Marcie and I looked alike, much like our father and grandfather. Many of my military associates called me "Rob or "Robbie", which our father was called by many. When my grandfather passed, and probably after seeing his photo and my likeness posted in the local Columbus Dispatch Newspaper Obituary, I received several calls from friends and classmates to give their condolences, hearing of what they thought was my demise. The arrival of my family traits and features lay dormant until someone noticed that *"I look like Rock"*.

"EDWIN, NOT EDDIE"

I was born Edwin, not Edward. For years, as a young child, I already had issues with my name. Not my first name, but my middle name is Drew. I never cared about it and always thought of changing it to Duane, Dwight, or something close, but Drew was never a cup of tea for me. Maybe it could have been that I knew of no one named Drew until I was older, and I accepted it. "Edwin Drew Robinson", I can still hear my mother calling me from the streets when she needed me to come home from playing. She would call all of us by our full names. How embarrassing. I soon grew into it. It seemed Edwin just rolled off the tongues of those who knew me. It was a sweet sound to my ears whenever the schoolteachers performed their daily task to ensure all their students were present, and they announced my name. I had never had a nickname except in the neighborhood; my friends, the Peppers, came up with the name "Saba Abba". I never knew where that came from until recently, when I researched the name. When I returned from the military and ran into the Peppers, one of them asked me if I remembered being called Saba Abba. I never liked it, and without a pause, I snapped back and said, "It's Ed or Edwin". Then, I realized I didn't like being called Saba Abba. I didn't know why they called me that, and they probably didn't know what it meant. As a kid, I didn't like it and wished I had asked where they got it from and why they thought it fit me. Like the oldest, Richard. When he got his hair cut close, his head resembled a box, and "Box" was his nickname for years. Today, I understand that Saba and Abba are often associated with being a father figure. So, I wonder, were the Peppers knowingly calling me "Old Man," or were they honoring me as their elder? I think to choose the latter. Well, as it were, in the military and probably where most nicknames were generated, because many surnames were challenging to pronounce, people looked for shortcuts, as many did with my name, Robinson. Now I wouldn't tell many about this nickname of mine that was probably proudly earned and lavished upon me by my great-grandmother, Mama Ada (Champion) (Robinson) Patton, but knowing what I remember about her and my history with my grandparents, I must share the story.

Do you know how your nickname came up? Well, I remember how mine was. We all know how grandparents can put a name on you, right? Well, it happened to me. I lived with my parents, grandparents, and great-grandparents when I was born. They were Frank and Carrie Combs, my grandmother's parents, and Mama Ada Patton, my grandfather's mother. I was their first Great-Grandson, the first Grandson, and the first son of William and Barbara Robinson. The grandparents spoiled me, all of them, but mostly the greats. So, as I was told, the story goes, I was about two years old, and a Concord Grapevine was involved. It grew in the backyard of my grandparents' home, and my great-grandparents would let me run the gamut of the yard, and I would immediately run to the grapevine to help myself. On one of those occasions, I had my fill of the delicious forbidden fruit after being told not to overeat. However, I did, and soon there was a mess of residue from those sweet grapes that affected my bowels. Yes, all those grapes had quickly fermented and made their way to crap. Someone told me that while Mama Ada was attending to cleaning up the mess, she said, "Why you ain't nothing but a Dootie-Bootie" (yes, that's where my grandfather got that from). I'm sure whoever was in attendance laughed and shared the story because from that day on, it stuck with me like that nasty grape-filled diaper Mama Ada had to pry from my bottom to dispose of. There were no disposable diapers then, and I was told that my diaper was so saturated with the stain of grapes that it was thrown away. So, you see why I had never shared this story with friends. I feared that it might have made its way back into my life as a permanent label. I loved my great-grandparents, and I know that they loved me. Later in my life, Mama Ada came to live with us briefly. She called me Edwin, but now and then, especially when we were alone, she'd reach into her purse, hand me a piece of candy, and then she'd whisper, "You'll always be my Dootie-Bootie", I'd thanked her and smiled, but in my head, I was yelling, "NO!" I was so glad that name never made its way into my life in grade school, junior, or high school, like some folks have had to endure. There are grown people still answering the nickname one of their grandparents stuck them with, and some of them are horrific. My daughter was stuck with "Miss Piggy" for a few years. Which was cute, but as an adult today, I don't think she'd accept it.

I was called Rob, Robbie, and because it was associated with so many famed personnel, I was called "Sugar Ray" or "Smokey" of the Temptations, and I accepted them all. However, as I matured, I began to take on the nickname of Ed. When I married, though, and we were expecting our first child, a son, the importance of what he would be called for the rest of his life landed on me. We decided to name him after me, Edwin. Well, at that time, there were a lot of Eddies in the family. My mother-in-law's brother was Eddie, her two sisters were married to an Eddie, and my mother had remarried a man named Eddie. I was the only Edwin in the family, and everyone at that time called me Edwin, not Eddie. So the day came, and I had to rush my wife to the hospital to deliver our son. While she was in labor, I was comforted by many of my in-laws in the waiting room. My parents-in-law, sisters-in-law, my mother, and other relatives accompanied me. It was a family affair for sure. As we waited to hear of a successful delivery, the conversation turned to my mother-in-law. She was excited for her youngest daughter's first child and became a grandmother again. She said, "Thank God, we will have another Eddie". Hold your horses, Mrs. Armstrong, his name is Edwin, not Eddie.

You all call me Edwin, and I have never gone by the name Eddie, and I wasn't about to start to, nor call our son Eddie. My son will be named after me, and you will call him Edwin, just like me. I was so adamant about what I had just said that I think the room was silent for a short time until someone changed the topic. Usually, my sister-in-law, Linda, who we called "Lindy". And true to form, she broke out into her streak of laughter, and said something in the effect of "Well, okay, Eddie, we'll call him Edwin". A few smirked and laughed with her. This was another time I was very adamant about my stance. And they saw that I was unhappy as I commanded and repeated, saying, *"Edwin, not Eddie"*.

NEVER GETTING MARRIED AGAIN

This could and should be a very long story, but then I wouldn't be able to qualify it as a short story, yet here it goes. Allison and I, along with our children, had moved into our newly built home to be later joined by foster sibling brothers, Corey and Shawn Jenkins. Later, we were blessed with their adoption. There are so many stories in this part of my life, but I will pass over them until later. It was no secret that after thirty years or more, Allison and I were having marital issues, and her illness of being a hypochondriac; however, she was never diagnosed, probably was bipolar too. It was not much of a secret with her family. Here's a true story, one of many. One day, Allison had a doctor's appointment with Dr. Choe Rhee at the OSU East Hospital. Allison was very knowledgeable. She had copies of the most recent Nurses' Drug Handbooks (NDH), Physicians' Desk Reference (PDR), and the Pharmacist Drug books. She was well-read and would practice the symptoms and reenact them once she arrived at her doctor's appointments to secure the specific medication(s) she wanted. She scared me once during an appointment I attended with her when she suddenly and seemingly broke down while speaking with the doctor and started crying, tears and all. I was speechless because I wasn't warned of her theatrics. Once she received her win and we were going home, she was just as calm as anyone. No symptoms whatsoever. It was an act, and I was a part of the audience. Another incident occurred when she went to see another doctor. She scheduled the appointment, and once we arrived, I told her I would be sitting in the chairs outside the waiting room, where she had to wait to see the doctor. As I was outside the waiting room, about ten minutes later, a young lady came out and told her mother she was ready to go home. I overheard her telling her mother she had just heard a woman in the waiting room explaining her sicknesses and illnesses. The young lady said, "After hearing all that, I don't feel as sick as the woman telling everybody about her illnesses". I interrupted the young lady and described the woman she was talking about: Allison. I apologized and told them that it was my wife. The young lady looked at me with sympathy and said, "God bless you, sir, because you've got a lot on your hands. I'm going to pray for you." I thanked her, and she and her mother left.

Sure, Allison and I had other issues that I attempted to handle, and of course, her medical problems were among them. And if I told you that I didn't love her, I'd be lying because I did; that candle that lit for her began to dwindle out in our last ten years together. I'd be the first to tell you, I had my flaws as she had hers, and I attempted to resolve them with her, even addressed them and shared them with close family members of Allison's, especially her older sisters, one of whom is in the ministry. I sought counseling from the church, the Veterans Administration through the VA Clinic, and Allison was not having it. She informed me that she did not want to share our problems with the church. When I set up family counseling through the VA, she would cancel the appointments in the morning and tell me that she canceled them when I was preparing to leave. During that time, we left the church on the South end of town and started attending a closer local church near our new home. That cut down on travel time to and from church, which was about 30 to 45 minutes, depending on the traffic, and the new church was just minutes down the street. She stated that she was too tired to participate some mornings and soon
stopped attending church altogether. She stated that she was too ill to participate some mornings and ended up just stopping attending, so I continued with our adopted sons, Corey and Shawn, who were about eight and nine years old. Today, they are grown men alone (yep, another story). A year passed, and I started performing with the worship band. Slowly, Allison would make excuses for why I couldn't take

the boys to church with me. I was attending church by myself. After another year, I started asking the elders and members of the worship team to pray for my family and our relationship as I sought to mend it. I had joined the men's ministry and found a good friend in one of the senior elders. He was also our church attorney, and I felt comfortable divulging Allison and my marriage issues and problems. We met once a week outside the church, as part of our men's group, to speak freely about God and family. Many church members prayed with and for me and my marriage. Pam Dixon was one of those worshippers. She was a singer in the group. She would at times tell me that she was praying for our marriage and provide suggestions that might resolve our problems, such as church counselors or outside counseling. However, I had decided that nothing would fix what had been broken then, and I had to change.

I could fix it, but after a hard inner soul search, I realized I couldn't. I believed deeply that Allison did not want to be married and preferred to waddle in what hurt her; she felt I created or contributed to. I just waited for God to move. And lo and behold, one Saturday morning, I got up and told Allison, I'm headed out to take care of some things. I don't remember what it was, but she told me I shouldn't buy anything because her money had not been posted to her account. But why? We had separate accounts, and I know I had funds in my accounts. That should have been a red flag to me years ago. But I trusted our finances were in good hands, as Allison had worked for years as a Teller and Accountant for several financial institutions. She supposedly was good with money. That was not the case. In all cases, Allison was very good at "manipulation," and our finances were victims of it. I had retired then and received my annuities and VA benefits. That Saturday, I stopped at the gas station for a coffee, and my card did not work. I tried another, and another. All of my credit and debit cards were denied. I quickly called

USAA and Huntington Bank to inquire about the issue. Both banks informed me that my accounts had been blocked. I asked, "By whom?". They both said, "Allison Robinson." Thinking quickly, I told them I had forgotten that I had lost my billfold and told my wife to block the accounts until I found it. I continued to say the banks that I had seen that morning, but forgot to call them. Of course, that was not true. Allison had put a block on all my accounts so that I couldn't buy anything – even a cup of coffee. The bank understood and unblocked my accounts. I was agitated because I knew I had funds in all my accounts. I opened my USAA app on my phone and went to the accounts section. I found that Allison had opened numerous accounts in both our adult children's names and their children's and grandchildren's names. She even had an account under our son-in-law. The sad part was that I trusted her with our finances and was unaware of her siphoning our income into her vaults. I called the bank to inquire about the accounts and was informed that I was not on any of them; however, they did confirm that there were funds in all the accounts, but the only person with authorization to manage them was Allison Robinson. Now, the shit had hit the proverbial fan, and I was "Robinson Furious." Yep, I just made that up. But for giggles, can you imagine our father's reaction to that situation? Yes, "Wild Bill Furious" is probably more fitting, and I've seen that in some of my siblings with short fuses.

That was my last straw of her manipulation, and I was no longer concerned about hurting her feelings. Later, I was confronted by family members on both sides of our families who told me, "We were wondering when you were going to wake up." And yes, it was a very rude awakening, and of course, I was hurt, but I was emboldened to make the move. I opened new accounts, moved my funds, and called my father for assistance in moving out. He was the last person I wanted to call for help, but I did. And yes, those who knew our father know that's another story. But he came through. He had two workers meet me at U-Haul, and we went home. I immediately confronted Allison and told her that I was through, I was moving out, and that I knew she had blocked my accounts. She denied it, but the deed had been done, and the iron had been cast. I told the guys to load up all my belongings, which I had packed for some time, knowing we were close to separating; it was just a matter of time. The move was fast, clean, and quick. I didn't want to hear her voice or any excuses, as she assured me it wasn't her. That Sunday at church, I was there early because the band always showed up early for a rehearsal before services. We held two services. I informed my Christian friends that I had moved out of our home and asked them to continue their prayers for my family. After the last service, I received many concerns about my situation and circumstances, such as moving with my ill father. Pam was there to console me and tell me that she was so sorry to hear that things were not working out and that she would continue to pray for us. She was always sincere about her prayers. We had many conversations throughout the following years. I don't remember this conversation back then, but now my wife, Pamela, likes to rib me about when I told her I was *"Never Getting Married Again"*.

OUR CHRISTMAS CHILD

The ground was cold from the morning winter, with 40 knots of wind. Yet there was very little snow. It was Christmas Day, December 25, 1981, and that evening was scheduled for a hospital visit. Allison was in labor with our second child, whom she had named Ayrika (pronounced Erika), and I agreed. I was on my way to visit her on Christmas morning. Allison had been admitted the day before after several false labor alerts. Yet the "Braxton-Hicks" seemed to come more and more. Dr. Jefferson was Allison's doctor. He delivered our son, Edwin II (Ilyas S. Abdul-min), and our daughter. Our son was then 3 years old and very excited about the arrival of his little sister. "Little Edwin" was what his grandfather, Robert Armstrong, Allison's father, called our son. It soon caught on with most of our relatives. Now it was and still is a hospital policy that children were not allowed on the delivery floor with the mothers and newborns, in fear that the children could be carrying germs and cause an infection from colds, etc. Little Edwin knew I would visit his mother and little sister, although Ayrika had not yet arrived. I was just as excited about seeing his mother and meeting his little sister once she was there. Like most of my ideas for inventions and creations, I was struck with a creative thought. I would design a box cleverly disguised as a Christmas package that would easily and comfortably carry my son. Of course, Lil' Edwin was all for the idea. During my designing of his "Trojan Box", I explained to him that once we arrived at the hospital, he would then enter the box, I would cover him with the lid that was nicely designed with ribbons and a bow that aligned with the box, and he would have to be very quiet once we entered the hospital. He was tickled to death and on board the plane to go into the hospital to see his mother on Christmas Day. I told him that he would be his mommy's Christmas Gift and that she would be thrilled and surprised after he jumped out of the box and shouted Merry

Christmas, Mommy! The plan did not go as simply as I thought it would. Lil' Edwin and I finished the box with holes in the bottom for his breathing and a blanket lining the bottom for his comfort once he got in it. We tested the box size to ensure that it fit perfectly.

I assured my son that once I covered him and walked from the hospital parking lot, into the building, and to the elevator to his mother's floor, it would be no longer than ten minutes, and that he would have to be very quiet once we entered the hospital. He, of course, agreed as a 3-year-old understood, and even though Lil' Edwin was very bright at his age, he was just as clever, intuitive, and inquisitive at the most awkward times. And that Christmas night was no different. As much as we had rehearsed, it did not do us well because Lil' Ed was now in the box and on our way through the parking lot, he started asking me, "Are we there yet?" And I would say, no, not yet, but you need to be quiet when we get into the hospital, and he would giggle and say, "Okay". I hadn't planned for the turnaround door of the hospital and had to adjust the box and hold it upward, forgetting the end where my son's feet were located. I positioned the box upside down, and he let me know. It took only a few seconds to realize it, but by then, we had gone through the door, and I had re-adjusted the box. I quietly whispered, "You okay, Edwin?" he said like a trooper, "Yes, Sir, I'm okay." There was a lady at the front desk, and I told her that I was there to visit my wife, that she was on the maternity floor, and that I was bringing in a bouquet of roses. She directed me to the nearby elevator doors. She said, "Fourth floor, Sir." I thanked her and quickly headed for the elevator button, hoping the doors would open soon because my son was now whispering, "Daddy, are we there yet?" I hushed him as the entrance doors opened. I looked around for directions to the welcome center. As I asked for the maternal floor, an attendant jumped up behind his station with a book. I wondered whether he would ask about my package or its contents. He wasn't. He seemed more concerned about my disturbing either his sleep or his reading. It was late, about 10 p.m., and pretty quiet in the hospital. Just as soon as I smiled at him with a nod, saying, "Gift for the wifie", he quickly returned to his sleeping or reading. We advanced to the elevators. When I entered, it was occupied by a doctor and two nurses. I entered the elevator holding my package like a bouquet, smiled at them, and quickly turned around, facing the now-closing doors of the elevator. As the doors completely closed, a bell rang, and as if it were his cue, Lil' Edwin whispered, "Are we there yet?" Shocked and quickly reacting, I looked down at the closed package. I whispered, "No, not yet." I turned to the folks behind me and told them I was an amateur ventriloquist practicing my act and would quickly present roses to my wife.

They were amazed, and our clever son heard me and thought of enjoying himself by saying, "I'm a Christmas Gift for my Mommy." The doctor and nurses gave me a round of applause and a couple of kudos for my talent. The elevator doors to the fourth floor could not have opened any slower, and you hear, "Are we there yet?" and not so much as a whisper this time, as the voice came from the box. I stepped from the elevator, turned and looked at my audience, returned attention to the box, and replied to my son, "Yes, Christmas Gift, we're here." Please, "At Ease" and be quiet until we get to the room, okay?" And my son said, "Sir, yes, Sir." The laughter pursued. When we reached the fourth floor, one nurse exited just before me. I stepped out, and the doors closed even slower, in slow motion. My fans were still laughing as the elevator closed, and you could still hear them as the elevator traveled up to the next floor. I said, Luckily, no one else had heard me and the box talking. I approached the Nurse's station and asked for directions from Allison Robinson, who was in room 218A. She was engulfed in her reading, and without even looking up, she pointed in the direction for me to follow the number I had given her. I hurried to the room, not wanting to prolong the conversation and give our son a chance to speak. Allison was awake. Before I could get the package to the foot of the bed or tell our son we were there, he popped the lid off the box, jumped up like a Jack-in-the-Box, and said, "Surprise, Merry Christmas, Mommy!". At the same time, Allison's attending nurse came into the room and caught us "Red-Handed." She laughed and told me she thought I was a ventriloquist but was still impressed. Then she politely recited the hospital policy and gave us 30 minutes before we had to leave. Allison was delighted to see her Christmas gift, her Lil' Edwin. But he would not be her only gift. On December 26th, 1981, Ayrika Daniece Robinson, our daughter, arrived. She was *"Our Christmas Child"*.

Edwin, with his 3-year-old son, Li'l Edwin, wrapped in a Christmas Box.

This is photo of our son as I took him to the hospital to see his Mom on Christmas Eve, as she was in labor with his little sister, whom he was excited to welcome.

PAMELA SUE

It was faith. As you've read in many of my stories, I was at the end of a rope, waiting for the other shoe to drop, at my wits' end, I had had enough, and had had the last straw. Then, in walked this tall drink of water of a lady. I watched her as she floated across the floor. I suddenly thought of the Latin samba, "Girl from Ipanema," and Uncle Charlie's hit song, "There Goes My Baby". I was smitten. Without going through the whole ordeal that I had experienced up until this period, I'm gonna tell you about the woman that God sent me when I thought that I would never get into another relationship. All I wanted to do was play my music, which was and is God's music. I had decided to throw myself into my music. By then, I had hidden from much of my family and didn't want to deal with life. No, I was not at that point. Some of you are thinking about it. Suicide, right? Nope! I was and still am far from taking my life. God still had more life and work for me, and my family still needed me. But what I had forgotten was that I needed someone in my corner. Someone who loved me for who I am. Someone who could see that there was a good person under all of the shit life and the world had put me through. I needed what God had made for me, and that was a help to me as my mate (Helpmate). And she was just served up to me when I was about to move because I could hear God telling me, "Get ready, Edwin, because when I move, you need to move". I've heard folks say, "God speaks to me" and all that. Yet, I am not claiming that is what I heard, but I think we can feel God telling us to do something, and isn't that just the same as hearing? It ain't that deep, but I felt something other than lust. Yeah, I know someone was thinking about it. What I saw and who I saw when this beautiful woman strolled into my life was my new life, and she was the angel we all know that God sent for me. Months before us officially getting together, we both were attending bible classes at our church and unknowing to me, Pam was staring at me and it must had been an during an incredible cold season because she told me later that I was wearing a black leather jacket and cap (on backwards), she couldn't take her eyes off me.

I remember seeing her stare, and I quickly turned my eyes away because I knew she was like that candy in the candy store, and I was told not to ask for or touch it. You know how you go to look at someone and they have the same idea, and you both glance and quickly look away? That was us for a period, and I looked forward to Sunday mornings more and more as I suspected she did as well. Yes, some of you are wondering, was I still in the throes of my marriage? Yes, I probably was, but I was on my way out, literally in with my father, then with my little brother, Marc. That's another story. I finally filed papers for divorce. It wasn't long after Pam and I started to see each other that I heard from my family and Pam's family that we were the happiest we had seen either of us. Yes, she was and is Pamela Sue (Stuck-Dixon), and we soon became a couple and then one. I told her this year that God took us two, Edwin Drew and Pamela Sue, and made us one. Now, being in the military, I have had very few issues dealing with being around white folks. Not so with Pam being around a lot of black folks, but I told her if she hung around me, I was going to indoctrinate her into the family, and if she stayed long enough, I would introduce her to some music. Most blacks don't have the problem that comes with being the only one in the room because we had to assimilate to fit in most societies that were and still are predominantly white. So, I have, for the most part, found it not that uncomfortable to be surrounded by a lot of white folks, no matter where I find myself. I want to confess that although my first wife was of a very fair complexion, as was my first date, it was never a conscious concern. It wasn't a prerequisite for me. I believed that all of the fair-skinned women in my life were kind and had good intentions, as I had. However, on the other side of the spectrum, many whites still harbored deeply ingrained stereotypes concerning black people or people of color, especially black men. And we all have heard them. "Black men are always angry", "They have a lot of women and kids", "They're lazy", and the list goes on. I've even heard white men say, "They want our women". Now, that is a true statement. I've listened to many of my brothers, both black and white, talk about that, but the truth be told, for centuries, their women have always wanted us. As the younger generation says, "I'm keeping it One Hundred". No, having a white woman had never been my personal goal. Yet, I found an interesting woman not from my tribe. And I had to take a passage to visit her village to seek their acceptance. Pamela, whom I lovingly call Pam, is a "Baby-Boomer," and she came from a very sheltered life, which she shared with me. She claims that her father may have had issues with me, but would have liked me soon. She didn't say love. But I would have accepted that. Did I tell you that Pam is a white woman?

Not everyone in my family loves me. On the other hand, Pam tells me all the time that her mother, had she met me, would have loved me. I took solace in that. Pam, when she and I were courting (you don't hear that much anymore), I assumed that she had been prepping her family to meet me. Telling them that I was black. She told me that when she was trying to inform her oldest brother, "Bobby," that I was black, she could hear his wife, Louise, shouting in the background, "Oh Bob, I've dated black guys before and they're lots of fun, get over it!". I don't know what Bob's reaction was to their conversation concerning me, but there was an agreement for us to visit. So, we made our pilgrimage to Peru, Indiana, where her eldest brother, Dr. Robert "Bob" Stuck, and his wife Louise lived. Bob had been a minister and pastor for some forty years, and Pam's only sister, Pat, and her husband, Dr. James "Jim" Walker, another forty-year pastor who also made the memorable trip to Indiana, all met Pam's newest love interest, me. Yep, I was going to be interrogated by two Bible heavy hitters in the heart of Indiana. The small but quaint home was now full of six Baby Boomers, one not like the others. It was a pleasant meeting, and I did my best not to speak about politics or religion. Although I was an Elder at our church, I didn't want to mix any of our conversations about either. My main thoughts were to get in and get out. As a habit would have it, whenever I'm entering a location that I'm not familiar with, I look for entrances and exits. And I did it once in their home, out of habit. After the informal meet and greet, I found myself with the men as the ladies huddled together. I don't remember all of what we talked about or the questions I probably received, but I do remember that Bob had served some military time, and so did Pam's other brother, Paul, who lived in Texas. Paul served in the Army Band as a Trombone Player, and we saw that we had that in common, other than his baby sister. After a short stint in the army, Paul, also a Baby Boomer, became a successful barber and owner of his shop. Now, while we men were getting to know each other, I recall them sharing what weapons they carried when traveling and at their churches. Some might have taken that as a threat, but I took that as an invitation: "I showed you mine, show me yours".

I felt very comfortable sharing my Glock, which I had holstered, letting them know their sister was in good protective hands. After sizing up each other and being indoctrinated into their biblical and political beliefs, I understood that they were staunch in their beliefs, especially their political views. Pam had asked that her brother, before we arrived, not play the radio while we were visiting because he and his wife were and are so far right and a "Trumper" supporter, that it even sickened Pam to hear all the propaganda that came out of the media radio stations. She did not want me to be offended. Can I say, "There Goes My Baby?" She had my back. While we started dating and trying to keep it a secret from the church members, Pam and I were fully engaged, talking to each other, discussing plans, and sharing church projects. One was donating to the "Peanut Butter Drive", which we did annually. Well, one Sunday morning, we both purchased several jars of the peanut butter and brought them to the church via the "Green Room", our worship band's rest area. I had asked Pam not to come in with me, saying that we didn't want folks to know yet that we were a couple. What does Pam do? As I was sitting and chatting it up with band members, Pam came in with her swag that she isn't aware of, but she has swag about her walk. Remember "Girl from Ipanema?" Pam swaggered in and stopped right in front of the coffee table before me, sitting on the sofa. Then, she looks at me and says, "Are you going to help me with these jars?" I thought, that's one way of telling anyone I was your man. I looked around, and only one person probably caught the vibe we were both putting off, that we were up to something. It was our keyboardist, Laura, and she said something like "Mmmmm, what's up with that?" I just knew the jig was up, our cover was blown, but Laura never said or let on that she thought Pam and I were an item. But I inquired afterwards, and she knew, saying, "Yeah, I felt something was going on with you two". Once I was legally divorced and the papers had been filed without a signature, the court granted me my release. I told Pam that it was time to inform the church, and the best way was for us to tell my partner in our men's group, Tom Berridge, who was also the Head Elder on the board. I called Tom and asked if Pam and I could visit his home. It was about four or five in the evening. He said, "Sure". When we arrived, Tom offered us a seat, Pam and I sat on a nearby couch, and after the "How you been", etc. I told Tom and his wife, Chris, why we were there. But before I did, I learned over and kissed Pam on the cheek.

We're here to let you know that we are dating (Our first date was when Pam asked me to borrow my computer monitor. I said sure and bought one). That's all I'm sharing about that. Tom and Chris looked surprised but were genuinely happy for us. They had no idea we were together. Tom thought that because we were both in the worship band, we were there to complain about the worship minister or the band. He was relieved. I thought it was time to introduce Pam to my family so she could experience our interrogations. It was all open arms from my ex-wife's family from day one. My niece asked Pam if she could call her "Aunt Pam". When we got into our car to leave, Pam was crying. I asked her why she was crying. She said my niece, who had never met her until that night, had asked if she could call her Aunt Pam. I told her jokingly, "That's how most black families roll". Maybe not those exact words, but close. That situation happened to me when we visited Pam's daughter (now mine), Tamra, her husband Chris, and their two sons, Sam and Max. Max said, "I love you, Edpa," when we were at the door to leave. Something like that touches a real man who cries, and I did. Now, the families were in it, and the church was in it. Of course, Pam was in it before me, to hear her tell it. She said that she had already asked someone to include me in it. No one asked me, probably because God told me. The marriage was swift. We purchased our rings at Macy's after I asked her if she would marry me at the Macy's jewelry store, right before the wedding bands. She said yes, no surprise there, and we picked out our rings with black diamonds. The day was September 5, 2016, and I arranged our wedding ceremony, the song "At Last," by Etta James, and our dance choreography. Pam entered from stage left and I from stage right during the playing of the song, "At Last" by Etta James and when Pam and I met in the middle, I took her in my arms, and we danced to the end of the song and afterwards did a little twirl ending up facing her brother and brother-in-law with our backs to the audience. They both married us. Yeah, it felt a little like a "Shotgun Wedding". Pam's brothers wanted me to make their sister an honorable bride, and I did my best. When Bobby asked me if I took his sister for better or worse, I could hardly hold back my desire to shout aloud, "Yes, I do take her to be my wife, *Pamela Sue*".

A SPLENDID BLENDED FAMILY

After our marriage, Pam and I wondered what our children thought about it. Although it's now the 21st century, and 10 years into our marriage, folks still are funny about seeing a bi-racial marriage. So, I took a step into the mind of one of our most inquisitive grandchildren, which they all are at one time or another. And I wrote how a thoughtful adult, a parent, would address specific questions that might linger in their little minds. In my mind, it went like this. Hi, my name is Niah, short for Jerniah, and I am four years old. One day, I asked my mommy, Why wasn't Papa Egwin (she couldn't say, Edwin) and Mama Allison not living in the same house anymore? My mommy told me that they don't live together anymore. My parents were in the army during the war, and Mama Allison and Papa Egwin cared for us until our parents returned home. My sisters and I, along with our dog Bella, spent a lot of time with our grandpa, whom we call Papa Egwin. When our parents had to leave home to fight the bad man for our country, we stayed with our grandparents. So when my mommy explained to me that her parents, my grandparents, could not get along, and one day they got a divorce. I asked her, "Mommy, what is a divorce?" She told me that divorce is when married people no longer live together because they cannot get along or do not love each other as they used to. She said they would still love me and my sisters and would still see us, but they might not be together. My Papa Egwin and Mama Allison live in different houses now, all by themselves. and I knew they were sad. It made me very sad, too. But one day, Papa Egwin brought a really nice lady to meet us. Her name was Ms. Pam. She made Papa Egwin happy again, so I was happy too. Papa Egwin said that God brought them together. I liked Ms. Pam. That's what we called her. She was pretty and she was nice.

And she had a dog too! His name was TJ. I had a funny feeling in my tummy at first about meeting Papa Egwin's friend. I don't know why I felt different inside. Mommy said maybe it was because she was different and not Mama Allison. That made me feel better. Bella and TJ liked each other and had fun chasing each other. Papa Egwin took Ms. Pam to meet other people in our family and his friends. Papa Edgin played the saxophone in his church band, and Ms. Pam sang. That is where they met. Papa Egwin and Ms. Pam enjoyed going to church and being in the band together. They were both happy, and that made my sisters and me happy too. Even Bella and TJ started wagging their tails. We learned fast that our family got a lot bigger. I now have another Grandma and lots more cousins, aunts, and uncles. My new cousins, my sisters, and I play together, and instead of being sad, I was so happy to have more family. Ms. Pam's kids are our mom's age, and they have kids our age who were happy like me for their Grandmother. They call her Mee-maw, and they call our Papa Egwin, Mr. Ed. We played together and laughed a lot. Papa Egwin smiled and called this a "Blended Family". He said that is what you call it when two families that are very different come together and make one big family. One day, one of my cousins asked Ms. Pam if she could call her Aunt Pam. That made Ms. Pam so happy that it made her cry. Papa Egwin likes being called Mr. Ed by the neighborhood kids and his new grandkids. Because it reminds him of an old TV show called "Mr. Ed" that was about a horse named "Mr. Ed" who could talk. Did you know that they gave the horse peanut butter, and when he ate it, it made him look like he could talk? Papa Egwin told me that. But I never saw the show because it was a long, long time ago, and kids today do not watch a lot of TV. Adults always laugh when they hear kids call my Papa Egwin Mr. Ed. It reminds them of that old television show they used to watch when they were kids.

Another time, Papa Egwin was visiting with Ms. Pam's family, and as they were about to leave their home, Ms. Pam's grandson gave Papa a high-five and said, "Bye, Edpaw, I love you". It made my Papa Egwin so happy that he cried, too, just like Ms. Pam did. Papa Egwin said, "It was the best gift he had ever received." Soon, our families visited each other a lot for birthdays and parties. The best of all was when we came together for no reason at all. All my family, my new cousins, aunts, and uncles, and Ms. Pam were a little different from the family I always knew. They probably thought the same of us. Yet, whenever we came together, we loved each other and had a blessed time as *"A Splendid Blended Family"*.

RETURNING THE RING

I left for the service in haste on the morning of July 7, 1974, carrying just the clothes on my back. I was wearing the only memory left of my days in high school, my graduation ring. My father had paid for the ring, even though it was more expensive than he had agreed to pay for. He was upset, but I was allowed to keep it. I proceeded through the in-processing and, all too soon, was on my way to the United States Naval Boot Camp at Great Lakes, Illinois, as my mother waved goodbye from the flight pad. I spent the next eight weeks there, wondering what I had done and how I would deal with my decision to join the military. On day one of my induction into the Navy, I felt like I was in a nightmare, hoping that one day I would awake, and it would all be over. Thirty-four years later, I retired from the United States Army, where I re-enlisted after my stint in the Navy. During my first time away from home, now at Boot Camp, I was privileged to " attend" the mandatory photo shoot. Afterwards, I purchased the photo to mark my military membership. I had no idea until years later that "joining up" was one of my most significant life choices. I had ordered photos and a naval ring that I paid for with my own money. While anxiously awaiting the delivery of the pictures and the new ring, I misplaced my cherished high school ring. I had lost the one most expensive item my father had ever bought for me. So, I was in Boot Camp, dressed in the mandatory military uniform, without my high school ring. For the first time, I had nothing to remind me of home. Graduation soon came, and I returned home from the start of many adventures and achievements, including the naval training. As a grand gesture to my father, I gave him my naval graduation ring because I had lost the ring he had given me. Yet, I never mentioned that fact to him until thirty-five years later. For over three decades, whenever my father and I had conversations, he always said, "I still have your ring. Do you want it back?" I would continually tell him, "No, I gave that ring to you". That question always reminded me of why I gave it to him. Part of me ached, wanting the ring back, but the other part still couldn't accept it. However, after a lifetime of wishing I could finally wear my Navy ring, I was finally ready to move past my reluctance to receive it. And when he did, saying, "I still have your ring, do you want it back?" I believed he wanted me to say yes. I said, "You have asked me that many times. But yes, sir, I'll take it now". As we walked into his bedroom towards his dresser, I spotted the ring box in which the ring was purchased, sitting in the center of the dresser. He handed it to me. I suddenly found myself wondering about the size of the ring. It may be that it no longer fits. I was only nineteen years old when I bought it. I was fifty-four at the time. I had, of course, gained some weight over the years. I weighed in at one-twenty-seven when I wrestled on the varsity team in high school, and I entered the Navy at one-thirty-five. Putting all my fears aside, I placed the ring on my right-hand ring finger, and it was a perfect fit! Dad seemed quite happy with himself, and I felt a sense of pride as he looked at it. "Dad", I said, "Before I take this back, I have something to confess. I gave you this ring because I lost my high school ring. You didn't want me to order it, but you paid for it anyway." He didn't say anything, just smiled, and he extended his hand to shake, but instead, I embraced him in a hug. As I turned to walk out of his bedroom, I thanked him. He patted me on my back and said, "That's okay, son, now I'm *"Returning the Ring."*

Edwin and Dad

RIGHT WHERE I AM

My life has been filled with acquaintances and some notoriety, with whom I am friends. Some I met and got to know for a very short time, and then they were gone. But I was blessed nevertheless during those brief moments, some longer than others, that helped shape who I am. I met Bobo Brazil, a once-famed wrestler, returning home from Naval Boot Camp. It was at O'Hara Airport. As he walked down the aisle with his staff chaperone, the closer his presence came to me, the darker the area became, as if the lights were shut off every step of his approach. He filled the area, and it was just as dark. I shouted, "Bobo Brazil." I'm from Columbus, Ohio, and I know you used to live or visit Stambaugh Avenue there. I extended my hand to shake his, and it disappeared into his enormous hand. He smiled and said, "Yes, I have people and have visited there." I mentioned that a friend of mine, Allison Armstrong (whom I married a few years later), used to play with your son Randy. He quickly said, "Yes, I know the Armstrongs, tell 'em I said hello". And his staff ushered him away, and he was gone. It seemed that all the lights were returning. And so it was for the rest of my life that I was blessed to meet and communicate with interesting people. After my combat days, I thought of myself as somewhat of a motivator, especially after reading several books that specialized in motivating folks. Les Brown was one of those folks. So, I attended when I heard he was in town for one of his seminars. After his spill, I waited for a few uninterrupted moments with him. I introduced myself and, with his big smile, said hello, Mr. Robinson. How are you? Knowing I probably didn't have much time, I quickly told him I recalled when he was here, and one of my biggest DJs on WVKO Radio. Again, the big smile brightened up the small conference room. I reminded him of the time he visited my junior high school and how he impressed me and motivated me to dream before he came out with his book. Then I told him that while I was deployed in combat, I read his book and showed it to him, battered from the wear of the desert sand and periodic folds that kept my place of reading. He was taken and appreciated that I kept the book, "Live Your Dreams." Without my asking, he asked me, "What's your first name again, Mr. Robinson?". I told him, and he autographed my book, which I still have.

I grew up in a popular area. I would not know much about its popularity until years later. Columbus was one of the homes of the Tuskegee Airmen at what once was called the Lockbourne Air Force Base, and many of them stayed and lived in Columbus. Music in Columbus, mostly at clubs on Mount Vernon Ave, Long Street, and The Valley Dale, was big and hosted many great musical talents. Talents like Nancy Wilson, Jimmy Smith, Hank Marr, Sam & Dave, Rahsaan Roland Kirk, and many others. Rusty Bryant was among them. He lived blocks away from where I grew up, and it wasn't until I was older that I found out again. I met him at a jam session called The Columbus Jazz Society, which many local musicians headed up. One of whom was Gene Walker, another saxophonist I also got to know and perform with. But back to Rusty Bryant. While attempting to jump into a session to "hone" my skills, he pulled me to the side afterward and suggested that I learn the song first. And if I wanted to, I could stop by his home, show me what I meant, and teach me a few things. Still, I didn't know he was the "Night Train" Saxophonist I heard my mother play at home. I was working the night shift at DCSC and told him I could stop by after work. He agreed. I showed up and played Amazing Grace for him, and he told me that I needed a little work, but he felt my soul in it. That's important, he said. "You've got to know and feel what you're playing." I returned a few times afterward, but it was short-lived, and I don't know why I stopped. Had I known more about Rusty

Bryant, I might have gleaned more of his knowledge and wisdom about playing the sax. What I do remember about Rusty is that he was kind and very willing to give his time to young musicians like me. That was an opportunity I sorely missed. Growing up in the South End of Columbus had its advantages; one was getting to know many of the great talents of neighbors or classmates. As many of my childhood friends can attest, we grew up with many. Eddie Milner, a player for the Cincinnati Reds, was one of my high school wrestling teammates, along with Andre Lanier, the brother of Kenny Lanier of the Kansas City Chiefs. As a "Newbie" to the wrestling team and at my first match, I sat next to Eddie, whom we called "Bogey." I met Bogey through our father's friendship. They were both auto mechanics. We weighed in and ate whatever we wanted before our weight class, and our names were called up. Bogey was laughing and joking as he always did. He was a very confident and assured competitor.

My time had come, and he encouraged me, as did our coach, to go and pin my competition. I was hyped up by the team and the coach, so full of chocolate and honey that it gave me at least 30 seconds of energy. I ran out, tapped my opponent's fist, and settled into the down position. A minute and 30 seconds later, I looked at the "Ref," who was now raising my arm as the match's victor. I was unsurprised because I had been informed by our coach that my opponent was a "Newbie" and that it was his first match. It wasn't. As I sat down beside Bogey, he congratulated me, and, as he was laughing, he said, "Robinson, that guy won last year's State Championship." I remember his last name was Davis, and he attended Central High School. After that match, we met again at the State Finals. He never pinned me, but beat me on points every game. Larry Williams, whom we call "Santa Claus" (I don't know why), is the older brother of Herbie Williams (NBA and Assistant Coach for the New York

Knicks). Herbie was a few years behind us, and I can recall when no one would call Herbie into a pickup game of basketball on the school grounds. I wasn't a basketball player by any means, but he was young and hadn't yet grown into his height or found his calling until years later. Santa Claus was a great guy, although we weren't close friends except on the wrestling team. I brought him up because the night he and his mother gave me a ride home from a Saturday evening match was late. When Mrs. Williams dropped me off at my house, just a few blocks from the Williams, I was met with a closed door. My stepmother informed me that my father told her not to let me in and to sleep in the car. She handed me a blanket and a pillow. I entered the car, and after waking up with the crying and feeling hurt, I left the vehicle, walked to the Williams' home door, and knocked. Herbie answered the door; I was so full of hurt and shame. Herbie called his mother, and Mrs. Williams took me into their home. Later, I told her my aunt lived just down the road, and I called her. I stayed with my aunt for a couple of weeks before returning home. The topic never came up, nor did my father apologize for kicking me out of the house when he found out that morning that I was attending a wrestling match. As I said, Santa Claus was a great and kind guy. He never asked me about what happened that night, and to my knowledge, neither he nor Herbie mentioned that incident to anyone at school. It may be over fifty years late, but thank you, Santa Claus and Herbie. Your kindness did not fall on unfertile ground.

They could have exposed my dysfunctional life with our classmates for a few laughs at my expense, but that never happened. Talk about having integrity. I didn't realize until years later that it was God who put people like that in my life. Such events like that kept me on the path he had set for me. I thank God for the families I was blessed to know in our village, where we grew up, we call Southfield, in the South End of Columbus, Ohio. Many families like that fostered many neighborhood kids. Those who grew up in the neck of our woods know that it was and still is a blessed village in the South End of Columbus. Sure, some bad things happened, yet I tend to say that more good came out of it than bad. The right path is typically the one that is chosen for us at the very beginning of our creation, and we soon conclude, after we've attempted many other avenues, to accept it. In my prime years, I had taken many decision-making paths towards various endeavors and dreams before I finally accepted what God had planned all along. And knowing he had placed those that I needed to meet as slight little nudges that kept me or put me back on track. Although many were just a moment and then gone, those minuscule moments left indelible marks of empowerment on me. Their wealth of education and knowledge, sound counsel and guidance, shared experiences and talents, desire to encourage, or proclivity to love and motivate me, all were part of God's desire to get me where he needed me to be today, *"Right Where I Am."*

SEX TALK WITH MY SON

Lil' Edwin was 5 years old, and his little sister, Ayrika, whom he later called "Birdie", was in her walker as they watched the Saturday morning cartoons, and this was the norm for our family. Allison or I would ask Lil' Edwin to watch his sister as Mom and Dad "Napped." That morning would be an educational opportunity for our son and me Edwin was always a bright and somewhat wise kid for his age and today he is still pretty knowledgeable in everyday matters. Even now, as an adult, Lil' Edwin is knowledgeable; if you want to converse more broadly with him about anything, you must be well prepared. Just as I wasn't prepared that morning to discuss a significant event that was to transpire, I had to talk to our little man about the virtues of love in the story of "The Birds and Bees." Of course, I thought I had years before addressing this subject. We lived in a two-bedroom home next door to Allison's parents, who owned it. It wasn't the best place to live, but the rent was affordable, and it put a roof over my family's heads. We were in a bad place and needed a home. I could have asked for assistance from my father and possibly rented one of the twenty homes he owned at the time, but everyone knows what that would have entailed. Plus, I heard our father would evict our relatives if they didn't do what he asked. I refused to put my family through that. As a federal employee, I worked the night shift as a computer librarian so that I would arrive home early in the morning. This was on a particular Saturday morning, after I had just finished a Friday night shift. I rushed to the bedroom to get undressed and jumped into bed. I wanted to get a quick morning's sleep so I could get up and do those things I liked: working around the house to make it livable or getting some practice on my music. Yet, that morning was the one Allison had been waiting for, and we needed a little "us time." As I mentioned earlier, one of us had asked Edwin to take care of his sister, and having gone through this routine several times, he knew we'd be up soon. As his Saturdays usually begin, Mom would start preparing his and his little sister's breakfast. I'd come down, joke with him and his sister, and watch the "toons" with them. Again, that morning was special because as Allison and I were taking our "nap," there seemed to be a nose at our bedroom door. As I said, the house provided a roof over my family's heads, but it needed many necessary amenities, like a new roof, windows, floors, plumbing, and electrical repairs. And all the interior doors need knobs. Hence our issue.

At the very least, there were doorknobs on the internal doors and a very apparent peephole where our bedroom door should have had a doorknob. But the rent that the in-laws charged kept us from asking for the repairs. So, we learned to live with them. And through the opening of our door, you guessed it. Lil' Edwin had probably gotten an eyeful of his mother and me trying to get "Some Sleep". I would imagine we were "noisy". I quickly lifted my head, looked at Allison, and asked her, "Did you hear that?" We were both still for a moment. The squeak came again, and I knew it was our door. I whispered to Allison, "I think that's your son". I said, "Lil'l Edwin, is that you?" and he very quietly said, "Yes, sir." I calmly told him to go back downstairs and look after his sister, and Mom and Dad would be coming down soon since we both knew that there was not going to be any more "sleeping" that morning. As Allison and I listened to his little footsteps as he descended the stairs, Allison asked me if I would talk to him or if I wanted her to. Of course, that's one of those wives' questions she already knew the answer to, and she just wanted to see if I'd step up and take charge. So, I gave the reply she desired and dismounted the bed that was beneath her. I quickly grabbed my robe, freshened up, and headed to the living room, where I found our little girl sucking on her binky, watching the quiet television with her big brother, who was dressed in his PJs, house shoes, and handsome robe that he had neatly tied around his small and narrow frame of a body. All he needed was a pipe and a book in hand to read because he looked every bit the part of a young, debonair Hugh Hefner. He was sitting on the edge of the couch, staring directly at the television. I quietly sat beside him. I opened our conversation by putting my arm around him and saying, "Hey, man, how are you doing this morning?" You could tell he had something on his mind, and I knew I had to get to it quickly. This was a delicate moment for both of us, and I didn't want to get it wrong. I was never taught about how and when to talk to my son about sex. So, I was very unprepared, but we were blessed because Lil' Edwin had the mind of a much older and more mature child at his age. For instance, there was an occasion when our paper boy, about 10 or 12, and Edwin was 3 years old. He befriended our son and often stopped by to talk with him.

On one of those days, the little boy was somewhat upset about something, and Allison found the two of them sitting on our small concrete porch, and our son was consoling him. The situation made me think about how my father-in-law would listen to someone explain their predicament. Once I approached Mr. Armstrong with an issue I had with one of Allison's past boyfriends. I was informed on good source that this guy was still "hitting" on her, and he knew we had married. That fool was crying at the ceremony. Anyway, he was telling her that since I was away, a sailor, telling her that I was "fooling around on her", and hinted that she could do the same with him. I talked to Mr. Armstrong about it, and he listened to my problem. After I finished, he said, "I understand, Ervin (I didn't correct him), that you may be upset, but when you see him, don't say anything to him. That monkey will always wonder if you know what he said to "Allie." So, I took his advice and never confronted the guy. I tend to believe whatever our son told his buddy was good information, like his grandfather. So, I knew that I had to be straight in my attempt to discuss what was a touchy subject about sex and what our son had just witnessed through the view from our bedroom door. I continued and asked our son, "What did you see when you were upstairs looking through our door?" He immediately replied without looking at me, in that he probably felt some shame, not moving his focus from the TV, "I saw you playing with mommy's vagina". Wow! I was not prepared for such a straightforward answer and truth. I told him, "Edwin, you don't tell anyone that you saw Daddy playing with your mommy's vagina, what Daddy and Mommy were doing was "Making Love." He parroted what I had just said, and I replied, "Yes, son, we were making love, but you don't tell anyone that either." And He said, "Yes sir." I told our inquisitive son that sometimes mommies and daddies do that. When we asked him to watch his sister, his parents would be making love. And he said, "Yes, sir". I hugged my son, thanked him for the talk, for being such a big man, gave him a dap, and thanked him for watching his little sister. I got them both a snack from the kitchen and told him I was going upstairs to dress and would return to fix breakfast. He asked, "Isn't Mommy going to make breakfast?" I said, Mom was tired and taking a nap. He said, "You're not going to make love?" I smiled and said no and hurried upstairs to give a report to Allison about my talk with our son. She was embarrassed more than I was because it took her a long time to come down those stairs. I don't know if she ever said anything to him about it that day.

Later that day, I purchased a doorknob and fixed the peephole, and I was glad to pay for it out of my pocket. Had I thought to do it earlier, it might have prolonged the premature *"Sex Talk with My Son"*.

MY SIBLINGS

You should have read about my brothers and sisters through some of my stories by now. But I would love to share a more in-depth look at who they are, and like most siblings, we are each individually different, but from the same physical fiber. The first five were of William and Barbara, and the last two were of William and Nathalene. When I say mom, I'm talking about my mother and will acknowledge my stepmother as such. So, many times, when meeting new people, I find it helpful to open a discussion by asking, "Where are you from?" And over the years, I will typically say, "My father and I are the only Hillbillies in our family, the rest of my family are Buckeyes". It gets a laugh. Of course, I go into the story about where we were born. I was born in West Virginia, just like my father, and my mother was born in Ohio, as were all my brothers and sisters. They're Buckeyes. After reading the first part of my book, you know I became a career man and musician. Mychaeltodd, early in his professional life, was coined by us as "Al Monday", from the TV show, "It Takes A Thief". All I will divulge about my brother, Mychaeltodd, is that he was good at his trade at a very early age. His gift, I believe, was gleaned from our mother, who could be intentionally misleading. It was no secret that my wonderful brother, also early in his life, came to embrace who he was as a gay man. I had always accepted my brother and his lifestyle, which was and still is fabulous. When he moved with our mother (years after her divorce from our father), I envied it because, before Michael legally changed his name, although he was my younger brother, he was already free from the life I was living at home. I know we all unfortunately carry traits from our fathers, good and bad. It's just the bad that I believe some of us had more of. I think a few of us lucked out. There was a time, while still living together at home on Moundview Avenue (before our father sent Michael away), Mychaeltodd (same person) and I had some heated confrontations and got into a few scuffles. Still, I believe most were instigated by our stepmother, who had a mean side to her personality. However, she stepped into her role as a mother to five kids, who were not her own. What a task to take on, and on top of it, deal with our father and his malicious behaviors.

I believe our sisters, Sheila and Angie, took after our father's mother, our grandmother, in the kitchen; they both can prepare food that, just looking at and smelling the finished products, could put two or three pounds on a person. What a task to take on, and on top of it, having to deal with our father and his malicious behaviors. She would strongly disagree that she could be somewhat mean, but her behavior towards us, William's kids, was questionable, especially when he favored her sons. My baby sister Angela, whom we call Angie, had issues with me once. Pam and I had been married about two years, and we were invited to Maryland, where Angie and her family live. When she heard I was in town (for only 1 day) and did not stop by to see her, she wrote me the nastiest letter, stating that we may be brother and sister, but we were only related by blood. Of course, I attempted to reach out to explain our trip and lack of time, that it was not deliberate, and that I loved her. She refused to reply. She went as far as to return a Christmas card I had sent her. That was straight out of the book of *"Wild Bill"* because our father did the same thing to me. Once, our father sent me a box full of all the accolades, photos, certificates, and military ribbons and metals that I had sent or that he had collected over the years. Pam opened our front door and told me I had a package from my father on the porch. We had not been communicating at the time. I yelled to Pam, "Don't touch it, it might be a bomb". I was serious because the old man had lied to me by telling family members that I had brought bed bugs to his home. Everybody knows that when William evicted a renter from one of his homes, he kept most of the things left behind. He had clothes and furniture piled up. So, Angie could have very well been following suit with our father. Years passed before we ended that misunderstanding and reconciled our differences on her side. She never apologized for her outrageous letter. The fifth child of William and Barbara was Marc, the baby brother (before our stepbrothers, Tunney and Keith). Like our father, Marc learned the trade and skills of a "Gearhead" (Auto mechanic) and is also good with his hands. However, like our father, Marc dealt with and probably still deals with issues that can flare up if triggered, and no one knows what that trigger may be. And there could be more than one. Even today, it is best to stay away from the trigger. But the primary trigger is alcohol, and there it is. I know that I will probably hit a trigger when he reads or is told about it. I love my brother and have told him repeatedly, as I had with our father, yet I feel it is possibly true about the phrase, "It goes in one ear and out the other".

Then there are my other little brothers, Tunney and Keith. Their mother was Nathelene. They both came later in my life. Just as he and I were reuniting after my return home from the war, Tunney took his life. His death was the first to crack my heart. He was our father's namesake and favorite, a gearhead and the spitting image of Bill Robinson. Tunney had the temper that we could turn on and off like tap water if provoked, and he could escalate it further than most, even his mentor. I heard when I was enlisted and away from home that he blew up someone's car because they had wronged him. You did not want to get on his "Bad Side", which many said about our father, Angie, and Marc. And that did not stop with them. Our other baby brother, Keith, was a bright, intelligent, and athletic child growing up. I don't know where he got his smarts, but he used them well. I want to believe that he peeked at my path when I started in track & field and wrestling, or my enlistments in the military, and saw he could pattern his own. I never talked to my brothers or sisters about going into the military. One of the proudest days of my life was when my baby brother, Keith, who had enlisted in the Army and currently outranked me, traveled with Vice President Dan Quayle from Washington to Bonn, Germany. Staff Sergeant Keith Robinson (has a nice ring to it, uh?) was a Financial Specialist and Advisor to the White House. I was stationed in Hanau, Germany, with my family. Keith contacted me to inform me that he was in the country, and a staff car would bring him to our home. That was a proud moment for me. Later that day, we drove Keith back to Bonn, and my little brother left an impression on me that I'll never forget. He was mature and in control of his life. As he departed our vehicle, he handed me all the German Marks he had left. I only pray that at some point in his life, there was a moment that I, too, impressed him as a man, a father, and his brother. All seven of William Robinson's children excelled at whatever we put our hands or minds to, and to a certain degree, I guess we owe it to him, if it wasn't but learning to be resilient. Like Viola Davis's quote in The Help, I will borrow and paraphrase: "We are smart, we are mostly kind, and we are strong." Sometimes it is said that the best way to influence or show people who you are is not by telling them, but by your actions. I know I have not led a perfect life, but I pray that I have mostly done that, especially leaving footprints in my children's hearts that they would want to follow. I know what I have placed within these pages and paragraphs may cause separation, but I pray it doesn't.

And as much as someone (maybe you) may feel a desire or urge to strike out, I hope you think about it by counting backwards from 100 thousand before saying or doing something that may be regretted.

These last statements contain my experiences, facts, and reasons for documenting and leaving a record for my family and children. They are intended to be preserved and hopefully shared by *"My Siblings"*.

Mychaeltodd, Keith, Angela, Dad, Sheila, Marc, Tunney, and Edwin

Marc, Angela, Edwin, Mom, Sheila, and Michaeltodd

THEY CALL ME MR. ROBINSON

Dad was well known and had many loyal friends who seemed to do anything for him. Although his name was William, he was called Bill or Robbie. But in our home, we mostly heard folks call the people he did business with. His close friends and work associates called him Rob or Robbie. My father was always good with his hands. He was an innovator, and that is where we all got it. He was always found working on something: the home, rebuilding an engine, restoring a car he had bought to turn around and sell, or working on improving our home. He always seemed to have a vehicle for sale and a second job. I remember he had a janitorial business and had a couple of locations where he would buff and wax their floors. I was young, but that was when I learned to handle the powerful buffer. I was a pro at running a buffer when I joined the military. I could easily control it with one hand. I guess I learned a few things from the "Old Man." I was good at watching how things were done. However, I felt that he always had us doing all kinds of work, like gardening, and I thought he benefited from our work. He was always busy doing something, but as I got older, or maybe once I left home because of all the work, I realized the family benefited. We always had food, a roof over our heads, and much more. But again, that was a realization until we grew up and became adults and parents. Benefits like working all day in a local garden where we had to plant vegetables like tomatoes, greens, onions, carrots, beans, potatoes, etc. We grew a lot of food for a few years and sometimes enjoyed the harvests. Our father would take us to an area he had rented or purchased for us to plant and pick once there was a harvest, and while choosing the food, he'd give us a saltshaker for the tomatoes and let us eat as many as we wanted. When I was of driving age, he brought a red 1955 Convertible Thunderbird with a white soft top, and I was allowed to drive it to school. Talk about a Classic, man... I wish he had kept it and let me have it. Of course, I didn't know much about cars then, but I wish I had. Our father seemed to be a mover in every business, and those who would see him respectfully called him Mr. Robinson.

He seemed to draw people, white or black, into his presence, and most of them were businessmen and those with talents that our father could use, such as an electrician or plumber. Our father worked for the sanitation department for a time. He'd bring home some items and repair them, such as power tools. Two items were my sister Sheila's and my first instruments. I got a tenor saxophone, and Sheila got a clarinet. That's where I probably got my zeal for second-hand items. My children would hide whenever we passed a pile of discarded items on the road, as I would slow down to check out the possibilities. Dad also worked for the Ohio Department of Transportation as a truck driver. One summer, the city's big yellow dump trucks arrived on our street and repaved it. Our father was driving one of the trucks, and all the kids saw him and yelled, "That's Mr. Robinson." It was a proud moment for me. Dad would run into folks everywhere, and they all knew him. They'd talk for hours, so it seemed. I was a teenager, and unlike most of the dads on our street, who were military veterans, our father had a sixth-grade education. He was the oldest of eight and had to help support the family. That is one thing no one can say that he didn't do. He was a great supporter. As I think back, I recall we always had food, fruit, and a roof over our heads. We were the first on our street to have air conditioning, a color television, and an addition built onto our home with a two-car garage. Most of the work was done by our father and his friends, who called him Mr. Robinson. I didn't know until years later that he was a self-taught mechanic. I remember Dad had paid one of his trade-taught friends to perform some work. Dad would watch and, most of the time, assist his friend while asking questions. Soon, he had no use for calling folks he knew to do the work, but they were always ready to lend a helping hand if he ran into an issue. Our father was a frugal man, but he was not a cheap man. That was why he had such a reputation as a good businessman. My father had so many projects going on sometimes that I used to make sure that I had something or somewhere to go before he got home from work because if he had something to do, he'd say, "Come on, boy," and that meant my day was over. That happened more times than I wanted on Saturdays. We would jump into his F-150 Ford pickup and head out to the lumber yard, warehouse, or somewhere to get material for his project. He would run into someone who knew him, and they'd talk, it seemed, for hours. Unsurprisingly, he would hear someone shout, "Hey, Mr. Robinson," while in one of those places.

Our father soon started flipping houses, and he never failed. On one of those Saturdays when I didn't want to work, I knew better than to look at my watch cause if he saw me, he'd say, "Got somewhere to be?" Of course, I'd say, "No, Sir!". That is probably why I couldn't wait to leave home and get out on my own. I was an artist, and he couldn't see me doing anything but labor work. Yet my father's experiences with people of all backgrounds showed him a certain respect; sometimes, he could be just as reciprocal. It was then I thought of the role Sydney Portier portrayed in "They

Call Me Mr. Tibbs," and that prompted me to give homage to him; however, it quite possibly is an unconscious tip of the hat to my father and his dad, my grandfather, Carlton James Robinson, who imprinted the family pride in being a Robinson in us all. And why I selfishly had myself inked, tattooed, *"They Call Me Mr. Robinson"*.

TUNNEY'S WELCOME HOME

The family and I had just returned home to Columbus, Ohio, after another stint in the military. This time it was eight long years in the army. We thought we could save money and opted for a "Ditty Move" (moving on your own, using services like U-Haul). That is when you forego the military moving you, packing your household goods, loading them up into a moving trailer, and transporting them all to your Home of Record, and you do it yourself. We made a few dollars from the move, but didn't realize how much time and effort it would take traveling from Fort Hood, Texas. It was well over twelve hours before we hit Louisiana. Traveling through Texas was a bear, especially when we had two vehicles plus one in tow. I drove the U-Haul 12-footer, and Allison drove the car. Both of our vehicles were vans. Although Allison, the kids, and I had done a few of these moves before, none were as rough as this move, nor as long. It took us two days to reach our destination. My discharge orders were cut for my release on March 10, 1995, and we arrived in Ohio on March 12, 1995. We were never so glad to be home again. Yet, we had left behind some good friends, as we had in other posts during my enlistment. Some of which were Fort Lee, Virginia, and Hanau, Germany. Little Edwin and Ayrika also had friends who were "Military Brats" and experienced frequent moves and assignments. And just like our kids, they would probably not see many friends or associates again. As I did in my earlier military stint, we gained some great memories as we experienced our travels in Germany and foreign neighboring countries, like Austria and Switzerland, or throughout Europe. For that, I believe we owe the military gratitude because the education they gained from diverse people and cultures is priceless. The cost of moving from post to post may have at times been hard to swallow for our children because the leaving of good friends behind was outweighed at times by the cultural adjustments we all had to make in becoming used to our new locations and acclimating to the differences that were often very different from what we were used to. However, our children were very adaptable. Mainly because they were young. Little Edwin was thirteen, and Ayrika was ten. They followed me to Germany.

Edwin picked up the native language of Germany within months and was speaking fluently by the time we left Germany. Yes, moving into the military has its pros and cons. But all of that was coming to an end. You see, Mr. Armstrong, my father-in-law, Allison's Dad, had been diagnosed with Alzheimer's Disease. He was now living with his wife, Mrs. Mary Elisabeth Armstrong, who had passed away just a year before. So, Allison wanted to care for her father, and I was ready to leave military life. So, I was at the end of my six-year enlistment, and we decided to go home to Columbus. It was the best feeling when we crossed the West Virginia bridge into Ohio, noticing the "Welcome to Ohio" marquee. And no longer were the kids asking, "Are we there yet?". It wasn't until a couple of months later that I returned home and was united with most of my brothers and sisters at our mother's home. Shelia married an Air Force "Lifer, "Mac. Sheila is a year younger than I, and now lives in Montgomery, Alabama. Michael, 2 years younger than Sheila, was still single. He had lived some twenty years in San Francisco, California, where he ran his hair salon business. He returned to Ohio to live and help with our mother. Angela, my younger sister, was also married. Her husband, Dennis Norman, was an Engineer for one of the nation's leading television companies. Angie, whom we called, had started her own catering business and was doing very well, contacting several television stations. She is 3 years younger than Mike. Then there is Marc Allen. Marc had been married and divorced, but still had a relationship with his ex-wife and their daughter. Marc was a year behind Angie. William was the next youngest, followed by Keith. They had a different mother than we did, but they were our brothers. There wasn't any half-brother stuff. We just had different mothers and the same father. William Dana was named after our father and had also married and divorced, but continued supporting the son he and his ex-wife had. William's nickname was "Tunney". The youngest, Keith, was also married and now has two kids. He had been with one of the nation's leading automobile factories for over 15 years. It was in Tunney, though, that one night and time when most of us were together, that I felt I was home. Tunney and I had taken a short walk outside into the driveway of my mother's home to talk. It was then that Tunney informed me that he had sent me many packages during my deployment to the Persian Gulf War. I had been calling our father back home and thanking him for them.

Although he sometimes funded the packages, it was Tunney who shopped and sent the packages. I thanked him that night, but it wasn't at all what he wanted to talk about. When I left home, he was only 5 or 6 years old, and I had left home without saying goodbye to anyone, except for his mother, my stepmother, "Toni". Nathelene was her given name, but Toni was her nickname. Tunney was hurt because I had left him behind. He and I cried and hugged as I apologized. It was the first time he and I embraced as brothers, and I believe a heavy burden was lifted not just from his shoulders, but mine as well, because it was then realized that I was missed and loved by my little brother, no matter how devilish he could be. We looked around to make sure there weren't any witnesses, wiped our eyes dry, and returned to the mini family reunion that was going on inside. When I think of him, those tears easily return, remembrance of his love, his brotherly embrace, and those special times with my little brother. I'll never forget *"Tunney's Welcome Home"*.

WHERE I BELONGED

I don't know when I started searching for myself as a fixture in this world, but now that I think back on my long journey to find my calling, I can tell you that there was a call in my life, but I did not come into it until I realized it was never my call. It was God's. I remember attending church with my grandparents, who were my mother's parents in Cadiz, Ohio. I was very young, but I remember having to get dressed for church. Back then, you had play clothes, school clothes, and church clothes, which consisted of a black pair of pants, a black suit, a white dress shirt, and a tie. I remember my grandfather was a deacon at the church. He was a stern fellow with very little to say, but when he did, it was like, "When EF Hutton talks, people listen." Our grandmother was a "God Fearing" woman, and I believe she was the first person to plant a seed in my soul about who and why I should know of God's will for me, instilling the importance of knowing who Jesus Christ was in my life. She knew that one day, someone would come along and water it. As I grew up, like many, I was searching for something. I joined the Cub Scouts. I was later a Boy Scout. In school, I joined the band and the choir, and in Junior high school, also. I was involved with Junior Achievement and track & field. And during that time, I was a Paperboy. In high school, I signed up for the wrestling team. I joined the Student Council Board. And during all those things, I was striving to find my place; I was back and forth, attending church as a teen. When I was old enough to be hired, I worked for the local IGA, and still in school, I worked part-time jobs at the Marriott Inn as a Busboy and Dishwasher. In my adult years, between my military stints (Navy and Army), I married and worked various civilian jobs. I was at the Ohio Historical Center for about 2 years, along with my wife at the time, Allison, the photographer in the Village. At the Ohio Historical Center, I received information concerning our grandparents (my father's parents). Their home was listed as part of the Underground Railroad and was eligible for a grant to bring it back to its original appearance, however, they didn't believe the grant was a good thing and it wasn't until years later that my Aunt Donna applied for the funding, and she started the project to restore the exterior to its original. I was still in search of my niche in my career.

I spent about two years at the State Data Center in downtown Columbus, then temporarily worked with Battelle Industries as an Entry Operator. I was still searching for my niche, and before returning to the military, I worked at the DCSC (Defense Construction and Supply Center) Depot. There, I held a few job positions, a Maintenance Worker and a Word Processor, where I developed my typing and proofreading skills. Before re-enlisting in the army, I was in an internship program for Computer Programmers. Yet, I was still jumping from church to church, holding various positions as a member in the choir or band (on saxophones and electric bass guitar), the Minister of Music, Deacon, and Elder. Later, I received my minister's license for Ohio and quickly recognized that it wasn't in my wheelhouse. However, it wasn't until the many significant events that took place in my personal life that I knew that something was waiting for me to do with my life, and that was to give it all over to Jesus Christ, honestly. I was all over the place, and I could go through all of those things that had me there one at a time, like the death of my favorite aunt, who was like a big sister to me, the things I regret, my struggles as a black man in the military, the death of my little brother (who took his life), the act of violence that almost stole our son's life and then his incarceration, my separation after forty years of marriage, the loss of my children's mother, the history with my father before his demise, and the list goes on. The prayers of those believers during all those times kept me. The times I wasn't in the Lord as I should have. When I needed protection, God was there. I know that I was not always in God's life, but he always was in mine. It wasn't until I finally gave up and gave in. I stopped looking for purpose. When I thought I was at my lowest, I gave my life to God as humbly as possible and said, "Here I am, Lord, use me wherever you will." That was when I knew "Only God Can." I found my purpose, a new life, and a new wife. He sent me Pamela Sue Dixon, a praying, devoted woman of God and a person who saw me for what God saw me as: a man of God. I had never tasted human love as sweet as her love for me. Pam often reminds me of when we talked early in our relationship, when I told her that God was first in my life. She teared up when I said that because that was the first thing she had written on her "Husband List of Requirements." And she had wondered to herself, "How many men would say that early into a relationship? He just said it, and I didn't even ask him the question! That was when she knew God had sent me to her.

I vaguely recall the conversation like a man, so I smile and agree. I was the one she'd been praying and waiting for. I made her husband's list. However, I recall telling her, "I'll never get married again." She told me later that she smiled inside when I said that. I guess we both knew then, *"Where I Belonged"*.

MILITARY EXPERIENCES

A SOLDIER'S CHRISTMAS

The date was December 19, 1990, when I was deployed to Saudi Arabia for combat service during Operation Desert Storm in the Persian Gulf War. My family and I were stationed in Hanau, Germany, at Fliegerhorst Kaserne. I was assigned to the 3rd Regiment, 20th Brigade, 42nd Battalion Field Artillery, and Bravo Battery. Because of my family's need for special medical attention, we were not assigned to a company until a hospital with doctors who would be able to address their special concerns and needs as patients. I completed my cross-training in field artillery in July and was shipped to Germany without my family. They soon followed and arrived in Germany the first week of November. Rumors of our being deployed had already reached our company, and orders were published at the end of November. We were to be shipped on December 19th, 1990. Christmas would have to be celebrated before I deployed. I had applied for housing for my family, but we had not been approved yet, so we had to find housing in the economy, which was not cheap. The wall that divided the East Germans from the West had fallen, and the Eastern Germans' search for housing raised the cost of rental, especially for the soldiers. So, it was somewhat expensive, and we didn't have much, but we had each other, as most military families were being deployed abroad and away from their stateside. However, and our children can attest, I was and have always been resourceful because of the German customs of "Junking." The rule was that if they purchased a new item and did not pay more taxes, they would have to rid themselves of the older item. I believe it was because of their rigorous taxation laws. And what was so lovely about how they got rid of those items was that on a specific designated day, they would place those items on the curb for anyone to take for free. The best part of it was – if the item were a shelf or cabinet, which they called a

"Shrunk", they would dismantle, place all the parts, screws, nuts, and bolts in a bag, and neatly stack it all on the curb.

So, before my family arrived, I had found a double rental just below German tenants, and I had outfitted our home. It was home. The first night I ventured out to junk, I was helped by some of the military wives I met who were also junking, and some were veteran Junkers. They were more than pleased to assist me as I informed them that I was being deployed, and my family was due to arrive in a few days. Within a week, I found rugs for all the rooms, a dining room table with chairs, a coffee table, and lamps of various types. I also found creamed colored glass shelving units, curtains, and drapes. I was ready to pick up my family and bring them to their new home away from home. Our van had not been shipped, so I had to rely on a brother, Minister Kenneth Hicks (PM Alan S. Webster #153), whom I had met at a church service and ended up playing with his gospel group. He played the piano, so we had something in common. Of course, that's another story to be told. The most memorable part of being stationed in Germany was the brotherhood between soldiers and their families. We still communicate with families we met while in the service. The date was November 19, 1990, a month before I would ship out on December 19th. So, as we settled in, we knew it would be our first Christmas apart. Money was short, and we had no transportation, but many military families offered to take us to shop for groceries and other essentials. Of course, I had also done some of that before Allison and the kids arrived. Now, back to the resourceful part. Since we didn't have time to decorate a Christmas tree, I thought drawing a picture of a Christmas tree with ornaments and lights would be nice. I persuaded the local German Butcher to give me some brown butcher paper long enough to go from the floor to the top of our ceiling – about 8 feet. We made gifts, and some were purchased for the kids, all placed at the bottom of the drawing. As I said, it was an early Christmas day for us. Still, we attempted to make it a happy occasion because we were together as a family. That Christmas day was over thirty years ago.

I'm sure my children appreciated that time we shared a month before Christmas, before I was deployed on December 19, 1991, to a war that was afoot, and combat that was inevitable and had called me away from my home, my family, and my loved ones, nor knowing if I would return. That was probably the most unforgettable, not the saddest, time as we celebrated a *"Soldier's Christmas."*

DEATH VALLEY

It was a glorious night when I watched from our perimeter and foxholes the bombing of Iraq. We couldn't see the bombers, but we were sure enough to hear them and the dropping of their bombs on Saddam's regime. Now and then, we would notice the sky as if it were lit up from ground attacks that didn't seem to hit anything but the dark clouds that were late at night. Our battalion's mission was to be in place for ground support and ready to move should the command come. We were excited, scared, and nervous, yet we were prepared. Although I was a gunner, I was appointed NCOIC for our Ammo Section, which consisted of six HEMMT cargo carriers and eleven soldiers. I made up our section of twelve, which meant I had two men per vehicle, a driver (A) and an assistant driver (B). We transported a mixture of projectiles, from high-explosive to white phosphorus projectiles, DPICMs, and RAPS, along with various powder bags that were red, white, and green. The colors identified their potential explosive properties. Red burning is the hottest. These were used for our M109 self-propelled 155 mm howitzers, which have since been upgraded to today's M109A6 Paladin. When times were slow, and there was no imminent danger, our team doubled as a supply support team, retrieving and transporting necessary supplies between companies, and we many times supported the whole brigade. The following month after the bombing of Iraq, our team was tasked to travel through Iraq to a SA, Supply Area, to pick up required uniforms, water, and MREs (Meals-Ready-To-Eat). While waiting for the trucks to be loaded, my soldiers and I took our lunch break and sat in the rear of a duce and a half truck. I had removed my Kevlar and web gear that held my canteen, extra ammo cases, first aid case, etc., so I could sit comfortably as we prepared our meals. After we had finished, I turned to reach for my helmet, and it was no longer the green and black camouflage that it was when I set it down. It was now completely black. It was covered with flies. And where we had stopped was in the middle of where our Air Force Bombers had demolished Saddam's soldiers. Bodies covered the area, as did the flies. So, you could understand my hatred for flies. If I hadn't mentioned it, I dislike flies. As I had completed my meal, I had time to walk the perimeter and saw many of the burnt and charred bodies.

Some were burnt and frozen in movement, as you could see a body that had attempted to leave his vehicle and was burnt in the midst of his trying to escape. His arm stretched out, and the door opened with his hand on the doorknob, one leg out of the vehicle pointed toward the ground, the other still on the floorboard of his truck, and his right hand still on the steering wheel. He didn't have a chance. He had to have been hit with the heat from a blast, so that he just died in motion. His truck was split in half; all the tires had melted, and all of the plastic parts of the vehicle. Even some of the metal melted. Can you imagine what it must have felt like to be devastated if the fire was hot enough to melt steel? I saw the body of what looked like a small young man with his right arm raised as if he were trying to reach for safety from the fire. But he was burned beyond recognition. Just as the truck driver froze in place, the stench that accompanied the sight was unforgettable, and there were times when I could still smell it. When something was burnt on our kitchen stove, the sight of smoke, and recently, the scent returned when I was watching a television show where a combat situation was taking place, and a bombing of a small village was taking place. I turned to my wife and asked her if she could smell it. Yell, it's like that. Something you don't forget. You overlook it and hope that it goes away soon. Although these bodies were our enemy, I felt a sense of sorrow for those who may now be missing their loved ones: father, son, brother, uncle, nephew, cousin, or best friend. And just as I was thinking about those mourning their loss, a young American soldier called out my rank, "Hey, Sergeant, come on over and get your picture taken". He had broken off the arm of the soldier I had seen earlier on the ground, reaching for help, and now this soldier was holding his arm in his hand, raising it over his head as if it were a trophy. I immediately said, "HELL NO!", turned quickly to my side, and bent over to discharge my lunch. After I regained my posture, I yelled at the soldier who had his battle buddy take his picture with his arm in hand and stepped on the back of the dead soldier. I told him, "Don't you know that a soldier is someone's father, husband, brother, or son? How can you desecrate that soldier's body?" I didn't know the soldier. He wasn't one of mine, but I told him to get the f**k off that soldier, put his arm down, and get the hell back on your vehicle, that could be one of us, your assholes. As he and his partner were leaving, I shouted, "You f**k'in vultures!"

It was a time when a calmer voice was not suited. I needed to get his attention and a quick and acceptable response. It was then that I wondered why some people were such animals. Where was the compassion for life? Who raised those young men who were now U.S. soldiers and thought it was okay to desecrate the dead of our enemies, take pictures, and then thought it was a great idea to send them home to loved ones? I later found out that many dumbasses were attempting to send such things as hands and unexploded DPICMs (Dual-Purpose Improved Conventional Munitions) home. Experiencing the smell of burnt flesh of mutilated and scattered bodies, and seeing the horrifying images of human parts, was probably one of the most significant events and moments I had on that day in Iraq. However, it wasn't. It was the inhuman act of the two soldiers I encountered, and their disregard for human life. That alone could easily cause a soldier to suffer from PTSD (Post Traumatic Stress Disorder), especially after what I saw in *"Death Valley"*.

THE DOWNBEAT

I was the designated driver for the band on this day. We were scheduled to perform for a High School in Richmond, Virginia. I was the designated driver during this mission. After doing my due diligence in signing for the bus, which I had done so many times when I was scheduled as driver, I did the maintenance on the 44-passenger bus to ensure it was ready for the task of traveling, in operating condition, checking the fluid levels, the air brake, etc. And of course, the vehicle was clean. Usually, the soldier that had signed the car out before me had done that but as in any employment, you have some lazy asses and that day, I had to clean the bus out and take it to the Post Car Wash, which was fit for trucks and buses where you could drive in and wash and spray them down. That took some time, and it made me run a little late getting back to our station, where I knew the band members and commander would be waiting for my arrival to load up and hit the road. I was always good at being on time and never late. This was my first task with this unit. I was the new sergeant to the band and did not need anything to be seen as incapable or unable to handle a task. I was on time with very little time for much else. The band loaded their equipment and instruments, and we were soon on the freeway to Richmond. While whistling and enjoying the drive, I was suddenly hit with some reality. I had forgotten to load my instrument. I had my mind start brainstorming in overdrive mode. A few soldiers drove their vehicles to Richmond, and a few followed the bus. One was an alto saxophonist, James Devine, who was new to the band. He and I are each other as Christians. We performed a dual solo earlier at another school event, playing a jazzy version of "Go Tell It On the Mountain". My thought was to borrow his car and find the nearest music shop or store, rent a sax, and get back to the school where we were to perform before the commander missed me. I parked the bus and ran over to the soldier. He had a station wagon. I quickly told him my predicament and that I desperately needed to use his car. He was very gracious and handed me his keys. I ran to my platoon sergeant, who is also a believer. I explained my issue and what I had planned to do. He gave me his blessings, and I was on my way.

We didn't have smartphones then, so I stopped a student on the stage and asked him if a music store was nearby. Wow, all was going great. He said, "Yes," and told me where it was. I asked someone in their office if they would call the store for me and ask if they had a tenor saxophone that an army band musician could rent for a few hours, since he had left his at his post. The manager said yes, come, and they would have one waiting for me. I had only 45 minutes before the band was to perform. Now, the reason I had to have a horn was if I were to be seating in my chair without my instrument on the down stroke of the commander's baton, I would be found not prepared for duty and written up on an article 15 (a provision in the Uniform Code of Military Justice (UCMJ) that grants commanders the authority to administer non-judicial punishment for minor offenses committed by military personnel). Missing the downbeat fell in the category, so I was safe if I was in my place of duty and prepared to perform. As I stated earlier, I did not need to start my stint off with this band, especially with the commander, who seemed not to like me. Remember, I was only 1 of 5 black band members in a 42-piece band in Virginia. And the commander was a red-headed, bearded white man. I had to deal with red heads of authority throughout my military career. I had a Lieutenant Colonel in the Navy who was a redhead. He gave me grief. Later, I would have two others in my career. One was in Germany, and the other was back home in Ohio. They all had it out for an outspoken black man, me. No, I wasn't one to take everything said to me, about me, or attempted to be done to me, without speaking up and protecting myself, even if no one else would. Sometimes I had black sailors or soldiers who would say, "Rob or Robbie, you ought not say anything, just let it go". But I couldn't, and sometimes it got me in trouble. However, once I knew how to read and comprehend the "Regs" (Military Regulations), they got me out of a lot more than less. Anyway, back to the story. I got to the music store, and at that time, I carried a checkbook (people don't do that much today). I asked how much the store owner would charge, and he told me they usually rent for fifty dollars, but if I leave my ID card, he will return it when I return the horn. However, I was ready to pay anything not to receive an Article 15 for the redhead. Then he asked if I wanted to try it out. I didn't care if the horn played or not as long as I had a horn. I asked for a 2 ½ reed, quickly put it in my mouth, and rubbed it with my tongue to condition it as much as possible.

I jumped in the car and headed back to the school, which was about a ten-minute drive as fast as I could without drawing the attention of a police car. The traffic was clear because school was in, and no buses were slowing it up. I got to the school, pulled the sax from its case, put the neck strap over my neck, hooked the sax, grabbed the mouthpiece and ligature with no time to condition the reed, and ran into the school to the stage as the other band members were all set up. James had set up my chair and music stand. I thanked him for that as I handed him back his keys. I quickly grabbed my music folder while watching the commander's movement, and as he was watching me. He probably was informed of my issue after inquiring about my whereabouts. He looked like he was in a race to get started as fast as possible to start the concert without me. Oh, I wasn't having it. Luckily, the school principal gave me a reprieve as he walked up to the mic stand next to the commander and introduced the band. I could see in the commander's eyes, and as he turned even redder, that he was a bit perturbed. I hurried with music in my hand, sat down, placed my folder on the stand, put the music in order, forced the mouthpiece on the dry cork of the sax's goose neck, and tightened the ligature while setting the reed. I quietly blew the sax to see if I could get a sound out of it to tune the horn, having missed tuning up with the band. I only needed the commander to hear my first note. As he stepped up to the podium, he looked at me with amazement at my prowess, because he knew I was hell-bent on beating him to *"The Downbeat."*

DUTY NOT REWARD

After about 4 months in the Saudi Arabian sands, I had become relatively acclimated to the change of temperatures between daylight and dawn. I had also adapted to the surface of the land with my troops. If you've ever been to a beach and walked or run along the shoreline in the sand, then you're close to knowing what it might feel like. Now, multiply that experience by several months without the pleasure of walking on a hard and stable surface, and then you'd be on the money as to what it felt like for us as we dealt with carrying an addition of any amount of weight from 20-40 lbs. daily. The weather was hot starting around 10 am and getting even hotter throughout the day. It was a shock for many of us who had never been in the desert for such a long time to know what to expect in the early mornings. The temperature would drop drastically by midnight; by early morning, 2 or 3 o'clock, it was a bitter cold of 40 to 50 degrees. I'd sometimes go to sleep in my long johns with my all-weather sleeping bag opened, and by 2:00, I would have to either slip into my uniform or cold-weather jacket. Had I gotten into my extreme cold weather bag, in my long johns or uniform, I'd have to peel them off because the bag kept me at body temperature. Yet, by morning, I reached for my uniform to dress inside my sleeping bag because it was too cold not to come out of it with something warm on. And there didn't seem to be a difference between winter, spring, or summer. It was around March, and the commander approached me. He told me he had a mission for me and needed me to gather six of my men: 3 drivers and three assistant drivers who were licensed and experienced cargo truck drivers. I was also instructed to report for the safety briefing before our departure. When we reported, we were met by a young lieutenant and warrant officer who would lead our mission to the rear to pick up three brand new fuel tankers, have them filled, and return to the brigade. The word was that we were running low on mogas, a type of diesel. I was assigned as the NCOIC (Non-commissioned Officer in Charge) to ensure we got those tankers back to the brigade immediately. After our briefing, we returned to our tents to load up on MREs, water, and one duffel bag that carried our personal needs, such as a change of clothing, etc.

We received our orders at noon, and by dusk, we were on the trail to Port Dumond, where "Tent City" was located and where we had first deployed in preparation for moving forward toward Iraq. The trip was reportedly to take us anywhere from two to three days. If we had any danger or a vehicle failure, we'd make it and our turnaround, making it back within 4-5 days. While the live fire broke out that evening, about 30 minutes to an hour after our departure, the brigade jumped and moved to another location. We did not have that location, and communication became problematic. We were on our own. The young lieutenant and warrant officer were younger than I; however, they oversaw the mission since they were commissioned officers. For the most part, I was in charge of our soldiers from my section, so I never had many problems with them understanding the chain of command. I learned early that if you were put in charge and new to the men you were to lead, there was always one or two who felt they needed to buck the authority. When we realized that the live fire had been announced, the troops started to question my ability to keep calm and challenged my ability to have a plan. I assured them we were on time and on the right track to our destination. I explained that everyone deals with fear differently, and I was just as concerned about our future and the possible outcomes of our mission. I chose the positive, and that appeared to help. We finally reached our destination after about 2 days and a night. One evening, we found an abandoned airport and pulled into Dammam Port, also known as King Abdul Aziz Port. I briefed my soldiers, set up a watch schedule, and then released them to make calls home. There was a hospital nearby that had working phones. I called my family as well. When we returned, I had to "Take One For the Team". The officers did not like that I released the soldiers and felt they needed to reprimand me. I played the part of an apologetic soldier and concurred with their tongue-lashing. They did threaten to write me up or report me, so I apologized and took it. It wasn't necessary, but one of them had it out for me from the beginning of the mission. I was too outspoken and needed to be brought down a peg or two. Okay, I thought it was worth it. The soldiers were happy after speaking to loved ones, which brought my leadership respect. However, I didn't have to since they knew I was for the enlisted and had always looked out for their welfare and never asked them to do something that I couldn't or wouldn't do. But we had nothing else to perform that night, and I made "The Call", which I explained to my superiors.

The case was closed, and all were happy. The following morning, we packed up our gear and travelled to the supply area to sign for the three Fuel Tankers to be filled. Once we filled the tankers, we headed back the way we came. However, we did not know where our people were. As we conveyed over the arid desert sands, we would periodically get communication with an element that might have known our brigade's location, and they would forward it to us. We continued to move with our new information, only to find out that they had jumped again. About 5 or 6 days had passed since we first left our camp, and we ran into a company that put us up for the night as their command attempted to locate our command. The next day, while resting in the GP Large tent, which comfortably housed 30-40 sleeping cots, we were hit by a sandstorm. I was lying in my cot listening to "Baghdad Betty" on the radio and recording a message to my family on a portable cassette recorder they had sent me. Suddenly, we heard shouting about finding the cover and tying down our gear, as there was a sandstorm on the horizon.

Sure enough, as I got up to look over my shoulder and through the net of the tent, the whole horizon was a dark line of wind and sand. Some moved as fast as forty miles an hour. I quickly jumped up along with everyone and ran to the outside of our tent to take down the outside tarp of the tent and make sure the pegs were securely in the ground. Some soldiers made additional sandbags to lay along the bottom of our tents, and some removed clothing they had hung out to dry after washing it. I had my men roll up the windows of our trucks and the Hummer, lay tarps over the front windshields, and secure them with sandbags. I'm not sure how long it took us, but we were all prepared. We had zipped up the tents on both ends and pulled our cots close to the ground so that you could lie between them. And I'm glad I did, along with several others, because our tent came down as the strongest part of the storm hit, and the long beam at the top of the tent fell onto the sleeping cots across from ours. Those who stayed on top of their cots were injured. I believe that there were two with broken legs and one with a broken arm. The storm left us just as fast as it had arrived. And it left its mark behind. The evidence was seen when we inspected our vehicles and noticed that paint was removed from the metal. Loose items had flown across the camp, and many items were outside our perimeter. After we accounted for the vital gear and items, we mounted up and rolled out to rejoin our brigade later that evening.

As we rolled into and through our secured perimeter, Command Sergeant Major Curtis Williams and others of our command met us and said they were glad we made it back safely. And from the CSM's mouth, "We had you guys listed as MIAs". I don't know if that was true or not. Yet, I found out later that our vehicles were all nearly empty or had low fuel levels. If they reported us on the MIA, the experience was such that when I heard those words, I became overwhelmed with fear, although we were home. Missing in action meant we were lost, and they had given up on relocating us. It wasn't until we had redeployed back to Germany that I found out that I had been nominated for the Army's Bronze Star for that mission. And the truth is, I have felt and still do to this day, that I did nothing more than what was expected of me, or any other NCO who cared for their soldiers and the task given to them would have done. We are only as good leaders as those who work with and for us, the soldiers. It's our *"Duty Not Reward"*.

MIA

It was the 3rd of March 1991. I had just sat down to write another letter to my family, as I usually did whenever we had downtime, with no mission or anything pressing to do, until there was a mission and something someone wanted us to do. I had written many letters, and just as soon as I got into writing them, a mission would hit us, something someone decided our team needed to do. And that would entail traveling outside our perimeter for supplies or fuel. So, I had a lot of uncompleted letters, but just as I finished my train of thought on what I wanted to write home about during those times, I would send them out as soon as I found a mail drop. And there had only been a few uncompleted letters to her like these because I usually would complete them and get them off to her and our children, Edwin the second, and Ayrika. It was about 0330 (3:30 am), and I was experiencing some discomfort sleeping from back pain. Of course, my letter mentioned that I missed her and the "kids," which was an ongoing feeling. This day was Friday, on the 22nd of February, and the day that President Bush issued to Saddam Hussein a 24-hour ultimatum that Iraq must withdraw from Kuwait to avoid the start of a ground war. I was tasked with heading up a team to return to Port Dammam, approximately 250-300 miles away, to procure 3 Fuel Tankers full of Mogas (Diesel fuel) for our vehicles running close to empty. About 2 hours after receiving my orders as the Non-Commissioned Officer-in-Charge, we were on the road back to Port Dammam Pier 30. The ground war had started. Our team was on the road, but in imminent danger of live fire. We arrived safely at the port the following morning. It was Saturday. I continued in the letter to my wife, Allison, by telling her that our team consisted of two officers, LT Logan and CW2 Viera, and six subordinate enlisted soldiers: SGT Michael Hamm. I remember his first name because he reminded me of my brother, Michael, before he changed it to

Mychaeltodd. He and I were assigned to the 3rd of the 20th. SPC Law and PFC Weeks (1st of the 27th), SPC Kelly (42nd Bridge Head Quarters), PFC Francis and PFC Folk (2nd of the 22nd), and SPC Welford (the others, I had forgotten and therefore, never wrote them down). I wrote to my wife that we had 6 hours of personal time. That consisted of personal hygiene, changing into clean clothing, or cleaning our uniforms for our return home.

Many soldiers weren't given time to change into a clean uniform before leaving and may have already been wearing their current uniform for a week or more. I had made it a personal choice not to go that long without a bath or changing clothing, especially underwear. That was a pet peeve of mine. You had to keep your sleeping area clean. My superiors, the Lieutenant and the Warrant Officer, informed me that we were not leaving our current location. However, we did have ample time to travel to "Tent City," which was set up for incoming soldiers. Since I was in charge of my soldiers and thought of their welfare as I was trained as a junior NCO, I broke ranks to improve my soldiers' morale, although I was told not to leave our area for any reason. Tent City was about 30-45 miles from Pier 30, our location at Port Dammond Airport. In my letter to Allison, I informed her that once we reached the PX, I attempted to call her, but I could not make a connection, but I did connect with my mother, Barbara Cobb and brother, Michael though and hoped that they would call her to let her know that I was okay, safe, and healthy. In the correspondence to Allison, I admitted that the LT and Warrant were upset with me for leaving the area. It wasn't because we had items to secure, because we had all our personal and sensitive items with us, yet I knew they'd get over it sooner or later once they felt good about chastising me. Yet, they knew that I knew they could call their family members and more than likely find a decent place for some decent chow. So, I didn't feel wrong in caring for my men, knowing that we all wanted to call home and eat something other than the issued MREs (Meals-Ready-To-Eat). We picked up the three new Fuel Tankers and returned to the road at about 1400 that afternoon. As I wrote to Allie, her family nickname, we were all happy about that. Because we were all from various units, we were all in a hurry to get back to our respective companies, which had all jumped (moved to a new location) on the day of the ground war, that Friday, the 22nd of February. Before leaving on our given mission, we all met up at the 42nd Brigade, where we rode out with 2 "Hummers". That Saturday, we departed from Port Dammond. We had no idea where our companies had relocated to, and therefore, for the most part, we were lost. Later that afternoon, we ended up at the 194th Replacement Company and stayed the night and the following day.

I documented in my letter to Allie that my LT and Warrant headed to the TOC (Tent of Command) to try and find out where the 42nd had jumped to and connected with them for further information and directions. They returned, saying no one had any information on the 3rd AD's location, which the 42nd was attached to. However, a day later, we received a message that a Reservist Unit was headed out to meet with a unit with the 3rd AD. So, we tagged along for about 24 hours before we realized that the 50 Tankers and several buses full of reservists, led by three LT Colonels, were also lost. Now, on our 3rd day of not knowing where we were in Iraq, nor where our companies were, we were tired from sleep deprivation coupled with a certain amount of uncertainty. The bad thing was that we were getting low on water, but we were full of fuel, with the 3 Tankers full of 2,500 gallons of JP-4 fuel. We had topped off the tankers that Saturday in port, and it was an all-day event. We took Sunday to recover and prepare for our convoy back to our unit. We left the following Monday. We were all glad to get back on the road. By the time we found where we were in Kuwait, we were near the 3rd AD, the 42nd, and the 3rd of the 20th. The ground war had ceased on the 28th or 29th of February. President Bush declared Kuwait was liberated on the 27th. We had missed the heavy stuff. I wrote, "Praise God!" he planned it that way, and I believe that our convoy was never intended to be a part of it. When we arrived, the Command Sergeant approached me and said, "SGT Robinson, we're glad you guys are back. We had you guys listed as MIA". I never saw the report, but believe they did prepare one the day they lost contact and thought the worst of our demise. Of course, I wasn't about to write that we were missing in action, *"MIA"*.

MILITARY INJUSTICES

After reading through the following paragraphs, you may think these things cannot be true. But they are events that framed my ideas about justice for those of color, like me. However, before I go on, let me tell you that I have always thought that the military is an excellent place for a person, especially a kid right out of high school, to experience. It's not the military I had issues with concerning the color of my skin; it was some of the people in the military who were prejudiced that gave me grief. My first encounter with injustice in the military came from a Petty Officer while I was assigned to the USS Nimitz aircraft carrier. I knew that there were some prejudices among many of the white sailors, but there were just as many whites that I could and did call friends. They saw me as an equal, probably because we grew up in the same economic class or lower, and or the same type of neighborhoods and schools where some whites and blacks got along, much like my high school, where there were just a handful of whites who didn't like their lives, living in predominantly black neighborhoods. We didn't use the term African American until years later. The event that opened my eyes was during an assigned task to assist another fellow sailor to clean the head (restroom), where I realized we needed another sponge. I had told "Sly" Copeland, a shipmate and Homey from Columbus, Ohio, who was assigned to clean the head with me, to inform the Petty Officer where I was, if he asked. I wasn't gone for more than 2-3 minutes. As I returned to the head, the Petty Officer was present, and before I could say a word, he asked me where I had been. I told him that I went to get a sponge, which was still dry and flat as a pancake. That was how new sponges were packed, and once they were hit with water, they would blow up into a large hand sponge. The Petty Officer told me he was writing me up for an Article 15, "Missing from the place of duty, under the Uniform Code of Military Justice (UCMJ). It was a lie! A week later, I found myself in front of the ship's Captain for my first Captain's Mast (small court), where you are brought for judicial punishment. As I stood before the Captain and the Petty Officer who brought me to this stage of my life, I listened to the charges being read by the legal clerk.

I interrupted the clerk and told the captain, "Sir, that is a lie!" He immediately replied, "Shut up!" I endured the rest of the reading and accepted my demise as the captain gave his judgment without allowing me to defend myself against the lie. I received a pay deduction for 6 months and lost one grade. I rendered the curiosity return salute, and at my about-face, I noticed a deliberate smirk from the Petty Officer as he nodded at me. I returned to our sleeping area (Birthing area), where we slept and watched TV, and informed my partners of the outcome. They all knew that the Petty Officer was out for blacks, and I just happened to be the one in his crosshairs that day. The following morning, during our daily training on the Fo'c's'le (also spelled "forecastle), it is the upper deck of a sailing ship forward of the foremast, or, historically, the forward part of a ship with the sailors' living quarters, and it was where the chains are stored and attached to the ship's anchors. I told Harper, a close partner, that I would take that Son-of-a-B!t@h out! And I meant it at that time. A few days had passed, and Harper and I had just returned from morning chow. As we returned to our workstation, we happened to walk by the Petty Officer who lied about me. His back was to us. I managed to get close to his coffee mug and reached for it. Somewhat concerned, Harper grabbed my hand and asked, "Rob, what are you gonna do?" I was surprised because he was the one with a quick temper. I opened my closed hand, which was hiding a Pixy Stick of drain cleaner. I told him, "I'm going to put this in that ass-holes' coffee". I was just a few steps from the cup when I told Harper. I had already opened the package and was about to pour the chemicals into the cup. Harper pulled my arm from the table where the "Cup of Joe" was located. The Petty Officer turned and looked at us and asked, "What are you guys up to?" Harper told him nothing and ushered me away from probably taking that Petty Officer's life. In hindsight, Harper saved two lives that morning. You cannot tell me that God was not watching over me, or that no one was praying for me. So, let me tell you how God was watching out for me. About a year later, I was still on the ship. I ended up in front of the same Captain again. But it was my fault, and I deserved the punishment. I was caught sleeping during "General Quarters", which was punishable under the UCMJ, "Sleeping on Duty". But because I was into my drawing then, I had just drawn a portrait of the Captain with Rear Admiral bars, which he was promoted to before my Captain's Mast.

It just so happened that I handed it to him on my way off the ship as he returned. As we were about to pass each other, I just gave him the rolled-up canvas of his portrait. I did not stop to chat with him, but I kept walking. I wish I had taken a picture of it for my portfolio, but I didn't. It was probably one of the best works I had ever drawn. It was the only one I had ever drawn. During the proceedings, he asked me if I was the sailor who drew his portrait. I replied, "Yes, Sir!". He handed down his judgment and then suspended it. I was told later that he did that because of the drawing I had sent him, and he had it framed and was quite proud of it. I only lost one month's pay reduction and no grade reduction. I was happy. I realized that I had to learn to read and understand the UCMJ. I was a "Deck Ape", a Boatswain Mate, and the work was like hard labor. I knew I had the skills to find a more suitable job, and I did. In the Navy, they called it "Striking" when studying for or applying to a different job or at a different rate. That rate would be Yeoman, or Administrative Clerk. I took a typing course in high school, which paid off. I was typing more than 35 words per minute. That was good, especially for a man. You had to type at least 25 words per minute to pass the Yeoman Test. I soon took the written examination, passed it, and found an OJT position on the ship. I was part of the Deck Department of the Boatswain's Mates, but it was an office job where I learned to type various types of naval documents. I had to utilize my understanding of what I learned from reading the UCMJ. Before taking on the office position, I volunteered as a Look-Out in Operations. We were a team of sailors who stood 24/7 with personal visual equipment outside the ship's bridge in search of oncoming unidentified aircraft and vessels. Seeing a Russian ship with the crossed hammer and sickle on the smokestack was amazing. I was 19 years old. And the only other time I had seen anything Russian was on television. That duty was a 6-month obligation. I imagine the Lieutenant I was working for, CMR Robert Yule, an all-red-headed and bearded Texan, did not know I knew about the 6-month obligation when I requested leave to go home to marry. He declined my request and informed me that I was being sent to fulfill a 6-month volunteer duty as a Mess Cook. Everyone had to do at least one duty in the Mess (Chow Hall, Cook) or Operations. I had already served my obligation.

I located the chapter in the UCMJ that covered the duty and found that I did not have to accept the duty as a volunteer in the Mess Deck because I had satisfied my volunteer duty in Operations. So, I resent my request to the commander, who was mad as hell but approved my request. When I returned and married, he replaced me with a new clerk who had just graduated from the Yeoman course. But it was fate because a month later, I was offered a position in the ship's Legal Department, X-4 Division. I worked and learned the duties of a Legal Clerk and recorded several Captain's Mast – ironic, ah? The Navy was not the only branch of the Armed Forces from which I received injustice from its members, enlisted or commissioned personnel. I re-enlisted years later, back into the United States Army as a Saxophone Player after an enlistment with the 338th Army Reserve Band. Then, into the active-duty band, the 392nd Army Band. My contract for active duty stated, "No Training Required", meaning that I did not have to attend the Army, Navy, or Marine Corps School of Music. I was already a sergeant but was re-enlisted as a PVT; however, I regained my rank within a year because I had time in service and graded over the other privates and some specialists (E-4s). When the time came a year and a half later for me to be promoted to E-5, the commander, another all-red-headed and bearded Warrant Officer, had it in for me. He had done his best to keep me from being promoted before some of his junior Non-Commissioned Officers (NCOs) were waiting to be promoted to E-5. However, I had time in service and grade, which meant that if I met all prerequisites, I would be next in line for promotion. The way that the commander attempted to block my promotion was to document my file with Article 15 of the UCMJ falsely. I knew how to address it from past experiences. Case in point. It was a Friday, and the band had been dismissed except those who had duty, such as the Sergeant of the Guard. I didn't have the duty, so I headed home. Our family had planned to go to the movies or something that evening and did not return to our quarters until late. We didn't have cell phones or pagers then. And we didn't own an answering machine. The following morning, I received a phone call around 11:00 from the Sergeant on duty, and he stated that the commander had him contact all band members on Friday evening to inform us that we had a "Photo Shoot" scheduled at noon. We needed to be there in Dress Blues with instruments.

I told the sergeant to inform the commander that I didn't get the message until that morning, and I'd get there as soon as I could get dressed and obtain my instrument, which was locked up at the band hall. I showed up around 12:15, right after a couple of other band members hadn't gotten the call until early that morning. The following Monday, I was confronted by our section leader, who told me that she was to document my tardiness and write me up for Article 15 of the

UCMJ, "Missing from the appointed place of duty". Knowing the regulations, I requested a Summary Court-Martial, where I would go before the commander's boss, the Colonel, and if found guilty, I would have accepted the punishment. But my section leader had never given me an Initial Counseling on what she expected from me, and could not counsel me without it. I informed the commander and told him that I didn't think the Colonel would like to go through a proceeding about being late for a "Photo Shoot". Oh, I'm sure I was called "A Smart-Ass N*****" behind my back (it wasn't the first time) as I rendered the appropriate military courtesy to the commander as I was dismissed from his office. Yet, I knew my time in the band was short. I was one of only four or five blacks in the band, with about forty-four members. I was right; I was forced to attend the School of Music and later told that I could not re-enlist in the band field, so I had a choice of either the Infantry or Field Artillery. I received my next promotion to Staff Sergeant a year later. I was headed for the Gulf War. Again, I saw it as fate. I received information from the band I had left that the commander had a friend at the School of Music and that I had been lied to about the promotion, but it was too late. But God had plans for me and used those who thought that they were blocking my upward mobility in the military to my blessings. I received a Bronze Star from my deployment to Southwest Asia, Saudi Arabia, Kuwait, Iran, Iraq, and Baghdad. Over the thirty years of military service, I have witnessed various acts of prejudice from mostly those of higher ranking than myself. I can only think of one occasion that a black person stood in my path of upward mobility, but there could have been others. I met many who did not stand for themselves or others. However, I am sure the acts were not specific to any branch. Still, I only served in the Navy and the Army, so I can only speak of those who targeted me.

I am positive that other black sailors and soldiers endured to achieve their set goals toward receiving their retirement, as

I found out as a member of the Ohio Army National Guard. I had heard stories about how prejudiced or racist some members of the Guard were. I learned of those descriptions from service members of the Army Reserves in the 70s, when I was still young and impressionable regarding the ways of military life. Yet, I had some life experiences dealing with them. In 1995, when I was discharged from the active army, I found myself wanting to continue my military career, back in service, but in the Guard. And soon I found out that the stories I heard were true. I re-enlisted in the 122nd Ohio Army National Guard Band, and like many of the military bands, I noticed only a few African American musicians. We were no longer known as Black. Blacks had collectively accepted a new label, bringing our culture from N***** and Coons, to Negros, to Colored, to Blacks, and now to African Americans. However, the Guard, which was born from the Militias, still harbored some of the old stereotypes concerning African Americans and our place in the military. Promotions, let alone selections and exceptions, were still slow. As far as I can remember, blacks have always been exceptional musicians, and it seemed that recruiting high school musicians among blacks was never a concentrated effort for the Recruiting Department. If so, you couldn't prove it with the percentage of black musicians in the bands I was a member of. I was far from an extraordinary musician; however, I held my own because of "My Ear". I learned to play by ear before I could read music, which came hard for me. Many of my counterparts could read circles around me, but most relied heavily on their reading and therefore had difficulty ad-libbing, playing by ear. So, here I was in the Guard band, 1 of 4 or 5 blacks, and the senior African American was a "M-Day" soldier. He worked as a civilian during the week and only drilled with the Guard on scheduled drills. During our annual two-week training, he was the First Sergeant. His full-time civilian job was that of a prison warden. Yet, I didn't see him as an enlisted soldier's soldier. He was more supportive of those in positions of higher offices, and his interest seemed more favorable to those of higher grades, commissions, positions of power, and primarily white. Being raised in a predominantly white neighborhood and school in Circleville might have done him a disservice, which kept him from knowing how white folks saw him, and his being a prison warden didn't help.

He likely never saw that he would never be seen as an equal. And therefore, he took every opportunity to belittle his people to prove he was. Of course, that's my observation of him and his "Napoleon Complex". I came up in the military, learning to care for my soldiers. We were enlisted, and as a leader and a non-commissioned officer, I cared for the welfare of enlisted, not commissioned personnel. They cared for themselves. I was the "Go-Between" and stood up for my soldiers, especially when they were right. I did not see that character in this African American senior enlisted soldier. He was for himself, and it later showed after he retired from the Guard and threw his hat into the Republican political race. To date, I have not found an African American who is a Republican who stands for what is right for our people. He was no different. And why did I face another attempt at injustice in the military? As I stated earlier, I have always believed and said that the army is not a bad place for employment; it's the people you have to deal with who have personal agendas against you. And you can find that person in any other organization, be it your local church, school systems, local or private businesses, etc. Here's the problem I saw and my experience with the 122nd band. As I said, I had been discharged from active duty in the army and re-enlisted with them just weeks after my discharge. I was a Senior NCO with work experience as a Section Leader and Platoon Sergeant. When I reported to the Guard band, I found that I was the senior Staff Sergeant with time in grade and service, which the military used to determine who was put into leadership positions. I confronted the leadership about my being posted as the platoon sergeant and was informed that they would be making changes, but these changes never occurred. Already, I got vibes that I was a troublemaker because I wanted the organization to operate as a military organization and not a "Club-Med". Yet, it was who you knew and hung out with. Just as my opportunity for upward mobility came faster than others when I was in the active-duty band, it came for my chance to advance to E-7 (Sergeant First Class). And again, I met with opposition from the commander, who had his sights on someone other than me to take the First Sergeant slot soon to be open with the retirement of the First Sergeant Warden. The band had just completed a week's tour of Ohio during my first Annual Training with them. The commander gave us a day off, and we were to return the following Sunday to complete our tour of the band throughout Ohio.

I had left my Garrison Cap in my saxophone case, locked in our "Batmobile" (Transport Truck), knowing that I would report early and obtain my horn in case and remove my cap for formation. However, most of the band had reported early, and the commander called the formation early. The truck driver had not shown up, and he had the keys to it. So, all of our instruments were still locked up. I informed my platoon sergeant, first sergeant, and assistant squad leader that I would not be in formation because my garrison cap was locked in the Batmobile, and my assistant squad leader would be accountable for our section. They were satisfied and nodded in agreement. As the commander called the band to formation, I stood alongside the First Sergeant and our Readiness NCO. The commander looked at me and waved his hand to me to enter the formation. I gestured back that I was not in uniform, pointing to my uncovered head. He then vigorously gestured again, insisting firmly that I report to my position as the Squad Leader out of uniform. I quickly marched to my squad as they covered down (moved to make room for me), allowing me to report to the commander. The following Monday, my Platoon Sergeant (Dave Sams) confronted me and stated that he was ordered to write me up for an Article 15 of the UMCJ, for "Not being in the appropriate Uniform". Say, this was too familiar, right? After reading the document of the so-called infraction, I immediately told him that he knew, the First Sergeant knew, and the Commander knew that it was "Bullshit!" and that I wasn't signing the document. And he needed to inform the First Sergeant and commander that I requested a Summary Court Martial for obeying his order to stand in formation out of uniform. Although they didn't require me to sign the bogus charge, they didn't have a leg to stand on because they knew that I had never been given an Initial Counseling (Required) as to what was expected of me as a new member, and a year had passed. Sound familiar? You've heard the saying, "Reading is fundamental." Yeah, well, Documentation is essential." And they had none on me, so those who know me, you guessed it. My dropping the boom on them, requesting the Summary Court Martial, probably had them wondering if they all wanted to confront the Colonel (the commander's boss) on such a bogus charge. They didn't. And I knew my days with the band were numbered. Moments later, the First Sergeant returned and called for me. I reported to him to see what he wanted to discuss.

Of course, I knew what it was about. He asked me why I wasn't signing the counseling statement. I told him that it was bullshit because he knew that I had informed my platoon's Sergeant and him why I could not stand in the formation. And my assistant would stand in my place. They all agreed that it was okay. We were taking "Head Count", ensuring everyone was in attendance to complete our tour. Seeing that I was angry and was not lying down for it, He quietly called me to "At Ease". That was funny because they all were going by first names, and up until then, it had always been informal, not by the book when it came to speaking with subordinates, addressing seniors, or vice versa. So, I said, "Oh, we're playing that now?" I immediately went into parade rest and said, "Yes, First Sergeant". He attempted to address me as his subordinate or dress me down as if he were now the warden. He said what he had to say and left, seeing that I was about to be a real N-word. I followed him just minutes later, giving him time to report to his buddy, the commander, who was currently in his office, adjacent to the Orderly Room (like a waiting room). The Commander, First Sergeant, Readiness NCO, and my Platoon Sergeant were in the office. The First Sergeant was doing all of the talking. I sat outside the closed door but could hear the whole conversation. The First Sergeant told the commander he had me at parade rest like one of his prisoners and read me "The Riot Act". Then, minutes later, he exited the office. I was already standing by the entrance at parade rest and nodded as he passed, saying, "First Sergeant", letting him know I heard the whole conversation. He quickly strolled out of the Orderly Room, not saying a word. The Readiness and Platoon Sergeants exited and informed me that the commander wanted to see me. They closed the door behind them, and I knocked on it 3 times. The commander said, "Enter". I marched in and did a Right-Face pivot toward his desk. I went to a stance of attention and saluted as I said, "Sergeant Robinson, reporting as ordered, Sir!". He said, "Have a seat, Robbie". I sat, and the conversation went that the counseling would not affect my record as if I had agreed to it. I told him in so many words that I still requested the summary if they wanted to charge me for the bullshit, and he knew it was. From that day on, I knew they, the commander and First Sergeant, would be out to destroy me or, at the very least, keep me underfoot, so the brother started making plans.

After I finally made E-7 (Sergeant First Class), I left the band to two other bandsmen whom the First Sergeant and Commander had identified as potential replacements for the current First Sergeant. While enrolled at the School of Music in Little Creek, Virginia, where the three of us attended for points for promotion to E-7, I found halfway through the course that the two soldiers who were fighting for the First Sergeant position had been given notes from a member of the band who had completed the course. One was a graduate of the Conservatory of Music at Capital University, and the other was a music major graduate from Ohio State University. I didn't have a degree then, but I had more promotional points, time in service, and time in grade. All I needed to do was graduate. I didn't have to worry about getting a higher score than the other two. We were in an open-book examination, and I overheard them talking about some notes that they both had, but I could not make out what they were saying, so I asked, "What's that you guys are reading?" And without hesitation, one guy replied, "Oh, they're notes we got before we left the band from someone who had taken this course last year." I looked at them as if they didn't just tell me that they were prepared to pass this course with support from someone in the band. And I wasn't. I told them both to say to that person once they called back about how well they did, and that Robbie said thanks. I'm sure they got the drift. Of course, I wasn't surprised cause the course required that we have conducting experience to pass the course. And during my preparation before attending the school, I knew this and requested from the band commander several times for some "Stick Time" (opportunity to conduct the band) with the band. I didn't care if it was before the concert, jazz, or combo band. And his response was always a denial, yet later. Well, later, I was looking at 2 weeks before the course. So, I asked a good friend, Joyce Robinson, a Music Teacher, Director, and professional pianist and organist. He introduced me to the Music Director at East High School, Mrs. Martin. I informed her of my dilemma and what I needed to pass the course. She set me up with an orchestra chart, introduced me to the band members, and we set up days that I would come in and direct them through the chart. Their band director had deliberately made changes to their charts for me to find and correct. It was a learning experience, and what got me through the course.

I never informed the band commander that I was receiving "Stick-time" elsewhere, but I should not have had to, especially when he allowed my two classmates ample stick-time during our scheduled drill weekends. The piece our class had to direct and correct within ten minutes to graduate from the music school was "The Star-Spangled Banner". I took what I had learned from working with the high school band. I purchased a piece of plexiglass the size of a regular music stand, and I would place it over the chart. As I directed the band, with a red grease pen, I would circle anything that did not sound correct during the performance. Once the score was played, I'd point out the measures and have the sections play their parts to pinpoint the culprit's errors. I had the saxophone section, trumpets, and clarinets, until every section played their parts, until I found the incorrect notes or rhythms. Then I'd play the section to ensure it was corrected. Then I'd start the score over to the end of the chart. That plexiglass was a great idea and a lifesaver. During my final exam as a conductor, I made all the necessary corrections to the chart and successfully directed the band from start to finish without an error. I was informed that I had about 10 seconds to spare. I passed, and when the points came out for promotion to E-7, I was number one among the three. While I was at the School of Music for the Advanced Course, I never let on to the other two that I had no intention of accepting the First Sergeant position in the band. I knew the "Kemosabe" and "Tonto" wanted one of their "Good O'Boys" to take the helm. I believe I had made my statement that they could not break or stop me, and that whatever I put my mind to, I was going to make it, and I did. I transferred without informing the commander and moved on. I accepted a new position as the Senior Enlisted Officer as EO Advisor for the Ohio Guard. That position was once commonly held by commissioned officers only. It was ironic that I was elevated in my military career to the point where I could fight for others' rights to receive equal rights, equipped with knowing how to maneuver around those who sought to block and contain upward mobility opportunities to those of color with their blatant *"Military Injustice"*.

PAYING IT FORWARD

Most people now are aware and understand the meaning when they hear someone say, "Paying it forward", the famed phrase and act that was the plot and title of a movie. As a soldier, I have been the recipient of such gratitude from our nation's citizens, especially during peacetime, when our fellow countrymen and women come together after either a natural or plotted disaster in one of our nation's states, their cities, or at one of our children's schools, etc. During such devastating events, we all understand that no one stands alone, and most Americans seem united. There are no white men or women, black men or women, brown, red, yellow, rich, or poor men and women. We hold each other dear to the fact that we are all Americans. We have become stronger as a nation and are proud patriotic patriots of this land we call the United States of America. Our soldiers are shown this nation's gratitude by folks who once were strangers. When these times come to us, I find myself again answering my obligation to the call to serve in the capacity that I've been trained. I responded to our nation's call to support or defend, never asking why. I say as I did when I served in the Navy, "I, I, Sir, where do you need me?" I answered the call to ship to Lebanon when our ship was part of the mission to rescue civilians in harm's way. I answered the call and deployed during Operation Desert Storm and Shield. I answered the call when our troops were called to Grenada, and our reserve unit was assigned to replace the deploying units at Fort Bragg, North Carolina, until they returned. I and our daughter, PFC Ayrika Robinson, and I answered the call as members of the Ohio Army National Guard when our nation was attacked in New York by the terrorists, who flew two commercial aircraft into our nation's World Trade Center and the Twin Towers, and a third that targeted the Pentagon. They would have us all dead for the privilege to die in their belief that they would be rewarded by their "Maker" with 15 wives.

That was, again, another significant personal event for us all. We all remember where we were or what we were doing at the time the first plane hit the towers. I answered the call and deployed to Mississippi and New Orleans when their state was hit by the devastating storm of Katrina in support of those who found themselves homeless and in need of food, water, shelter, and personal protection from what would be looters.

We paid it forward for our country during our military obligations, sworn duties, given tasks, and appointed missions. Our soldiers, Marines, Sailors, Air Force, and Coast Guard personnel unquestionably have given our nation's states and cities continued unselfish service in protecting and defending the freedoms all American citizens enjoy, whether they've served in the armed forces or not. Now, I said all that to say, it is then that we as Americans show our appreciation to soldiers like me, my daughter, and her husband, who also served in over four deployments to Iraq and now suffer from brain trauma, for our service. During those times of answering the call, I recall that strangers would come up to me if I were in uniform and thank me for my service. They'd attempt to force money into my hands or pockets, and I would say, "Thank you, but no thank you, it was my duty." They felt obligated to pay me for what many of us would do for free if it meant protecting our family and loved ones. And we do it for our country. I've been protecting our way of life for over thirty years. I often took my troops out for lunch and picked up the bill. But this time, Post 9/11 (After the attack on our Twin Towers in New York), we were sitting at our favorite location, eating lunch, and "Shooting the Bull." An elderly couple, I assumed were probably husband and wife, came up to our table and laid a twenty-dollar bill on the table. As usual, I'd thank them and tell them we appreciated the gesture, but it wasn't necessary. However, I gave in, did not argue with them, and accepted their gratitude. They stood over our table, and the wife told us that their son, who was a Marine, was stationed in Germany and was soon to deploy. She said she wanted to pay it forward for him so that someone would likely appreciate his service as we did. I told the soldiers that lunch would be on me again the next day. We, of course, were all touched by the mom's love for her son, and our service as she noticeably fought back her tears. I stood and assured her that their son was in delicate hands and, since I was a praying man, as some of my soldiers were too, that we would keep him in our prayers. I thanked them again, and she hugged me. I shook the husband's hand. He looked me in the eyes. We both nodded, and I saw he, too, was fighting his deep love not just for his son, but for us all. My soldiers were Black, White, Latino, and Latina men and women, and one of my soldiers was Native Indian. I guess you could say that my section represented our nation's melting pot. As they walked off, our table was silent, and I noticed no one was eating.

I said, "Hey, guys, y'all eat up; I'm paying for that food." And as they laughed, I told them we had lunch money for another time. We continued to talk about what had just transpired. It was a great feeling. I told them that whenever I saw a soldier who served in other wars, especially in Vietnam, I made it my mission to thank them for their service and welcome them home. Something that many of them never received for their sacrifices. I have an uncle who served in the Army and was in Vietnam at nineteen. He was severely wounded and hospitalized for over six months. He later shared his story with a group of veterans while we were on an Honor Flight. He said a sniper shot him three times in the back. He received a Purple Heart Award for his wound, but I'm sure he would prefer returning home without being shot. Although he was drafted, I still love and appreciate his answering the call. Many people enjoyed our service, and many merchants, stores, and restaurants also showed

appreciation to our troops by offering discounts on their purchases. Yet, these discounts never last. It seemed patriotism sometimes forgets, and slowly, over time, the accolades and "Thank you for your service" decreased. I asked the store owner at the fast-food store if they offered a military discount. Some places still do, all year round. The other discount trills are gone once the thrill is gone. I recall that in the summer, I had requested a summer vacation from my station in Fort Hood, Texas. My family and I traveled from Texas to Alabama, where my sister, Sheila, her husband, Israel "Mac," and their family lived. Israel, Mac was a lifer Air Force Command Senior Master Sergeant. Then, we traveled to Maryland to visit my wife's oldest sister, Phyllis, and her husband, Willie, and their family. Willie also served in the Air Force. We continued our vacation trip home to Columbus, Ohio. And everywhere we traveled, I wasn't too proud to ask if the restaurant offered a military discount. I was on a tight budget while traveling. We had finally reached Ohio and decided to stop in the Port Clinton (Puttin' Bay) area to have dinner. There were six of us: my wife, two teenage children, and the two foster children we planned to adopt. So, I had a lot of mouths to feed. Once I reached the cash register clerk, I overheard our son say to his sister, "I bet Dad is gonna ask if they have a military discount". I turned to him, laughing, and said, "Yes, I am." The clerk asked if she could help me. I asked her, "Do you offer a military discount?" The young lady looked puzzled and said, "No, sir, we don't".
And it just dawned on me that when I worked for Walmart as the manager of a Class 6 store, Lube Express, I offered the police and fire personnel a 10% discount all year round. So, I asked the young lady, "Tell me, do you offer a discount to the local police or fire department?" To my surprise, she quickly replied, "Yes, sir, we do." Now somewhat miffed, I had to ask, "Why?" And just as quickly, I could see that she was very proud of her answer as she smiled and said, "Because they protect our cities." I let it sink in for a second and

answered her in return, "Well, we protect the country." Already, I held up the line, but I heard some applause from the line behind me. The little girl was frazzled and said she'd have to go and ask the manager. I told her not to worry about it, but maybe she should explain our conversation to her manager as soon as possible. I paid for the six trays, and my family and I found a table to eat our meals. It wasn't long before an older lady approached our table and said that one of her associates had been told I had a question about her. I quickly repeated the conversation and the discrepancy that was practiced in giving discounts to uniformed personnel. She paused and said, "Um, I never thought about it that way". She immediately offered to "Comp" (complimentary) our meals. I told her nicely, thank you, but no thank you; however, if she would "comp" the next military family that came in, that would be satisfactory for me. She agreed and apologized for the oversight of our armed forces and our contribution to protecting our country. I told her that it was our way of paying forward. She smiled and said, "The movie, right?" She was referring to a movie that had come out, titled "Paying It Forward". I said, "Yes." I told the manager it might be a blessing to the next family. She thanked me for my input and insisted we stop in again to ask for her as she handed Allison her business card. Then she walked away. We never passed through again. But I'm sure she kept her word in *"Paying It Forward"*.

POTUS #38

As a band member, I was one of approximately 40 sailors who volunteered and performed aboard the first US Armed Forces nuclear-powered aircraft carrier, the USS NIMITZ. It wasn't exactly what I had envisioned for myself, a volunteer bandsman and still having to work the job, which was being a full-time Boatswain mate, a "Deck Ape" (I wonder who came up with that?), we were called. Nope! I had other loftier goals as a musician, but it was a start. It allowed me to do what I enjoyed doing, playing the saxophone. As a graduate, Class of 1974, from Marion-Franklin Senior High School, a school that had given birth to many successful students pursuing their dreams, I was on a quest to do the same as a musician. Yet, my recruitment from the great state of Ohio was less than pleasing because I was among the many recruits who were lied to about having the opportunity to work in the field of choice and signed a blank check to serve in the United States Navy without representation. It wasn't in the band's corps, but aboard a ship, where the military best thought they needed me. And it was as a Boatswain mate, painter, anchor and chain repairer, ship janitor, "Deck Ape". So, when the message was announced from the ship's announcements that they were looking for shipmates who played instruments and were interested in playing for what would soon become the USS NIMITZ SHIP BAND. I jumped at the chance to get away from the anchor & chains, and the cleaning of bulkheads and decks, to play the sax as I entered the area where auditions were being held. I scanned the room for friendly faces; someone I could relate to. Yes, black faces. There were four of us. Later, I realized that one of the brothers was Hispanic. I remember his name was Juan, and he played drums. The other two were Edward Harper and Ronald Houston, whom I had already met. We were Boatswain mates in the Deck Department, which had four Divisions. We were in the First. So, we bonded not because we were shipmates, but brothers, fellow musicians, and it wasn't long before we became good friends. Harper was from North Carolina, and Houston was from North Dakota. Damn, I told Houston, I didn't know there were any black folks in North Dakota. I don't remember his response, but as far as I can recall, they mainly were flip-it responses.

Harper and I never put too much into Houston's antics because that was Houston, nonchalant about everything, and never took much to heart or seriously. His thing was that he was never around, and someone would ask, 'Where did Houston skate off to?" That name stuck, and we called him "Skate". Houston could get out of waking up in the morning. He had a Chet-sheet (excusal from duty) almost every week, which seemed like every other day. He may have been printing them up, but whatever he was doing to get 'em, he was never around when there was hard work to do. He always found a way to skate out of it legally. However, when it was time to prepare to perform with the band, "Skate" was present with his horn in hand. The ship would have the band flown from the carrier's flight deck in an H-60 helicopter to the port where the boat would dock. We'd form along the port and play as the ship pulled into the pier. It was a great time. The band's director would schedule the band to play in small towns near the ports where we docked. And they were Edinburgh, Scotland, and Portsmouth, England. Later, we'd hit Tunisia, Morocco, Africa, Barcelona, Rota, Spain, Naples, Italy, and Germany. Houston seemed comfortable and at home in new environments, no matter where we ported. Harper, on the other hand, was somewhat more of the primitive type. He was a hunter, and women were his prey. Yes, that phrase might not go over well in today's climate, but he was never short or shy on words or animation in his briefings about how, when, and where he got on with one of his dates. But boy did he pay the price when the following day, from some of his explorations of the native women, aboard or stateside. Let's say that Harper made numerous visits to the clinic for personal examinations, and penicillin was the dose of choice. Yet, Harper was the "Party Guy". He believed in having fun and was never short of it. He was never too serious about "little Shit", as he would say a lot, that's why I remember it. Harper was looking for the next adventure. He later became a cook on board the ship. Houston soon signed up for the printer shop. Now that I think about it, he probably had been printing copies of those requests to be excused from duty. I was their "Go Between Guy". I kept the peace because of both Houston and Harper. They were both stubborn, and neither wanted to give in to the other. Not to say that I didn't have my time with either one of them myself, because I did, mainly with Harper. He and I would get into it, but everyone knew we were friends and expected us to argue, usually.

That was our thing. If you let him, Harper could convince you both that your shoes were left feet. I wasn't one to give in. Some of our shipmates called me "Professor" because I had an excuse for any given cause and was very knowledgeable about specific topics. It might have been because of all of those "Psychology Today" magazines that I had always found reading. I was always looking for the neutral zone. It was probably something I got from my mother, a non-violent parent. I don't recall her ever giving me a beating, but that subject is for another chapter. Well, May 5, 1975, had come about quickly as we had been practicing our parts on the Naval Hymn, The Military Concert, and marches like the "Washington Post", "Hail to The Chief", and of course "Ruffles and Flourishes" for the arrival of the 38th president of the United States, Gerald R. Ford. It was a momentous occasion, and I was proud knowing that my mother would be able to attend the commissioning of our ship as I performed in the band for the president. Little did I know I was accomplishing one of my personal goals: playing in a military band. Playing for the president was "Icing on the Cake". I would later experience performing for three other sitting presidents: Reagan, Carter, and Bush Sr. Did you know that P.O.T.U.S. stood for "The President of the United States?" I didn't until I inquired, and I did the research. It was May 3, 1975, a memorable day at Naval Station Norfolk, Virginia, when our ship, the USS NIMITZ, was commissioned. The sky was clear, the weather was warm, the festivities were grand, my mother was there, and I was dressed in my Topical Whites (all white uniform) and performing for Gerald Rudolph Ford, *"POTUS #38."*

POTUS #44

I was, as usual, running late and needed to obtain my tickets to the rally and my volunteer pass to see who would most likely be the first African American president of the United States. I did not want to miss the opportunity to see him, Barack Obama. The crowd was electrifying, and everyone was on pins and needles in wait to see this "well-spoken" change bringer. I got to the official headquarters for the Vets for Obama, and everyone had left for the rally. I signed in, and the sheriff who was posted for security handed me my volunteer pass, which got me through the security faster and up close to the action where Obama would be coming in, giving me a great chance to shake his hand and possibly get a photo op. The photo op did not pan out, but when he entered the staging area and approached our group of now very impatient supporters, I presented my hand in hopes that he would not overlook it as he shook hands with each of them. As Mr. Obama provided his left hand, I took the opportunity to raise my camera with my free left hand. I gripped his hand and took the shot. Not knowing if I had a good aim or not, but later that day at self-help photo shop, I eagerly awaited to see if the camera would divulge that I did capture that moment that I held the hand of possibility what I had hoped at that time, our first black president, which he was, and served under him as my last Commander and Chief, as member of the armed forces. And I did. I had a picture of Barack Obama with my hand in his. It was a great feeling, and I was proud to share that moment with family and friends, a moment I will never forget. He would be our first African American President, and I had decided to stay in the military until the election process was over. I hoped he would be our first African American Commander-in-Chief. He was sworn in on January 20, 2009. I resigned my commission in March, and I officially retired from the Ohio Army National Guard on October 30, 2009, under the leadership of the First African

American President of the United States, Barack Obama, *"POTUS #44".*

PRIVATE WAYNE HAGWOOD

I joined the United States Navy in July, right out of High School, Marion-Franklin, in Columbus, Ohio, along with friends I later found out had also enlisted in the military. One was Wayne Hagwood. He was on the track team at our junior and senior high schools, as I was. However, Wayne excelled in track and held several records for our school and the city. I later found out that Wayne had joined the Marines. That was like him. He trained hard as a runner, and the Marines seemed to follow his routine in becoming the best. It wasn't until my tour to Barcelona, Spain, that I ran into Wayne. My buddies and I visited the USO club for military personnel. I was standing at the bar, looking out into the main floor where several tables were set up. There sat Wayne in his Dress Blues, as I was in my navy uniform, which we called "Cracker Jacks". I called out his name, and he looked up, laughed, and said, "Edwin Robinson, I heard you had joined the Navy". Wayne grew up just down the road, a few blocks from my aunt's home. My Aunt's brother, my uncle, "Tony", was dating his soon-to-be wife, Fran, who lived closer to Wayne's house. Everyone knew everyone in the South End of Columbus, especially if you lived on the same block, unlike today. No one knows or even attempts to get to know their next-door neighbors today. So, it wasn't hard to believe someone mentioned my enlistment. Although we attended the same schools, I lived further south of Wayne and hadn't heard about his enlistment. I approached his table, and we sat and got comfortable as we asked about others who graduated with us, if they had entered the military, and which branch. As most "Homeys" (someone from the same hometown) would do, we tried to catch up with what was going on at home, depending on who had been home the latest, and what the others were doing that we ran with or participated in sports, track, wrestling, football, band, or basketball with. That was the small talk. We mostly talked about our new wives. We had both just married, and he informed me that he was expecting a child. Little did I know then that he would never see his daughter or wife again. He continued to tell me how much he was enjoying being a Marine.

We compared our duties and training locations, as the hours seemed few, and before we realized, the club was closing – around 11 or 12:00, and it was time for us to say our goodbyes and depart from each other's presence in hopes of seeing each other again. Yet as I stated earlier, that was not to be. As I arrived at my liberty launch to return to my ship, I talked about how that night had been good. Compared to some other ports we had pulled into, where I had spent time alone, I hadn't run into any other hometown friends, especially one in another service branch. About a week or two had passed since that night at the USO Club and on a particular morning as I usually did during chow (eats) or once I had arrived at my workstation, I pulled out my monthly copy of the Naval Times and as I read through the articles, I came upon one that quickly caught my eye. It was a photo of Sailors and Marines searching for fellow members. As they bent over the liberty launch, they were trolling the harbor for survivors where the collision had taken place. Their launch was hit by a Spanish oil freighter. It was titled, "Launch Collision Toll Is 49". I felt sick as I distinctly recall our ship being in Barcelona that night, and Wayne's name came to mind. I quickly read through the paragraph and froze as I read over his name, as another paragraph of Marine casualties started. Of the more than 100 servicemen aboard the launch, he was one of the fatal casualties from the collision. They were headed back to their ships, Guam and the amphibious transport Trenton; I believe Wayne said he was on. I stood in place for some time as everything around me could be seen, but I couldn't hear them. My fingers suddenly went numb and lost their strength to hold onto the paper, and my heart felt heavier than usual as I recalled our conversation and laughter that night at the club. We talked about plans for our futures with our families, our children. I finally lost hold of the paper as my head felt like a spinning top. The ship felt like it had taken a sharp starboard turn, and I felt dizzy as I tried to balance my body on my feet, as my legs began to give way. I had gained my "sea legs" the first day I boarded the ship and had never gotten seasick from the ebbs and flows as the vessel was on an even keel. But that day I did. I was sickened by the reality that my friend was dead, I felt dizzy, and was led to a chair by a sea mate in my department. I believe he was asking me what was wrong, but I couldn't find the words to explain that I couldn't swallow because I couldn't yell or cry out. After all, the pain was too hurtful.

The tears were there, but filled my eyes as if they were behind a dam about to burst through the wall of pain. I had lost a friend and had no one to share those feelings with. No friend or relative who had him in common. So, I remembered him and held onto the article and later the picture of his little girl, Shimell Natasha Hagwood, who had yet to be born. Unknowingly, my wife had become friends with Wayne's wife, Sharon, back in our hometown of Columbus, Ohio. They both worked in the same area, and Allison was a child photographer. She had taken pictures of Wayne's daughter and his wife, who gave us a keepsake photo of Shimell. I put her picture with her dad's information in hopes that one day I could share it with her. And it happened. When search engines and platforms like Facebook were introduced, I was able to find her and send her the information so she could hear and share my story of her brave father, who was a classmate, a comrade, a good friend, and someone remembered, *"Private Wayne Hagwood"*.

RELIEVED

One very hot afternoon, while sitting inside our tent trying to stay cool, I heard my name being summoned by our Captain. "Sergeant Robinson!" I exited the tent and replied, "Yes, Sir, what can I do for you?" He looked frantic and said, "I want you to triple load one of your HEMMITS with the 'Joes' (projectiles) and ride it around the perimeter to see how sturdy the load will travel". By then, my assistant Sergeant and a few of my soldiers arrived to see what the mission was about to be. I was already hot because of the heat; sure, the captain was too. And he probably was also suffering from heatstroke, in that what he was asking about was a suicide mission. We were taught to stack our Joes no more than two high. I said, "Sir, that shit will get someone killed." We had HEs (High Explosive), and White Phosphorus, and we could not stack them together. "I continued to tell him, "Hell no, Sir, I'm not doing that and not going to have one of my soldiers do it. You guys sit over there in your tents thinking of shit that's gonna get one of us killed." He looked at me, turned, and walked away. My sergeant said to me, "Damn Rock, you're gonna get court-martialed for that. I told him that all they could do was send me back home. But once the command heard about that crazy ass-shit he wanted us to do, they'd slap my hand and send me back. They ain't gonna waste time, not during wartime. We laughed and headed back into our tent. The next day was like the days before in the desert sand. The sun was relatively high, the heat was again unbearable, and the humidity was so dry that it was hard to breathe. Even the warmest water would quench the thirst and relieve the driest of cotton mouths, rejuvenating the tongue. Suddenly, we got a call to jump camp, meaning we were about to move out to another location. Of course, we would start packing our equipment and gear before we knew where we were headed. We were told that the captain wanted volunteers. Most of us know that you don't jump up and volunteer for a task, especially during wartime. So, I didn't. However, my Platoon Sergeant approached me and said I was selected to volunteer to assist in a mine sweep of our newest location. Of course, I was not feeling my latest task, and I vocally made it known to those within shouting distance and in a commonly universal language most were familiar with, with vigor. I recall that I shouted out, "Whose dumbass hair-brain idea is this"?

That ain't our f**k'in job, and whoever's idea it is, that Son-of-bitch is suffering from some severe heat damage and is gonna get someone killed". We were all inexperienced soldiers, and the leadership, just as inexperienced, was too impatient to wait for the assigned trained members of the bomb squad to arrive and perform their duties. They forced us (Junior Non-commissioned Officers) to sweep by walking 2 locations shoulder by shoulder, for explosives using hand knives, shovels, poles, sticks, etc., before our companies jumped to that location. It was 30 minutes into the sweep. An explosion went off from the other perimeter - about 100 paces from my stance. I froze in place. Our leadership halted, who had been sitting in the safety of their vehicles while we swept. We all stood quietly in place as if standing on a mine. We watched the smoke and dust rise from just over the man-made mound that separated the two locations. There was silence that seemed to be forever. The bomb team showed up, relieved us after their sweep, and made a path to safety for us to follow off the field. The soldier lived, and the chain of command was *"Relieved"*.

DANGEROUS EXPERIENCES

DAMN UNDERTOW

Up until this family outing, I had faced several life-threatening experiences, not that I was a person who strived for such things then, yet those types of events also seemed to find me, and believe me, I didn't know then. Still, most of them could have seen me in a close-to-dead, if not fatal, predicament. One incident that comes to mind is, to this day, very vivid. I can recall the day I again attempted to show off my swimming skills as I leaped into Hoover Dam late that Saturday afternoon. I was an avid swimmer at the local community pool. So, not ever swimming in a river, lake, or even a creek, I figured it wasn't that much of a difference in swimming in the damn. I was already in shorts, the sun was warm, and I thought the water was too. After I had ensured that my father was looking on, I girded up my courage, ran toward the damn's bank, and plunged into the murky, muddy water with eyes closed. Man, it was colder than I had imagined. As I waded in the water, I turned around to wave at my family. They were yelling, laughing, and cheering me on. I turned and swam out further. Although the water was cold, I didn't want them to think I could do it. Swim out into the deep. Once I arrived where I felt I should stop, I looked into the water. Once I dunked my head with my eyes closed underwater, I opened them, thinking I would view the bottom. It was darkest, and I quickly resurfaced for air. As I did, the safety patrol boat found me and beckoned in a very authoritarian manner, so I withdrew from the water and returned to shore immediately. Not one to disobey the authorities – hell, I was on my way out anyway- I waved as if I was saying okay and turned toward shore and swam like I never swam before. I feared what I didn't see in the water or on the bottom. But I attempted to swim as though I were a pro. I wanted my father and the safety patrol to see that my strokes were smooth, and the kicks were strong, the form of a good swimmer. Relieved, I finally returned to safe shores, the safety of the bank beneath my feet. Looking over my shoulder from where I had just swum, I swam about 50 yards more than I wanted and was glad to be on land. I dried off as I continued to walk toward our picnic table to rejoin the family. When I finally approached the table, there wasn't much said about why I was told to get out of the water, and I believe that my parents saw the boat and heard the bullhorn as the patrolman ordered me out of the water.

I always looked for approval from my father, and that day, I could see that he was happy with my ability, but he didn't say a word. He wasn't a swimmer, and I had swum for a couple of years now and had several ribbons and trophies for my individual and team wins. Of all the awards and ribbons for my accomplishments, my father never attended one race, so I took every opportunity to showcase my talents. Later, after a long, hot day at the park, we packed up the old Ford station wagon, one of many, and headed home. I felt good about the swim, even though I was forced to exit the damn. The conversation on the way home was about how I jumped into Hoover Dam and swam until the police told me to get out. I was proud of it. I was the oldest and, at that time, was the only swimmer in the family. I felt like a hero that day. As we pulled up into the driveway of our home, I woke from the long drive home, during which most of us had fallen asleep. After Dad opened the door, I grabbed a couple of lawn chairs, took them to the back of the house, and was the first to enter. As usual, I hurried to the living room and turned on the television – we didn't have remotes then, so I was the human remote. I dropped to the floor, lying anxiously in front of the television. I was excited about watching a good TV show, but the news was on, and the newscaster was talking about the Hoover Dam. The news reporter was reporting that just hours ago, at the same time I was swimming in the dam, there were two deaths there. Unfortunately, although they were experienced swimmers, the undertow was so strong that it pulled them under and drowned them at the Hoover Dam. I sat up in front of the TV, probably in mild shock. I thought, "I could have been one of those people who drowned at Hoover Dam". I believed that my face showed it. As my mother entered the house, she stared at me; her arms were full of bags with the leftover chips, hot dogs, hamburger buns, and other items from the outing. She laid the bags on the kitchen table without taking her eyes off me and released them. She asked, "What's the matter, Edwin?" as if she knew something was wrong. After that encounter, I know that only a mother can sense when one of her children is in trouble or when something is wrong. Maybe it's that thing they call 'Women's Intuition'. I don't know, anyway, I recall saying, "Nothing", as most children do today when they see that they've done something wrong. Anyway, a pause seemed to last for minutes before I responded. She had just missed the newscast.

Like most kids, I answered questions about our goings on, "Nothing". She hummed and turned toward the kitchen to continue unpacking the bags she had just laid on the table. It wasn't until some years later, as an adult, that I revealed that occasion to my mother, and she remembered that day and said that she thought I looked worried but didn't know why. But I do. I was scared to death by hearing the TV news about the two swimmers' deaths at Hoover Dam. I know I thanked God because I had survived the *"Damn Undertow"*.

MY FRIEND JOE

My first experience with water was at our community watering pool, the Marion-Franklin Recreation Center Swimming Pool. I had just graduated from the sixth grade to the seventh. My friends and I, supposedly best friends, gathered and walked up to the pool. We walked everywhere, unlike the kids today, who drove. Anyway, while at the pool and now in the water, I met a young lady who was probably 4-5 years older than us. She was very friendly, to say the least, and I was the boldest of the group, hoping to prove to them that I was the man. The girl was flirting with all of us, and I was her first victim, and I was glad to be. If you have ever experienced the foreplay in the pools, you know what I attempted to do, what we did (could get away with), and how far I could get. Let's say I could not get out of the water as quickly as I usually did once the whistle was blown to exit the pool for recess. Yep, I was the "Rock of Gibraltar" and "The Man" in the eyes of my male peers. When it was time to leave the pool, the lady wanted to meet me after we left. She disappeared into the girls' side to exit. If there's such a thing, I casually rushed, trying not to show my excitement (mentally and physically) in the boy's locker room. Then I ran through the shower, grabbed my clothes, and threw the lock key at the attendant. I exited the turnstile gate, and she was waiting for me, along with her angered grown-ass man (probably a high school student). He looked like an adult. All I recall is him swinging a short-bladed knife at me. I took my towel, as you've seen on TV during a hand-to-hand fight, and someone suddenly pulled a knife out, and the other took his shirt or jacket off and wrapped it around their forearm. I did that. I didn't know what I was doing, so I ran back into the locker room and asked that the attendant call the police, "There's a guy out there trying to kill me." The attendant said or asked me if I wanted the bat he had picked up, and then handed it to me. I said, "Hell no, I want you to call the police." I stayed inside for a while. Already forgetting about the girl, I peeked around the turnkey gate to see if he and the formed crowd were still there. They were all disbursed. I never saw the police. I exhaled and headed on my long journey home, thinking, "The Close was Clear."

But it wasn't. As I started walking down the road of Lockbourne, still in a panic over what had just transpired, I heard a voice hollering, "I'm gonna kill you, n*****." The voice belonged to the guy running towards me over the hill across the road. I started running, and he was gaining on me. Fortunately, I was in pretty good shape; I ran track and tried out for the Junior High School I would attend if I weren't killed. I also wrestled, but I didn't want to try out any of my takedown moves on this guy. It seems that my feet had made up my mind for me. So, I ran into the street trying to flag down and stop oncoming vehicles, which wouldn't stop. I ran down to the corner gas station at the end of Lockbourne and Groveport Pike. I entered the station's front door and went directly to the phone as if to call someone. I didn't have a dime. The guy caught up with me. He came in and sat down in a chair behind me. I looked at him with the phone to my ear and acted as if I was talking to the police and explaining my situation. I didn't have a dime for the payphone, but he didn't know. He sat with the gun in his lap, hidden by his other hand. He quickly showed it to me and said, "Yeah, n*****, I'm gonna kill your ass." The fear heightened, and I was desperate. As we played the waiting game, I frantically searched for someone to help, and out of the blue, there was a friend, Joe Robinson (no relation). He just happened to be riding on his Stingray bike. Back then, we had the small 24-inch bikes fashioned with butterfly bars, banana seats, colorful streamers, and sometimes a card in the spokes for sound. I stuck my head out of the doorway and yelled, "Hey, Joe." He rode over and said, "What's up, Edwin"? Without saying a word, I jumped onto the back of the banana seat behind him and said, "I'll tell ya later, just go!" I started assisting Joe with paddling on the bike as I helped him steer east on Groveport Pike Road towards our homes. As we sped off, I glanced back for a quick second to see where my assailant was. He was pointing at me and saying something, but I couldn't hear anything. I stuck my tongue out, gave him "The Finger," and quickly returned to my peddling. I don't remember Joe saying anything. I do remember telling him when I thought that we were at a safe distance that if he saw the guy back by the gas station, he had a gun and was going to kill me. I thanked Joe for the lift, and he was more than glad to help, although he probably thought I was out of my mind. I was. I was scared for the very first time in my life of losing my life. I did not venture into the pool for a very long time.

Swimming no longer appealed to me, and my thing for the girls slowed down. To this day, I can remember another "life's enlightening advice" my father once gave me. "Boy, (my father would call me), "Never fight over a woman." I don't recall the content of that conversation, but I remember those words, which rang true that day because they almost got my ass killed. If it hadn't been for Joe, I might not have been able to tell the story about how he saved my life. But I have another thing to tell you about my friend Joe. As I said, Joe and I were not related, but we hung around together. He was probably a year older, but we were all childhood friends, especially when we started to drive, and Joe was a mechanic and loved cars. I had not gotten my license yet, so I was the guy hanging out the window of my best friend's ride, but I wasn't yelling at anyone. Some will get the picture. Joe would give me a lift to or from school, or we would ride around the neighborhood because he was always tinkering with his engine and was very proud of his ingenuity. One summer, while riding around, Joe put on an 8-track. It was the Isleys' "Summer Breeze," and I loved that song. I asked

Joe if I could hold it, but he said he wanted to play it more that day. I took the tape when he dropped me off at home that afternoon. When I returned from school the next day, my stepmother informed me that Joe had stopped by and asked for the 8-track I had "borrowed" from him. Of course, I was worried about our friendship. The next time I saw Joe, he said nothing about the tape. I felt embarrassed, knowing he had retrieved it from my home without telling my stepmother that I had stolen it. I was more ashamed and didn't know how to express it. He never brought the topic up. Years passed when friends told me that Joe was getting married, and I was invited to his bachelor's party. It was mostly just those guys we grew up with in and around our neighborhood: me, the Peppers, and others. I suddenly remember a very embarrassing event when Joe and I were younger. And I had to make it right. So, when I reached Joe's front door that evening of the party, I took a deep breath and knocked. Joe answered the door. You could tell that he was glad to see me. I told him he would come outside to the porch before I came in because I needed to talk to him. Being the Joe most of us knew, a kind-hearted and quiet-type guy, he said, "Okay, Edwin." We sat in the chairs on the porch, and I handed him a cassette tape of the Isley Brothers' "Summer Breeze." I looked at him and told him the story I just told you.

I apologized for stealing his tape and asked for his forgiveness. He immediately said, "I knew you were just borrowing it, Edwin. That's okay, man, come on in the house". He ushered me into his home as if it were yesterday. Joe passed away years later, and I was the only one from our neighborhood who attended his coming-home service. During the service, I shared with his family how he saved my life and who he was to me. As far back as I can remember, he was always "My Friend Joe."

NO FEAR

Looking back on my life's experiences, I recall the saying that black people could not and did not swim. My father and mother weren't swimmers, and that was all I heard on TV and mostly from black and white folks alike, that black people did not swim. Today, with every turn (opportunity), I show them that one black person can. When I was a kid, every summer, the kids in the neighborhood played outdoors, in vacant fields, for a chance to defeat an opposing neighborhood rivalry team in football, kickball, or baseball, and visited the community recreation centers and pools. Of course, in the summer, the pool was the place to be, and I always teamed up with a few friends from our street and headed to the pool as usual. My best friends, the Peppers, Richard, the oldest, David, and the youngest, whom we called "Jamie," were very competitive and were the first to display our swimming abilities. Soon, it was their courage and ability to climb the high dive and demonstrate their diving skills. I was still standing on my tiptoes in the pool's deep end, which was 6 feet, just before it parted into the 12-foot end of the pool, where many swimmers dove into. The 6-foot end was roped off to prevent anyone from entering the deeper end of the pool. I was cautious but curious and wanted to see where my friends were. They challenged me and encouraged me as I watched enviously. The day had come, or should I say, I finally got up the nerve to take the plunge. I was tired of watching my friends dive off the diving boards, including low and high dives. I was confident in my swimming ability, although I had no training or idea of what to do once I was deep in the water. We called it "12-foot", which was the end of the pool. Yet, I had girded up the courage to approach the diving boards. And it wasn't the low board that I went for, it was the high dive. As I ascended the ladder, it seemed to have no end. I could hear my friends egging me on and telling me I had this. That was all the encouragement I needed. I could jump off the high dive and swim out of the deep end to one of the available exit ladders on the side of the pool. As I ascended higher, the encouragement got denser and muddled, and all I heard was the wind blowing across the springboard. I cautiously walked out to peek over its end and into the abyss awaiting me. It was 12 feet of clear, beautiful, ice-cold water, where I could now see the very bottom.

I had stood long enough on the board that my body had dried off and welcomed it to goosebumps and many shivers, which was probably more from the fear of jumping, not drowning, which was not my fear at that time. Suddenly, I heard a whistle as it broke through the silence that had engulfed me with fear. The lifeguard was now urging me to climb down or jump. I now had a line of capable swimmers and divers waiting behind me, and they, too, had started yelling at me, "Jump Already!" I was now in a quagmire, to jump or embrace my embarrassment for my failed attempt. Remember, I was an overachiever, which sometimes got me into trouble. That day was no different. So, I once again approached the end of the board, took a few bounces to look like I knew what I was doing. As I said, I had watched my friends on the dives, and they all would take a few bounces from the board and look good at doing it. I'm sure I wasn't as gracious, but I did it anyway. After the board and I came to a rest, I once again looked over the board, took one big bounce on the board, and jumped. As I hit the water, I quickly continued to sink like a heavyweight to the bottom of the pool. As much as I thought I was trying to get back to the top of the water, I could not reach the surface of the deep end. I remember frantically looking towards the surface and attempting to push myself from the bottom of the pool, which I thought would get me to the surface, but it didn't work, and I was running out of oxygen. The next thing I remembered was the lifeguard who had blown the whistle for me to get out of the pool, but it was too late. I was in deep, and he had to pull me out of the pool and perform the lifesaving procedures. When I came to, I saw the lifeguard bending over me and telling me that I had to stay off the diving boards until I could swim. Yeah, that did happen. My friends were good friends. They did not make fun of me but told me what I had to do to get to the surface: kick my feet and do the "Dog Peddle". The pool had stopped because of my incident, and when recess ended and everyone was allowed back into the pool, I waited for my moment. The moment the lifeguard who rescued me was relieved for a break by another, I took a chance to use what I was now equipped with to get back to the top of what looked like a bottomless chasm from the high dive. I hurried to the high dive. Why not the low dive? I don't know. Maybe I was "Fast Tracking." I figured if I was going to defeat my fear, I had to show that I was fearless and could jump off the high dive and swim my way back to safety.

Again, my friends, who knew me, were not surprised to see me heading towards the dives because I had always been somewhat fearless and had to prove it. I fiercely marched to the high dive. My friends were watching. I climbed the ladder with certainty, tested the bounce with more vigor, and once at the top, before heading out to the end of the board, I waved at the crowd that had built up to watch me sink or swim. As quickly as I climbed the ladder, I gave a powerful bounce before confidently jumping into my awaiting abyss. I hit the water and quickly, before I started to sink, I began to kick with a purpose and used my arms and hands to pull the water down below my body. Yep, I know I looked like a dog swimming, doing the famed "Dog Peddle", my friends had instructed me how to perform. It worked! I hadn't tested it before I took my leap of faith. I was that confident and went with it, and I got to the side of the deep end without incident. I pulled myself up from the ladder on the pool's side and felt a sense of accomplishment. I had conquered, and it was to master the diving techniques. Richard and David were good swimmers and divers, and I admired their diving finesse, which they incorporated into each dive, and their ability to improve their execution as they progressed. And it must be said, although I do not recall the name of the lifeguard who saved my life, he was a young black man, years older than we were, but he was a great diver. The guy was beautiful when he launched from the high dive. And the Peppers started to copy his moves from the diving board, starting on the lower board. We all marveled at his command and skillfulness as he delivered some dives we never learned to master because they looked and probably were dangerous moves. Still, that guy had no fear as he almost made the board bounce so that it would relocate once it rested and had to be relocated. He would gain such a height on the board before he drove off that he had to have had some powerful legs to get the height to perform the dives he did. I thought the guy could have competed or tried out for the Olympics. Richard and David soon moved their act to the high dive, and before long, they were emulating the guy's departure off the board even more gracefully. I was a fan and eager to dive, if not better. As you know, I was very new to the world of swimming. But in time, I joined ranks with the Peppers as a capable and fierce competitor and soon performed impressive dives with the best. I started with the Front Dive Pike, turning it into "The Dolphin." It was a pretty sight when done right.

Then I went on to perfect dives like "The Front One", a "Half Pike", and a "Cut Away". It wasn't long until we welcomed each other to challenge each other with more complex dives. We were all about the competition, and I believe it was a healthy one. And all that while, I was improving my swimming skills, learning how to wade in the water once above the surface. I exchanged the "Dog Peddle" with the breaststroke and exited the twelve-foot pool more confident in my capabilities. I had arrived by conquering my inability to swim because I was always of the mindset of *"No Fear"*.

NOT ONE TO BE BULLIED

I'd say, as kids, that most of us had our share of bullies, at least one that probably could be recalled. I had three. For privacy reasons, we'll call them MB, CT, and FB. For one reason or another, I seemed to have had a bull's eye on my back starting in grade school, as if I were vulnerable. I probably wasn't the most feared person, nor was I someone who had a reason to flex my muscles, but I was never one to back down. Some found that out soon enough. Yet, I thought I was pretty shy and docile when I was younger. However, after a few encounters, I gathered my anger and could protect myself if pushed hard. My first exposure to dealing with a school bully was in grade school with CT, a minister today – "Go Figure". Yet, many of us from our village accepted to follow Christ later in our lives. CT had thought that I had said something about his mother, or chanted the words, "Your Mother", which were fighting words, but I hadn't said such a thing. Yet, he took the opportunity to display his power by telling me that he would be waiting for me after school once the 3:00 bell rang, and damn-it, that clock for once in my life would not slow down as I watched it. What happened to "Watched paint won't dry"? The rest of that day flew by as I worried about how to escape what seemed to be my demise. The only reasonable plan was to run home. And with no shame, I did. In those days, everyone knew where everyone lived, so CT and his entourage of Cronies, those who edged him on, which he didn't need, came looking for me. There was something about CT that he had to show to be feared. I thought he was a bit crazy, and his family had a history of it, so I figured I wouldn't be a mark on his hit list. The crowd stood before our home for a period and soon left. Although I did confront him and told him, "I did not call your mother out". If that was what he heard, I asked him to forgive me, even though I knew I didn't say it. I don't know if my confronting him put him off and shocked him so that he didn't have a good response, but to say, "Okay". We never had bad words between us from that day on. Whatever the problem was, it just seemed to disappear. Years later, while enrolled at Ohio State University, I ran into CT, and he was pushing his self-published book of poems and asked if I could help him. I agreed. After some time, that short-lived relationship ended.

That was in 1978, the last time I saw CT. After all, he was a good guy, maybe just misunderstood, but I credit him for sparking my interest in self-publishing my book of poems, "My Reflections, A Collection of Poems". I later heard CT had accepted Christ and was now ministering. My second experience with a schoolyard bully was in the summer. I found myself on the opposite side of MB in a basketball pick-up game. He was every bit of sex-feet. At that time, he was taller than I was. He could have been only five feet, seven inches. I was short then and only grew to 5'7 for the rest of my life. He was tall for his age, and rumors had it that he had been left behind (failed a few grades), which explained why he seemed to be a bit slow and quick to anger. It was during the summer break. I had just graduated from the 5th to the 6th grade at Clarfield Elementary School, which was located on the corner of Groveport Pike and Clarfield Avenue in the South End of Columbus. I was just a few blocks from our home on Moundview Avenue. Most neighborhood guys had gathered at the school playgrounds for a daily basketball game. My father's brother, Uncle Tony, was with me that day. The school was within walking distance of our homes. Whether we lived on one of the three parallel streets that ran North to South: Clarfield, Moundview, and Augmont. Moundview was between Clarfield and Augmont. Then there was Bluefield Drive and what we called the Southfield communities. And of course, we sometimes had visitors from the Stambaugh area. We all would eventually show up at the court for a chance to be picked to play in the next game. My uncle and I were chosen to play for a team that had just lost two players, who had to answer a call from their homes just over one of the fences that divided the school, probably from theirs, which butted up against their backyards. During the game, as I said, I was on the opposing team from MB and was assigned to check him on his approach to the basket, and I unintentionally "hatched him", fouled him. He immediately dropped the basketball, stepped towards me, and pushed me. He started to swing at me, and in quick response, I held up my guard (my fists) to let him know that I was ready to defend myself. I looked over at my uncle and he told me, "You better Kick his Ass Edwin, or I'll tell William", his brother, my father, "And he and I both will kick your ass." I had no choice but to fight, which was a refining moment because it was probably my first fight.

Fearful of what may happen, my getting my ass kicked more than once, I recall what my brother Michael (Mychaeltodd), a few years younger than me, once told me. He said, "Edwin, you just gotta act like you're crazy and they won't mess with you". I may not have thought of that advice then, but as I looked around, I found a small bicycle frame, picked it up to protect myself from MB's attempts to hit me in the face, and swung it wildly at MB. He probably thought I was crazy. He soon gave up, but not before warning me that he would "Get me". My uncle was proud of me as we climbed the fence to head home, and I was too. Thank you, Mychaeltodd, crazy works. Although I didn't "Kick his ass", I put some fear in him, and I think my uncle approved. I believe MB always had it out for me before that incident. Later that summer, I began boxing at the Thurman Recreation Center and built some confidence. I was so glad I had taken up learning to box because that fall, a classmate approached me after school had let out and informed me that someone was looking for me. I had the distinct feeling that it was MB. As I slowly looked around the corner of our school on my way home, it was. I saw him standing and searching for the crowd of kids and knew he was looking for me. He seemed to be even taller and bigger. That dude was trouble. I had heard that he had been expelled from school, had a truancy problem, and attended a special school for kids with personal issues. Someone told me that he lived at the Marysville Mental Health Department. The guy had some problems, and one of them, he thought, was me. Well, I first sought help from our principal, but he was no help and told me to go home. So, I headed out to my home. The school yard had cleared, and most of the kids had, but right outside the school property, MB was waiting. He ran upon me and, as he approached, swung at me. I pulled my head back, and he missed, probably from knocking me out. It was a "Haymaker." Not moving from my stance, I automatically went into defense mode, and to his surprise, he started to back up. I was no Mohammad Ali, "Smokin' Joe", maybe, because as I slowly and methodically landed blow after blow to his midsection. I could see his whole demeanor changing as he realized that I was no "Pushover", and he was going to have to work if he was to save his "Street Rep" (Reputation). His retreat from my prowess encouraged me, as I kept moving toward him and backing him northward down my street on Moundview Avenue.

Within minutes, a crowd of classmates and neighborhood kids heard about the upcoming event. Some had lingered behind, knowing MB wanted to "Beat me up". Once they heard, others returned to witness what most thought would be my demise. I thought then that I wouldn't back down, and if MB wanted me, he would have to bring it. My friends, who also lived on Moundview, the Peppers, Jones, Halls, Gustus, and others who probably had their own experiences with MB, were all cheering in my corner, which was very encouraging. MB was a notorious neighborhood bully, and I felt I was fighting for our side. I began to throw more blows towards MB. Although he had a good reach for me, he didn't know how to protect himself from my entering into his midsection or from my upper cuts. By the time we rope-a-doped ourselves (both tired) and were close to Pepper's home, Mr. Peppers came out of his home for a moment. I could hear him telling me, "Kick his butt, Edwin". He knew how MB was a bully, and I felt him watching with a sense of pride, as if I were one of his sons. After MB looked as if he wasn't moving any further from his stance or attempting to throw a punch, and neither was I, Mr. Peppers broke us up and told us to go home. MB lived just around the block behind the Peppers on Augmont. As he left for his home, Mr. Peppers patted me on my back, saying, "Good job, Edwin, you did well, now you go home". I thanked him along with his sons, my best friends, Richard, David, and "Jamie", with a couple of "Fives" that later became "High Fives". I was a neighborhood hero that day. MB and I never had words again. That was not my last bout with a bully. Another came when I entered Junior High School with a much smaller and shorter person than I, "FB". It wasn't until years later that I knew what the term "Napoleon Complex" meant. However, looking back, this person suffered from it, and in my life, I have had my share of dealing with various men with that affliction. Back in those days, most families were extensive. It was no different for the three bullies I encountered during my childhood. My family was no different. As I've mentioned, there were ten of us at one time. It wasn't uncommon for a family to have four or more children. It was probably the average in the 50s and up to the 70s. I was told that FB came from a large family, and most of his older brothers were "Bad-Boys", with reputations for fighting, arrests, and incarcerations, which they perceived.

Plus, it was known that they would take up (protect) their baby brother, who started most of his issues with others, mostly someone he probably could not beat on his own. He depended on his brother's history of putting fear in anyone who came up against him. FB used that to his advantage against anyone who would face him or not bow to his every whim. By then, I had decided that I wasn't much of a follower, nor did I care for his company of friends, who probably feared him or his brothers. During recess in the gym one day, we played a pick-up game of basketball. Again, during a basketball game? Maybe that is why I never excelled at the game. I again was chosen to be on the opposite team of the person who would soon be my aggressor and foe. As history would have it, I accidentally scratched FB as we were both going for the loose ball. I recall forcefully snatching the ball from his hold by swinging it from the far right to the far left to take it out of his hands. He didn't like it because I showed that I wasn't fearful and didn't allow him to have the ball, as someone else might have. He may have felt embarrassed as his sideline buddies voiced their opinions about how I stole the ball from him. So, in retaliation, he felt obligated to approach me violently, looking to fight me. I had been training to box, but soon gave it up because I didn't like being hit and settled for wrestling. When FB ran toward me after seeing that he couldn't box me, he grabbed me around my waist, which was a bad move because I just reached over his tiny body from his back and locked my hands up under his chest and lifted him from the floor, which kept him from moving and possibly breathing. All he could do was walk into me, and I carried him around, and I could tell that his breathing was weakened every time I lifted him from his back. While backing up, I still had a tight hold on him. I was dictating where we would move in our dance. I suddenly felt a prick on my backside. I let go of FB, and he was too tired and more than glad to do nothing but walk away, and just in time, as the Assistant Principal showed up. Of course, the code was "No one Snitches". However, as the bell rang for the next class, I felt something warm running down the back of my right thigh and leg. I tucked my right hand down into the right backside of my pants and realized that I had been stabbed. Someone stabbed me with a small pin knife. I mentioned it to the Assistant Principal.

He had the nurse look at it, who told me that it had just broken my skin and that I should probably get a doctor to look at it to get a tetanus shot and possibly stitches. I had a feeling that one of FB's cronies in the crowd stabbed me because, as I turned around when I felt the prick, a couple of them reacted suspiciously. However, I had no proof. So, after that, I watched them, their hands, and my back. I never trusted the guys or FB's other cowardly friends afterward. To this day, I believe I know who did the deed, but never found hard evidence; however, the two I suspected, as I was informed, had "Done Time" some years later for other illegal actions. While I was in the Assistant Principal's office, they called my home, but no one was home, so I was released early to go home. FB never approached me again. I believe it was that day that I gained some respect from the would-be bullies who ran in packs, especially those who ran with FB. Junior High was my defining moment as an independent mind. When I entered Marion-Franklin High School, it was well known that I was *"Not One to Be Bullied."*

SERGEANT'S TIME

I was introduced to "Sergeant's Time" as a Field Artillery soldier in 1990 at Fort Sill, OK. Up until then, I had no idea what Sergeant's Time was. Let me explain. Sergeants' Time is when sergeants (section chiefs) were given a scheduled time to train their soldiers for wartime, typically once a week during the first four hours of the day. That training could include first-aid, combat training, weapons qualification, aircraft or enemy recognition, or time on unit equipment, landlines, etc. Many soldiers, like me, thought this was a waste of time, especially once the information and training material became redundant. After training at Fort Sill, I was deployed to Germany. As a sergeant, I was assigned to a section chief role and was responsible for training my soldiers during Sergeant's Time. Since I had already received training on most of the subjects in the Soldier's Manual at Fort Sill, I was excited to train others in what I had learned. Soon, I began to think, as many other Section Chiefs did, that we didn't need to teach a subject we had already trained on. But we did it anyway. We trained in the same subjects repeatedly. At times, it did become a bit boring to my soldiers. As for me, I knew the subjects well enough that I could instruct without the manual. I attempted to make the training more interesting by doing such things as going into a neighboring community for map reading, playing card games with the deck of aircraft/vehicle recognition cards, and so on. We continued to present the material through the *TASK, STANDARD, and PERFORM* methods prescribed in the Soldier's Manual. Yet, it still seemed that we all tried to get out of Sergeant's Time when it came around or just tried to get through those four hours as painlessly as possible. Several months later, on 19 December 1991, our company (2nd/20th Battalion, Field Artillery, Bravo Battery) was deployed to Saudi Arabia to support Operation Desert Shield, which soon escalated into Desert Storm or the Persian Gulf War.

There was no time for any Sergeant's Time training. During this deployment, I realized Sergeant's Time was a lifesaver. A soldier was injured while lighting a submerged tank heater*. As many know, this type of equipment is dangerous if you don't understand what you're doing...as this soldier found out when he attempted to light the heater and was thrown to the ground when the tank exploded.

There was no fire, but the impact of the explosion was enough to knock the soldier out cold. Nearby soldiers came to his rescue and began CPR (first-aid training from Sergeant's Time). Without stopping to ask for help or to read instructions, they provided immediate aid to the soldier and then got medical assistance. Luckily, it wasn't fatal. He was just bruised. It was later attested by the soldiers who were first on the scene of the accident that the training they had received during Sergeant's Time prepared them for what they had to do during an emergency. They said they never thought about what they should do; they just did it. They were confident in their abilities because they had practiced it countless times before, until it became second nature to them. If it weren't for Sergeant's Time (peacetime training), many soldiers would not have been so prepared for any wartime emergency with quick wartime reactions. Sergeant's Time wasn't just for the soldiers being trained, but also for the trainers. I should know because those soldiers provided first aid to their trainer, me, the injured soldier. I learned the importance of training my soldiers during *"Sergeant's Time"*.

Note: A submerging tank is a Heater Immersion (old type), NSN 4540-00-2666835, that was used to heat water. We used it to heat our MREs (Meals Ready to Eat). It consisted of a 36-inch galvanized trash can filled with water and equipped with a heating element that had to be manually lit. As fuel drips from the heater to another part of the system, you use a match to light it, much like lighting a gas furnace pilot light; however, it is a bit more dangerous.

RACIAL EXPERIENCES

BLACK LIVES MATTER

It was 1970. My sister, Sheila, and I were members of our Junior High School, George C. Beery Choir, under the tutelage of Mrs. Clara Ike. Her husband was a dentist. She was a good-looking black woman, and as I recall, seemed very sure of herself as a person and our choir director. However, there was something that I remember about her, and it was from my young perspective, she carried herself to the point that I thought her to be a little "Uppity", but she was a good person and teacher. Over the years, she and her good friend, a musician, became known only by their first names, Joyce Robinson and Clara. Mrs. Ike had taught our small singing group to sing several gospel songs in preparation to perform at Watkins Elementary during February in celebration of "Black History Week", now known as Black History Month, after being extended through the whole month. Since the elementary school was so close, we had decided to walk to the school. As I recall, the weather was cool and a little damp; however, it was a decent morning for February and still winter. At my age, I can only recall a couple of names other than my sister's and my own. Joe Freeman and Claretta Baker are the only two names I can remember from the group members. As we walked, talked, practiced singing our parts, told jokes, laughed, and just had a good time, we suddenly noticed a white Volkswagen that had now passed us a few times. Soon, it trailed us along the road we were on, Koebel, between Lockbourne Road and Fairwood Avenue, on the South End of Columbus. Racism was present, but not very prevalent. I noticed at least three white guys in a white Volkswagen Beetle who passed us. The driver was the brother of a white girl I knew from one of my classes, Carol Lambert, and his name was John. John was a student at Marion Franklin High School. Marion centered on Koebel Road, which we had just walked past. As the "bug" passed us, the passengers called us N*****s and gave us "The Finger". I remember telling Joe, whom we called "Big Joe," that we needed to protect ourselves, and remember him picking up a large piece of a dead tree branch lying on the roadside. He reminded me of Buford Pusser in the movie "Walking Tall". As Joe picked up the stick, the car returned, and they again shouted profanities and threats.

Joe pounded the stick into his hand, saying he would use it if he had to. The girls with us were as afraid as I was, but I attempted to assure them they would be okay if anything happened. I had by that time had my share of fighting and had been practicing and learning to box and wrestle. I felt that I could take care of myself. Before we knew it, Joe was jumped from behind. The guys in the car had stopped around a corner and doubled back around us as they came up from behind to attack us. I recall Joe swinging his stick as I was struggling with someone holding my arms from behind my back. I soon forced my release, and as Joe and I warded off two white guys from the car, one of the girls and Sheila ran back to the high school entrance for help. By the time a teacher returned with my sister and the other girl, the assailants had left just as fast as they appeared. The teacher, Mrs. Barnett, was my English teacher at the junior high school. Our parents were called, and when our father showed up in 'The White Ghost", our 1954 Ford Country Station Wagon, I felt a sense of relief and protection. He was agitated and concerned, asking obvious questions about what happened, why it happened, who they were, whether we saw or knew who they were, etc. I told the teachers and parents who it was and what type of vehicle they were riding in when they showed up. Soon, Sheila and I got in our car with our father and headed home. As he turned off Lockbourne Road and onto Groveport Road, heading East, towards home, I noticed the Volkswagen ahead of us. It was white and I shouted to our father, "There they are, that's the car that followed us and the boys that jumped us." Immediately, our father excelled and overtook the vehicle ahead of us and threw on the brakes. We stopped in front of the beetle, and it stopped too. Our father grabbed the .22 long rifle that he had thrown in the car. I knew what it was because he and I had practiced shooting in the woods with it. He quickly jumped out of the car and shouted to us, "Come on!". We slowly got out, fearing the worst, and headed towards the Volkswagen, which had suddenly stopped, preventing a rear-end collision with our car. As our father was headed to the driver's side of the car with my sister and me following closely behind him, I could see the driver attempting to quickly roll up his window as he saw our dad with the rifle. But it was too late, our father forced the muzzle of the gun into what was left of the open window, which kept the driver from continuing to close the window.

Our father turned to us and asked, "Is this the guy you saw who jumped you?" Sheila, without hesitation, said, "No, that's not him". She may have saved that white boy's life. I nodded and shook my head negatively, knowing it was. I do not recall the aftermath of that event, but I believe our father either filed a complaint or charges were filed against him. Either way, I remember that the Lamberts soon moved from the neighborhood. Years have passed since that happened. I recently asked my sister if she recalled it, and she had little to no noticeable, clear memory of it as I attempted to refresh her memory. I don't know if our father was charged with his act, yet had he been, he probably would have done some time for pulling a weapon on some young white boys. But they knew as well as their parents that their sons performed the racist act. Our father never questioned Sheila and me about the event again. It seemed to have just disappeared. I do know this. I remember it very clearly because it was among other racist events against me and our people. Recently, we have been shaken and "WOKE" by the nation's current race and racist events of our country, brought on by the racial follies of such foolery like that of the number forty-seventh

POTUS and his following cult. Their visible acts of the nation's justice system's systemic racism were brought to light, thanks to our national media and the movement of *"Black Lives Matter"*.

BROWN PEOPLE CARRY GUNS

I was a manager for Walmart Division VI in Hilliard, Ohio. I was, for a time, the only African American manager with the nation's largest retail store in the Columbus Area. I had just been discharged from the army. I was a student at Franklin University when I received a letter from the unemployment board stating that I was ineligible for unemployment benefits while attending school, which was being paid with my GI Bill. So, I applied for employment with several companies, and Walmart allowed me to receive an income that would provide my family with the lifestyle we had been accustomed to. As I waited to be called to the desk set up for interviewing inside the trailer where they were being held, I asked the other applicants about the positions offered. Since I was a leader in the military as a non-commissioned officer, having held several management positions as a section leader, I was looking for a position in management. Once my name was called, I approached the desk and answered the question about the position I was looking for: management. Quickly, the interviewer replied that they had several management positions in dog food, hardware, and appliances. I knew what that meant. I would manage and be responsible for stocking and setting up a specific retail line within the store, but not manage the store. I began explaining to the young interviewer that I possessed upper management skills and was looking for a position where I would be expected to manage personnel and their work performance. There was another table just behind me, and the interviewer must have heard my conversation and asked that I be sent over to his table. His name was Richard Bird, the District Manager. He interviewed me a couple of times and eventually hired me and two other African Americans, which at the time was not a very accepted practice – I soon found out later as our relationship turned into a friendship. Richard, a white brother and army veteran, had remarkable qualities as a person. He was a Christian, a family man, husband, father, and soon became a good friend. He and his family became outstanding, supportive friends of ours. But I digress. After completing my management training with Walmart, primarily on-the-job training, as a Store Manager for the Lube & Express Division 6 Department, Automotive, I was offered a choice of three stores to manage. I eventually took over the store where I trained in Hilliard.

Fortunately for me, the manager at the store decided to leave for personal reasons and asked me if I'd be interested in taking it. I had been given a store in Indiana, and boy, I was so blessed that the Hilliard store came through. There seemed to be much work at the Indiana store, and I would have to make some critical decisions to work over 100 miles from home. I visited Indiana to meet potential future work associates, and I knew that I would likely have to find an apartment and commute to and from Columbus on my free days. As a salaried position, I had to deal with changing the mindset of the employees at the Indiana store, and I would have been the only black associate at the store if I had taken the job. Plus, I would have had to deal with their having to take instructions from a black manager. Talk about having to change a paradigm. It was 1995, but all the signs and signals were very present, and I was just as aware. My military experience would have assisted me in dealing with the differences, but I didn't want to have to deal with it as I was also leaning into my new work position. So yes, my visit was not received very well. I soon realized that our presence as a manager at a smaller Walmart would be a hard pill for some. You could feel the stigma about blacks was still deeply embedded in many of the surrounding Ohio communities. For instance, during one of our monthly visits to fellow stores in our district during our training, trainees traveled with Richard, our District Manager, to meet & greet. It was Richard's way of introducing the diversity Walmart was talking about within the company. He wanted us to accompany him to see how the other stores were run and to introduce us to our new associates who worked in the other managers' Division 6 Tire & Lube Express Stores. As we sat by the visiting store manager during the morning store briefing, he introduced the associates to some of the changes taking place in the store's security policies, as outlined by the store's security manager. At the time, we were not introduced to the store associates because the manager had a couple of special announcements. Most of them did not know they had visitors in the store. But behind the employee's name tags are color codes assigned to the various store emergencies: red for fire, Adam for a child lost, and Green for someone with a gun. The store manager introduced the security officer and asked everyone to remove the green sticker for someone in the store with a gun and replace it with the brown stickers she had previously passed out.

The meeting was being held in the snack area of the store, which most of today's stores have replaced with McDonald's Stores. Some associates were facing away from where Richard and I, and the store manager, were because of how the tables were set. The other employees were able to see us as we faced up to them. As people began to talk and the question arose as to why the change, a thunderous response said, "Because it's mostly brown people with guns". Immediately, those who noticed and knew that Bill and I were present, the only brown people in the store, gasped. Richard immediately turned to me and said, "Edwin, maybe you might want to respond to that". I agreed with Richard quickly and stood up to respond. The snack area quickly became quiet, and before I could say a word, the young lady who had made the statement turned around and apologized for her insensitive statement. I kindly accepted her apology, but informed her that she was only apologetic because she was caught. She thought that she was in a safe place that accepted such comments or behavior toward brown people. And she probably was. The store manager turned to his visitors and apologized as well. As we broke from the meeting, many associates came to apologize for the young lady's comment. I accepted and reiterated my statement to the young lady about feeling comfortable saying or making such comments. For the rest of the day at that store, I walked around with a toy holster with two pistols strapped around my waist. I assumed some associates may have seen the humor, whereas others probably did not. But if that was the sentiment of the store and their community, at the very least, I had an obligation to give them something to think and dwell on after most of them found the girl's statement about brown people so humorous. They didn't mind me being offended. So, I made them see and feel the shame in how ridiculous it was to believe that only *"Brown People Carry Guns"*.

CHERRY VALLEY

It wasn't a great time at 1353 Moundview Avenue, in our home. Our mother, Barbara, had just received yet another attack from our father, William James, and for good reason, some called him *"Wild Bill"*. And it wasn't long before our mother packed the five of us up and we left Columbus. Our destination was our mother's home in Cadiz, Ohio. There we would live with her parents, so we thought. The five consisted of me, my two sisters Sheila and Angela *"Angie"*, and my brothers Michael *"Mike"* and Marc *"Marcie"*. That time of our life is about as clear as mud, discussed with Sheila and now Mychaeltodd. We probably blocked bits and pieces out because, as I will share with you within these pages, we came from a dysfunctional environment, and I blame both our mother and father. She was a partygoer, and he was a womanizer with a temper. And they did not mix well. This wasn't the start of it all, but let me tell you, I recall a pot of hot beans playing a role during a heated argument, mostly from our father. We were young children and didn't know what it was about or blocked it, nor do I care, but our mother suffered for whatever she did that made our father think that she desired what she received from him. I remember him throwing that pot at our mother as we sat at the dinner table, as did my sister and brother when I inquired to them about that significant event in our lives. It was the last abuse from our father that our mother would take from him. The bad thing about abusive spouses is that their families know how abusive their sons or daughters are or can be, and yet stand by and do nothing about it. This is the shameful part, especially when children are involved. And we were. We were in deep abuse as well. So, as I started to say, we traveled to Cadiz. Sheila recalls us taking a cab to Cadiz. I laughed at the thought and told her we took a cab to the Columbus Union Train Station. So, we both agreed. The Columbus Union Train Station was the first Union Station in the world from 1851 until the last passenger train left Columbus in 1979. Yeah, I will educate some of you as you decide to read on. I'll have to lay some mud now because I don't recall what happened between the train station and when we arrived in Cadiz, who picked us up, what mom had told her parents, etc. We were soon enrolled in Cherry Valley Elementary School, and our uncle, Calvin, was already attending.

He was only a year older than I, born in 1954. He and Mom were both born in Steubenville, Ohio. Calvin was called "Skeet" and was well known, so the kids didn't bother him. But we were new to the area, just having relocated from Columbus, Ohio, which was considered "Up North." Up until the first day I was in school there, I hadn't realized that I was much different from anyone else, even the white kids, because we had white kids at our school in Columbus. But Cherry Valley white kids were different. Uncle Calvin, my sisters and brother, and I were the only black kids in the school. There were no black teachers either. And we were the only black "kids" in our respective classes. We were alone. As I attempted to assimilate into the school, I was made quite aware that I was different. I recall during recess, when we went outside, a group of the kids, boys and girls, gathered around me, pointing at me and chanting, "N*****, N*****" and started running around me as they placed Ivory Soap stickers on my back. I had never been called that by any of the white kids back home until I got older. I was in what you could call culture shock. Their putting the stickers on me was their way of saying I was dirty because I was black. As soon as I removed one sticker, they placed another. This went on during the whole recess period. When recess was over, we returned to our classroom, and I sat in my assigned seat, which was directly in front of the teacher's desk. I now suspect that she purposely posted my desk there so that she could keep an eye on me. Inside, the chatting changed to "Edwin loves Ivory." The "kid" behind me kept reaching over his desk to stick an "Ivory" sticker on my back. They were possibly labels from the Ivory Soap Company since they all said "IVORY" and were shaped like a soap bar. I would hear the laughter, turn around, and then quickly attempt to remove the stickers from my back. That went on throughout the class. And the teacher acted as if it was nothing and took no action. There was a red-headed and freckled-faced boy who sat to my left, and when I looked at him, he called me a n*****! Now, I may not have been called n***** to my face, but I had heard the term before, and it was never in a nice way, and he was nasty when he said it. I immediately gave him the biggest right-handed middle finger as straight as I could and said, "Your Mama's a n*****"! All his freckles enlarged until his face was almost entirely red. As he quickly turned around and faced forward, he threw his right arm and hand up in the air and started waving them wildly to get the elderly teacher's attention.

"Teacher", he said, "That boy called my mama a n******r", forgetting to mention the fact that he had called me a N***** first. The teacher called me up to her desk, and without asking why I had called the freckled-faced boy's mama a n****r, told me to lie across her lap. I reluctantly obeyed and lay over her legs. She commenced to beat my butt with her open bare hand with crippled and deformed fingers. I later realized that she suffered from arthritis. I would guess that she was in her sixties or even seventies. I didn't cry, I just looked at the boy who was now laughing out loud along with the whole class. After she had finished, she ordered me back to my seat. As I think back, I imagine that her poor hand couldn't have taken much of her spanking me because she probably was more on the receiving end of the pain than she thought she was administering to me. The spanking hardly matched the beatings I received from my father or Custer Gregory. Custer Gregory was a hard man, and I later found out that he and our grandmother, Mary Gregory, had adopted our mother and Calvin, but they were blood relatives. They did that back then. I never could get the whole story of who their real parents were. Mom's real father was Emory West, and I know nothing else about him, and neither does my mother, from my inquiries about him. Anyways, my father and Grandpa Gregory could bring the pain. It was probably in the summer when we discovered how evil Grandpa Gregory could be. Mike was accused of starting a nearby field fire. All I remember about that was that the Fire Department showed up, and the town sheriff, friends of the Gregorys, allowed Granddaddy to handle the situation as he saw fit. A good old-fashioned ass whooping was in order. Custer did not play. Mychaeltodd told me he had no recollection of the event but confessed that it could have happened. Grandpa Gregory was furious and went upside Mike's head with the handle of a hammer. He probably thought that was his way of trying to knock some sense into my brother's head. That was Child Abuse, right? We got a lot of that *"Back in the day."* Mike ran away but showed up later. Grandpa Gregory was one of those old-fashioned Country Baptist Deacons. In church, he never smiled, and I don't believe he smiled much anytime. He was a coal miner, worked hard, and was a hunter. He dressed and looked the part. He was also well-known and respected in the community.

I believe my father was afraid of him, and I can never remember seeing them in the same room, let alone having a conversation. There had to be a reason why. Hey, I hope you are still following. I do jump around. Let me get you back on track in my classroom. So, I faked that I was hurt from the spanking, but from the kid's laughter, it hurt a bit inside. As I slowly returned to my seat with my head on my desk, I slowly raised my head towards the freckled-faced boy. I gave him a stare so that he never looked in my direction for the rest of the day, and he hurriedly ran to the school's only bus when the bell rang. I sat at the rear of the bus, where I found Calvin, Sheila, and Mike. I pointed my freckled-face foe out to them and told them what had transpired. Just as I had finished my story, the boy turned around, and without a beat, Michael mouthed to the boy, "Red, your mama's a n*****." Now, what do you want to do?" No one dared speak to Mike, and the whole bus got quiet. We started calling him "Red". Mike talked about what I should have done to Red and what we could do. "Freckled Face" was fortunate that he hadn't called Mike a n*****, because Mike would have probably been taken to jail that day. He was always a little bit more outspoken than the rest of us. Red didn't show up for school the following day. I'm not sure of the time; however, I recall the event where another older, red-headed, freckled-faced teenager bullied me and Mike. And what was with all the redheads? I have had difficulties with red-headed, red-bearded folks in my past. Even as I got older in my military career. I digress, back to the bully. I remember Mike probably taking as much as he could from that white boy and getting the best of him. And he did. It happened on a day I climbed up in an apple tree, as we did many times, and ate from it. Suddenly, I saw Mike running away from the red-headed, freckled-faced teenager. I shouted to Mike, "Come up the tree". As he started climbing the tree, I started picking apples and throwing them toward the boy as he tried to climb the tree after Mike. Mike was fast, and as Mike reached the branch I was perched on, he stood up, hopping up and down, causing apples to fall onto the boy. Then, the best defense I had ever seen and memorable, as I tried to remind Mychaeltodd (Myke). I told him, "You pulled his pants down and peed on the top of the boy's head". We laughed. I explained that as the boy had looked up the tree to see where the apples were falling from to dodge them, Myke started spraying him.

After hitting a few branches, Myke's aim improved as a steady stream splashed into our would-be attacker, and as he tried to look up to see where the water was coming from, he yelled and received a mouthful. Realizing it wasn't water, he quickly released his hold on the tree and fell to the ground on his back. When he recovered, he got up and ran away, cursing us, crying, "I'm gonna kill you n*****s." We laughed, calling him "Piss Face." Myke and I grabbed an apple and ate it on our way home. We later told Calvin. Calvin confronted him later with us and told the boy that if he ever touched one of his nephews, he would have to answer him, which would not be pleasant. We had no more trouble with that kid or any other redheads at Harrison County Hopedale Elementary School again. It was late at night when our mother was out, probably partying with family and friends, but we were home alone. The family members in Cadez were close and loved to get together, go to church, eat and drink, and have a "Ball". So, that night, it wasn't a surprise to us to find out that Mom was going out again. I was the oldest, but it seemed the second person in command was our sister Sheila, who is one year younger than I. She kept us sane while we were in Cadiz. She was the organizer, our cook, and the babysitter. You see, our youngest brother, Marcie, was just a baby. I think he was either 2 or 3 years old. Although there is very little I can recall about our stay in Cadez and attendance at Cherry Valley Elementary, I remember the night our father rescued us from the poverty we were living in. Mike and I would search for and pick wild berries, pick apples, and occasionally fish at a nearby pond for Bluegills. Sheila would prepare them (clean and cook) for dinner. She made blueberry pancakes and biscuits. I don't know where the food came from. Maybe our mother brought some food, but Sheila, for the most part, was the person who ensured we had something to eat. She reminded me of how we would go into our grandparents' garden and steal vegetables. She took care of our baby brother, who to this day denies it happened, but if there is so much that we can't remember, how can he remember that it didn't happen? It's called "Denial" for a reason. We all blocked a lot of our pain and experiences as children. Yet, we survived (play Gloria Gaynor, somebody). So, unbeknownst to anyone, an unscheduled visit from our father as he showed up, life again was about to change.

Mychaeltodd and I talked and tried to rehash what we could recall. He informed me that our father's brother had come with him to take us home.

There were no "Amber Alerts" back then. For years, I had believed it to be one of our father's drinking friends, Mr. Simmy Jackson. But Mychaeltodd assured me that it was our Uncle Jimmy. We also discussed how our memories differ and can be tricky or blocked. I don't know what time it was, but it was dark, and Mom was nowhere to be found. She later informed me that she was working at a local nursing home from 3 to 11 pm. Our father came in, and I believe at that time, we all sensed some sense of relief, a rescue of sorts, and were happy to go home. Yet, I don't remember if any of us were pleased. Probably in shock again. I don't know if we asked where our mother was and if she was coming with us. Our father and Uncle Jimmy packed up very little of anything, wrapped us up in blankets, got us in the car, and we were on the road within minutes back to Columbus. I asked Sheila and Mychaeltodd what they remembered that night. Our memories were all over the place, but one thing was for sure: we remembered the time and reason we left Columbus for Cadez and how we returned to Columbus. Along the way, I recall our father having to stop because Uncle Jimmy had to pee. Our father pulled the car off the road, and Uncle Jimmy jumped out and ran into an open field alongside the road. Soon, a police car pulled up behind our car. Uncle Jimmy shouted something about having to pee and then saying "officer". I don't remember much more. But I distinctly remember passing what seemed to be a long brick wall, which always reminded me of getting close to Granddaddy's and Grandma's home. And soon we were there, at 1032 Bryden Road, in Columbus. You have just read my siblings' and my memories of what we collectively recalled living in *"Cherry Valley"*.

DON'T CALL ME BOY

I was a grown man when I had the unfortunate opportunity to experience what I'm sure was prevalent during my grandfather's time. Knowing him, I could not see him being called a boy as a grown man. I was re-enlisted into the Army at 32 after 8 years in the Army Reserves. I had to take a grade deduction to go back in, so I was informed, and I did. The military had offered the medical benefits my family needed at the time. I had already performed in the Navy as a saxophonist aboard the USS NIMITZ in the ship's band for two and a half years and six years in the Reserve Band. So, it was natural that I went back into the band field. I flew out of Columbus, leaving my wife and two children behind until our family came up on the Family Housing Listing for Military Housing. And I was informed that it would take 3 to 6 months. During that time, I would stay in the barracks where most of the single band members lived. The atmosphere was much like that of a college dorm. Many of the evenings were wild, and since we were musicians, the dedicated ones would be practicing. You could hear soloing being transcribed from a boom-box – it was the 80s, a trumpeter ripping a high C, a flute rolling through a few flutters, and either an alto sax player sight-reading from the Charlie Parker Omni Book or a clarinet player attempting to play the intro to George Gershwin's "Rhapsody In Blues". I made myself known as much as I could. The band was predominantly white and remained predominantly white most of the time. I was in the Fort Lee, Virginia, 392nd Army Band. The blacks we had most when I was a member were about 5 or 6 of a 44-piece band. It has been over 25 years, and I've kept in touch with Bob Burford and his family and James Mullins, who ended up performing with the West Point Band. James was the youngest of us, and once my family arrived, my wife, Allison, and I took James in as a friend, and he had a place to visit. Bob and his wife Brenda were the same. Once I met

James and introduced myself, I could tell he had lived a sheltered life in Mississippi. He lived and was raised by his grandmother. He showed up in a brand-new Honda sports car, a vehicle most senior NCOs and some officers couldn't afford. James was 19 years old and straight out of high school.

And he had little experience dealing with the socialites of racism, as I was very aware of. And I felt it my duty as his senior and friend to let him know how it was in Virginia because folks at that time seemed to act as if blacks were to be subservient to their needs. I was so bad that even some black folks treated other blacks poorly, as if to show the whites that they had nothing to worry about because they were handling it for them. I experienced that firsthand the first weekend my family arrived, and we were asked to attend the base church outing by one of the senior NCOs in the band, Hilberto Rodrigues, and his wife, Roberta, and family. They had a son and daughter like us, who were about the same age, so we attended. They were both trombone players. Hilberto was the only Hispanic in the band. We arrived at the large tent set up and found that Hilberto had held a place for our family, and we sat with them. Hilberto and I introduced our wives and children. We were eventually informed that we would approach the serving table, where we would be served by the commanding staff, consisting of the base commander, the Command Sergeant Major, and his wife. They were black, and it was nice to see a black man in such a position, which was still a feat for us. As we passed the various pots and plates of food provided and served, Allison and I got to the Sergeant Major for our portion of ribs. Hilberto and I were behind our wives as they talked and got to know each other. I hadn't noticed, but Roberta was given a more significant portion than my wife, and I was given a smaller portion than Hilberto. Allison was behind Roberta. I was behind Allison and in front of Hilberto. Hilberto stopped the Sergeant Major and asked him to give Allison and me larger pieces of ribs, as he gave them to his wife and the others ahead of her, who were white. If you could have seen the expression on the Sergeant Major's face, you would have thought he was having a coronary. As we returned to our table, Hilberto told Allison and me that we had to watch people like him because he showed favoritism to those who were not black. Although the army had many bi-racial marriages and couples, Virginia residents still were behind the times and slow to change. Allison and I thanked them for the education. I soon found myself educating a fellow band member about our cultural differences and what was accepted in my neighborhood, instead of his.

You see, this soldier had a habit, and I wouldn't say it was nice because it was an accepted habit he learned from his neighborhood, among his family and friends.

And that habit was using the term "boy" when speaking to someone. I don't know if it was to everyone; however, if you're a black man, especially one who grew up before the "Baby Boomer" era or even after it, you know what nappy hair on your head that term raises. So, I waited for an opportunity to address my concern with the young man, about 19 or 20. That day came as we were scheduled to perform at a local high school and would travel in a chartered bus for the event. I sat by the young man after a few minutes into the trip. I soon told him that I wanted to share a feeling with him. Although I was giving him the benefit of the doubt, he probably never meant it the way I was about to explain why I didn't like to be addressed as a boy. I wanted him first to hear my explanation before he responded. I told him about what my grandfather had to deal with as a grown man and some white men desiring to treat my father as a boy when he was a man, and that he could from that day we were aboard that bus, he could address me as Specialist (E-4) Robinson,

Ed, or just Robinson but "boy" was not my title and I would not be accepted it and strongly recommended that he did not use that label with me. Because it offended me, and I would take offense if he used that term when addressing me. Although he'd used it all his life and meant nothing by it, as he explained, he didn't. But I made it clear that since I respectfully informed him of my desire and offense, he was informed, and I would have no problem addressing the issue legally. Of course, he was somewhat offended that I had the nerve to tell him that, especially since he was a grade higher than I at the time. We performed the concert and sat in different seats on the way back. Later that month, our combo band consisted of keyboards, drums, bass, guitar, saxophone, which I played, and a trumpeter, my friend. As we did monthly, we got to the officer's club and were scheduled to play for the Officer's Commissioned School graduation. And we had a standard list of songs we'd play: the official military songs, the ruffles and flourishes for the commander, and later, the dance music, ranging from standard jazz, waltzes, and some blues, rock, and popular tunes. One of the standard songs we performed was the Beatles' "Yesterday." Early in my life, I learned to play by ear and read in Junior and High School, but I was never a great reader. However, the younger trumpeter was an outstanding sight reader but couldn't play a note if it wasn't written.

As we set up our equipment for our performance, the young trumpet player noticed that he had forgotten to bring his fake book, which had most of the songs and lyrics we performed, and began to panic. He didn't have the written music and was going to have to fake it to make it. During the performance, when it came to playing "Yesterday," he said that he could not play it, even though we had played it numerous times. I could play the song before I could read the song. I told him it was in C and just ad-libbed. He shouted, "I told you 'BOY', it sounded like the whole club got silent when I heard him address me, and he continued to say, 'I can't play it without the music". Of course, all I heard then was "BOY". I finished the gig, but I don't know how I kept my composure when I returned to the band hall to unload our gear. I was still heated and waiting to get with this young white boy, who was a boy now, and I tried hard not to face him because I didn't want to hit him. He was still upset that he didn't have his music, and I took all the heads and started the melodies and rides (solos) for that night. I was entering the band hall door, and he shouted from behind me, "Hold that door open, BOY!" That time, I distinctly heard the bell ring. All I could see were his lips and the rest of the band members' lips moving, but there was no sound. I guess that is what people mean when they say, "I saw red". To this day, I can't recall what I had in my hands, but I dropped it. As it hit the ground, the sound returned. I found myself quickly on his face. However, he stood a bit taller than I, and it was on. I sternly shouted, forgetting where I was and that he out-ranked me, "Who the F***! are you calling BOY?" (continuing) "I already told you, my name." I was immediately physically pulled away from him by our band leader, the drummer, and the senior non-commissioned officer in the group. I adamantly informed him and anyone who happened to be in the shouting distance how I was provoked to anger and why I was about to kick his young ass. I continued to tell the NCO that if he didn't talk to his "BOY," and I didn't care, I prepared to lose what little boy stripes I had – my rank. After the chain of command and my brothers heard about the incident, I was revered or left alone. Nothing more transpired from it, and I never was called a boy on purpose or by accident again, at least not to my face. Yet I'm pretty sure I was called an "Angry N*****" thereafter to my back. Black men had been labeled that from birth, before people even knew us. Fifteen years later, I returned to Fort Lee for an officer's course and visited the band.

I had asked about the chain of command before the visit, and that young man was now the First Sergeant, but my subordinate. As a Warrant Officer, I was now his superior. One of his soldiers called "Attention" as I entered the room. As our eyes met, he immediately recognized me, saluting with "Welcome, Sir!" I could see that his mind had already returned to his experience of calling me a boy. However, I recall what my father-in-law had shared with me when confronting someone I had an issue with: "They know you know, so let them suffer wondering if you are going to mention it to them." We got to talk about family, what and where we had been doing the past fifteen years, and ask about others we served with. Along the way, I never hinted about the subject we had words over back when he was my superior, nor did he. We had a good time reminiscing about the old band times when we were younger. I'm sure his subconscious was constantly reminding him of when I told him, *"Don't Call Me, Boy."*

DWB

If you don't understand the acronyms, then you probably have never experienced it, or you're white because DWB (Driving While Black) is a real thing. It was when I first started driving, and I'm sure it was before I obtained my driver's license. My grandfather and father experienced it at some point during their lives. And so did my uncles and other men in our family. Funny thing, though, is I've never heard our black women complain about DWB. And I'm sure they have, but given the history of slavery, black men, white women, and the fear whites had and still some still harbor, relationships between the two, it has been the black men who get the brunt of selective "Pull Overs" by our local police force. My first pullover was in a small city east of our home called Bexley. It was 1973 and I was a Junior in high School. I had heard that the police would stop you, especially if you were in their area after dusk, not dark, just as the sun went down, sunset. I was leaving the area one night after visiting a "friend," and I crossed through the Bexley community. It was a beautiful night, a little after 9:00 pm, so I dropped the top of my car. I turned on my 8-track tape player to listen to some Isley Brothers and felt good. Wow, I'm so glad I didn't light up the joint that was given to me earlier. I was driving my first owned car. A 1964 Ford Galaxy. It was canary yellow with a soft black top. I had mag wheels and black racing stripes on the front hood and back trunk. And it was clean. I may not have known much about the car then, but I learned how to get and keep it clean. And I was clean. A clothing store got all of my money, Mr. Lee's. You were not in style if you didn't buy from Mr. Lee's. The shop had it all. That became the style when the Jackson 5 wore striped and multicolored knitted apple hats. Mr. Lee had them. When the Elephant pants and large collars with the "V" necks were in, that's right, Mr. Lee's had that too, and he had my money too. It was a race to see who was wearing the new styles, be it in shoes – platforms were still in, leather jackets with zippers up the arms and down the pants, pleats, and see-through silk tops. I was a good runner, figuratively speaking, I beat a lot of folks; sometimes, Mr. Lee's would have a small inventory, and if you didn't get it when it was hot, by the time he got another order, hot was something else. So, I'm dressed to the hilt, or as my grandfather would say, "Cleaner than the Board of Health," and so was my car.

I had just pulled away from a traffic light and hadn't seen the cruiser behind me or pulled out from a side road. He lit 'em up, slang for turning the lights on. I had an opportunity to experience a "Ride Along" with a police officer when I was considering a position with the Columbus Police Department. And by chance, his name was Officer Robinson, but he was a white officer. So, I'm sure that we were not related. During my 8-hour shift with Officer Robinson, he allowed me to "light 'em up" as we pulled over a speeder. I was somewhat happy that the driver wasn't black. I heard the short siren, and the officer announced over his speakers, "Driver, pull your vehicle over and come to a stop". I must admit, I was afraid. I wasn't scared of getting a ticket. I was fearful that I was going to be asked to step out of the vehicle, and the fear was of a possible beating. However, the police officer stepped out of his cruiser with a flashlight shining and reflecting off my driver's side mirror into my eyes. And all I could make out was his silhouette. I asked the officer as he approached my door. I had already pulled out my license. We didn't have to show proof of insurance then. I asked, "What's the problem, officer?" He had already taken my license, flashed the flashlight over my license, and then returned to his car. He took his time and, after about 5 minutes, returned to me. He asked me, "Where are you headed?" I replied, "I'm headed home. Then, he asked me, "Where are you coming from?" I told him that I was leaving a relative's home, which was hosting a party for my cousin who had just graduated from Ohio State. He looked at me, handed me my licenses, and said, - Now get this – 'Keep the music down and watch your speed. And a little nervous, I replied, "Thank you, officer!" He returned to his cruiser. It was then that I realized I had been stopped because I was black. I thought that I'd wait until the cop turned off first. Still, he out waited me, so I checked my mirrors, all 3, turned on my signal, put my left arm out to let him know that I was making sure the road was clear – hell, he and I were the only ones on the road – then I slowly turned my steering wheel and gradually pulled out and drove about 10 miles as hours, keeping his parked cruiser in sight. I noticed when he pulled off, and I slowed down even more. I had two blocks to go until I was out of Bexley, which was known as "Old Money". The area I was in mainly belonged to folks who had old money. They were wealthy. I didn't know then, but it was close to the Governor's Mansion. Nor did I know that I would perform there thirty years later with the Ohio National Guard Band in the garden.

When he pulled off onto a side road, I had just crossed into Columbus, and I blasted my radio, picked up the speed, and hauled my ass home. I never rode through Bexley late at night again until some years later, after I had enlisted in the Navy and was discharged 3 years later. Bexley was my first but not the last time I was pulled over for DWB. It was now 2007, and I was a member of the Ohio Army National Guard and a full-time federal employee as a Manager Analyst for the Maintenance Department. I was also just promoted from being enlisted to a commissioned officer, and I was the junior officer in our office. Our officer managed the maintenance community and briefed and answered the higher-ups and senior officers. And part of our duties was to attend monthly and annual Manager Meetings to brief the managers of the 20 maintenance shops that supported the Ohio Guard. Some of our meetings were off-site, and this particular meeting was in Cincinnati, Ohio, and it was an overnight stay. During the event, we were scheduled to attend a Reds game or take a cruise on the boat, which allowed gambling. I wasn't much for gambling, so I participated in the ball game. Because I didn't drink, I volunteered to be their Designated Driver. At the night's end, there were two groups: the gamblers and the ball players. The gamblers also had a designer driver. And the vehicles were GSA vans. We all met up at a designated point before returning to the hotel where we were staying. It was dust. As I followed the other Driver through the city from the stadium back towards our hotel, he drove through the traffic light that had turned yellow, and as I came up on the light that was still yellow, I stopped abruptly. In the passenger seat with me, the colonel asked, "Robbie, why'd you stop?" I looked at him and said, "DWB, sir." He looked puzzled and said, "What?". I pointed to the police cruiser in another lane adjacent to me, probably just waiting for me to go through that yellow light so he could "light me up." I was the only black person in the van, and I only heard a few chuckles from the back, who undoubtedly understood what DWB meant. So, I educated the Colonel. "Sir, DWB means Driving While Black, and until you can walk in my shoes, this damn thing is real, sir!". I don't think he knew whether to laugh or not. But I wasn't very meek when expressing my thoughts at times. But trying to keep it light, I said, "My blue-eyed soul brother" (as I pointed over my shoulder to one of the other officers in the back of the van, who was already explaining it to the other white officers), knows what I'm talking about."

I laughed along with them to lighten the shock on the Colonel's face, acknowledging that this was his first time experiencing a black man's truth and our fear of *"DWB."*

I WROTE A LETTER

Our father was a Ford Man for years, and just for context, I recall that my best friend's dad, Mr. Peppers, was a Chevy Man, and his sons, Richard and David, were as well. They had a Chevrolet as long as I could remember, and we always had Fords. My first car was a Ford. My father told me, "Boy, always buy American". He was a Ford and Quaker Oil man for the longest. It wasn't until I had served in the Navy and married that I could purchase my first new car, a Ford Fairmont. I drove up to our home to show the old man that I had purchased a Ford, and the first thing I saw in the driveway was an Audi. Of course, the first thing out of my mouth was, "What happened to buy American, Dad?" He said, "Boy, foreign cars last longer." I was hurt, but later, the real reason I was hurt was I found out that my new Ford was a "Lemon." Yes, that's right, the car was just two weeks from the dealer's (Dick Masheter Ford). And there was already an issue in which I had to take it back to have the water pump replaced. The dealership informed me there would be no repair or car rental cost if they had the car. When we picked up the car, we were told to pay $900 to cover the repair and rental. We wrote the check, and just as soon as we returned home, we stopped the check, and I wrote a lengthy letter to Henry Ford III. A week passed, and we soon received a check for $900 and an apology from the Ford Company. From that day on and until the car was paid off, I would park the car with signage in the back window that stated, "I brought this Lemon from Dick Masheter Ford." Sometimes because we lived just behind the dealership, I would slowly drive through their car lot so the dealers and the owner would see my signage. I learned from that experience that when an issue is hot, it is the best time to capture the raw feelings to attract the proper attention to resolve a disappointing issue quickly. I wrote a letter. I have had various problems that I had to "Strike while the iron was hot." It was 1995, and I was one of only three blacks hired into Walmart's Management Training Program to manage one of their Division Six Tire & Lube Express Centers in Hillard, Ohio. After my training, I was given the Hillard Store to manage. I had enrolled at Franklin University, and two other guys who had applied for management positions were also black. They had their degrees; one had a master's, and the other had a PhD.

After the training period, during one of our monthly managers' meetings, I asked the other Ohio managers how many a college or university degree had before being hired. Not to my surprise, most of them were hired right after high school. I digress. The issue that challenged me to write a letter to the company was when I left Walmart. I worked for Walmart for about two years and accepted a position with the Department of Logistics. After leaving the shop in the hands of the new manager, who had shadowed me for two weeks, I returned several weeks later to have my tires balanced and rotated. I did not have a copy of my receipt for purchasing the four tires with the tire protection program; however, I assumed that the manager who worked under me knew that I would have bought the tire protection plan since I got the tires there. He would not perform the service for me because I did not have my receipt. I told him to check their records because we kept yellow copies of customers' receipts. He refused to. Then I went to his assistant manager, who also had been my assistant when I managed the shop. She vouched for me and the bay manager who put my tires on my vehicle. He vouched for the service and knew I had purchased not only tires for my car but my wife's, my daughter's, and my mother's, along with the tire protection. The bay manager informed his new manager that I never purchased tires without the tire plan. This dude still refused to authorize the service for my vehicle. Finally, I told the guy I did not want to go home to get the receipt and asked if he could give me a professional courtesy, but he refused. I told the assistant and bay managers that I appreciated their stepping up for me and that it was a personal issue with this guy, and they both agreed. I knew the guy had a problem with me as he shadowed me and didn't care to take any instructions from me. Was it a racist thing? Hell yes! This cat had the biggest attitude and disliked taking orders from me. He hit the ceiling several times whenever a customer asked to speak with his boss and would quickly inform them that he was the new manager. And if I were around, I'd let the customer know that he would be my replacement and was shadowing to get the lay of the store and shop. I thanked the manager for his time and returned home. Home was a forty-five-minute drive, and I wasn't about to go home and return with the receipt. I had the receipt because I kept good records. Remember, I was a Yeoman in the Navy and a Personnel Clerk in the Army, and I will admit that I am a bit OCD when it comes to record-keeping and still am.

Ask any of my children or my wife. Once home, a bit peeved, I wrote a letter to the District Manager, Richard Byrd, and the Regional Managers of Walmart, explaining my issue with one of their associates at their Hillard store. I received a call a few days later from the Regional Manager. I remember his name being Jay. We met during one of our Manager's Monthly meetings earlier that year. He remembered me not because I was the only black manager but probably because I was the only one who ordered a steak on his dime. We didn't know he was buying until we had ordered. Several other managers thought I should have ordered a less expensive dish because they did. I told them that we always paid for our meals and planned to order a steak. Besides, I was born with a brown nose and therefore didn't have to "Brown Nose" the boss. I believe that year was when management had just introduced training concerning diversity, which was a big thing then. The two black managers in training with me had taken jobs outside Ohio, so I was the only black manager managing a shop in Ohio. After the niceties, Jay referenced the letter I had sent him. He asked me, "What can I do to satisfy the situation?" He was very interested in resolving the problem of all of us coming out as winners. I told him I knew the guy was married and had a family and could have easily gone straight to Human Resources with my complaint, but I passionately told him that I did not want to see him lose his job. However, I wanted to send a strong message about how he should treat all his customers, especially formal employees. I asked Jay to have the manager, not the bay manager or any of his associates, put four brand-new tires on my vehicle, and the cost came from his bottom line. Jay agreed and thanked me for not requesting him to fire the young man. I had read something about striking a good letter while the flames were hot, so I wrote a letter. Those weren't the only letters I had to write to "Upper Management" during my career. In the military, we called Upper Management the "Higher Ups". When stationed in Hanau, Germany, we had returned from a combat deployment to Southwest Asia during the Gulf War, I had to protect myself from a young captain, CPT Gary Hisle. Because he did not put me in to receive the Bronze Star Medal as he did for all the other Gunner Chiefs, he had an issue with my receiving the medal and made it a personal one with me. I was well-liked by most enlisted and commissioned officers.

One morning after the commander's staff meeting, one young lieutenant warned me that the captain told his staff, "If Sergeant Robinson ever falls, I'm going to do my best to keep my foot on his neck". Meanwhile, I arrived earlier that summer in Germany before my family and started attending church service, taking my saxophone. Before the service, I asked the keyboard player if he minded if I played. He welcomed me, and when he was done, he went to the pulpit to deliver his sermon. He was the preacher. He invited me to lunch after service and informed me he was not just a Masonic brother but a Worship Master. I had attended many Masonic events before the incident with the captain, and when talking to my mother on one of those long-distance calls (back then, there were no cell phones), she told me to seek out a well-known relative in the Masonic order. I did and found that he was a Command Sergeant Major (CSM) at another post. So, I addressed a letter to my CSM Morales and relative, CSM William Sayles, which covered what I felt to be a racial concern with the captain's threat toward me. I'm a firm believer in "Who You Know". It wasn't long before the captain informed me that I needed to report to the CSM immediately while I was still standing in military formation. He called me out, and I could see his concern about why I was being summoned. I reported it to the CSM. He suggested I take a seat. He paused for a few minutes and then informed me he had read my letter. He said it was well thought out and professionally prepared, addressed the appropriate regulations, and had a lengthy conversation with a certain CSM. He did not ask me to explain myself, which I covered in my letter. However, after another pause, he thanked me, said he would investigate the matter, and told me to return to my duties. That was the most of our conversation, but I felt assured I would have no further issues concerning Captain Hisle, and indeed, I had no further issues because *"I Wrote a Letter"*.

ROCKING THE BOAT

While stationed aboard the USS NIMITZ, a US Naval Aircraft Carrier, one particular Saturday morning, a shipmate, Edward Harper, and I were sitting on the pier enjoying a long-awaited break. Suddenly our chief, Larry Layman, came stomping down the plank and barking at us as he pointed at a pile of links from the ship's anchor, "Break down them-there chain links and repack them with some grease, but first, move them motherfuckers from over there to over here", which were just about 25-30 paces. Hey, I looked at Harper and said shit! that Son-of-a-Bitch must be drunk again - which he was most of the time. And he's a damn fool if he thinks I'm gonna move "them-there" chain links just to pack 'em." Hell, those bastards weighed about 250 lbs. each. As I started contemplating what we were going to do, I noticed a "Yard bird" sitting on his forklift eating his lunch, it was that time. I yelled and motioned to him, "Hey, can you help us and move these links over here," pointing to the spot where the old "Salty Dog" of a Sailor had told and shown us before he struggled to turn around and climb back up the plank onto the ship's deck. The Yard bird nodded in the affirmative and said, "No problem, just as soon as I finish my lunch". And he did. A couple of hours later, old Chief Layman, the epitome of the character Popeye, returned, and he came to a complete stop. His eyes got big when he noticed that all the links, about 25-30, were moved, and Harper and I were "Shooting the Breeze" as we were busy packing "them-there" chain links. The "Chief" was upset, as you could hear it in his voice. Pointing at the links with the mouth end of his pipe, he said from the right corner of his mouth, "How the f**k did you guys get them-there chain links over here so damn fast? I replied, "Good Old Brain Power Chief! He looked at me as if he didn't hear me and said, "Say what?" I repeated myself, then continued to explain that we asked a Yardbird (shipyard employee) to forklift them for us. He stood silently for several seconds and then repeated the instructions he had given us. I replied, "We did what you told us to do, and I didn't see why we had to break our backs, Chief". Harper and I hadn't done anything wrong - and here is where I probably went awry with him. I shouted aloud, "What the hell Chief? You trying to punish us for something or trying to win a bet with the other chiefs, that you could get us to move those links before you returned? "I'm a Sailor, not a Slaver!" He turned beet red as he silently stared at me and I was waiting for the "shoe to drop", but he just seemed baffled, probably because I spoke up. He turned away quickly and headed back up the plank stomping and cussing under his breath. He might have been calling me and Harper, "Smart-ass-n*****s". Smiling, Harper, said, "Damn Rob, you done f**ked up!" I said, "Hell, I don't care." I said, "Shit Harp, I'd rather use my head than my damn back." Then I told him that I was striking (applying) for another rank (job skill) because that Boatswain mate bullshit was for the f**k'in birds". It was months later, but I finally transferred from the Deck Division after passing the written test for Yeoman, an office clerk. And I owe it all to Mrs. Ward, my Junior High School typing teacher. Oh, it didn't hurt that she was a beautiful lady; the class was full of girls. I was one of the only two guys in the class. The other guy was a relative, Forest Stevens. I typed about 35 wpm and only had to type 25 to qualify for the Yeoman Navy test, but not until I received three Captain's Masses while in the deck department. The charges were bullshit charges that I didn't do…well, maybe one of them I probably deserved. I was young, still a teenager, and in the military; some teenagers still did dumb shit now and then. Let's say I forgot to say "Amen" when the duty guard came up on me while I was on watch, fast asleep. So, I took that hit. I soon landed a job in the Legal Department in the X-4 Division, the Ship's Legal Office. On the face of it, it probably was a good move for me cause I had too much mouth for those I worked for or with aboard the ship. The ship was full of folks who thought differently of folks like me, and I needed to know the law of the sea if I were to survive. It was the '70s, and still in some locations, people considered that a black person who spoke out against injustices had too much of a mouth, and that was me, "Robbe, the Boat Rocker", Harper and Houston, another shipmate, would jokingly call me.

So, I learned how to read the UCMJ (Uniform Code of Military Justice) Regulations as a legal assistant. I didn't realize it then, but God was moving me towards my fate in a future career. When Harper often told me, "Rob, stop rocking the boat, man; you're gonna get us in trouble." I would inevitably tell him, "If anyone deserves to rock the boat, it's us. Hell, they brought us over here in the boat". Little did I know that the phrase "Good Trouble" would be coined by the late John Lewis, Activist and former United States Representative. Harper, as always, laughs and says, "N*****, you're crazy." Harper eventually transferred into the Mess Deck as a Cook. He was just as crazy. When he and I returned from shore late at night, hungover, he'd sneak us into the mess hall and cook up some eggs and a couple of steaks he had hidden aside for us. Enjoying the meal, I'd pause and say, "You know you'll be in deep shit if we get...." Before I could finish my sentence, he'd laugh and said, "Naw, I got this Rob" I laughed with him then called him out saying, "Harp, now whose *"Rocking the Boat"?*

THE HNIC

Strap on your feeding bag, because this will be a good one. Yes, it was me. I was finally arrested; I had become part of the percentage of black men arrested in America, which I believe wholeheartedly could have and should have been avoided. However, we all know that when you throw in an "Uncle Remus" or "Uncle Tom", you can forget being treated equally because they don't believe you are equal in our society. The date was April 18, 2017, when I found myself in an arresting position while taking my 81-year-old mother to visit the Smithsonian National Museum of African American History and Culture and the statue of Dr. Martin Luther King. As I mentioned, I was apprehended by an African American Lieutenant named Gadson, an employee of the Smithsonian Police or Security Guards at the museum. Okay, let me start at the very beginning with the how and why of my predicament. My mother, Barbara, whom most of her friends call Barb, lived in Arizona. She was visiting me and my wife, Pam, in Ohio for a 3-week stay. During Mom's time with us, she shared her desire to see the National Museum of African American History and Culture and the Martin Luther King statue in Washington. I did not feel the urge to drive back that very same day. I soon caved to her request, and we traveled approximately 400 miles one way. We left Columbus after stopping for breakfast at "The Nutcracker," a local "Mom & Pops" family restaurant in Pataskala, Ohio, just minutes from our home in Blacklick. As it was a daily habit, after Pam and I had both applied and received training for applications for Conceal & Carry Licenses (CCL) in Ohio, I carried a weapon then and still do, to this day, regularly. I retired from the Army in 2009 and from the Department of Defense in 2012, and I volunteered for a non-profit organization, Nehemiah House of Refuge (NHR). I assisted and supported the reintroduction of men back into our communities after various circumstances that many of them had experienced and landed them in the prison system. Many had felonies and were looking for employment using the organization's multiple resources. It had been about a year since I had been steadily carrying my weapon, and it had become a part of my daily wardrobe to NHR, church, and areas where I felt it necessary. Of course, when it was not authorized, Pam and I would leave our property in our cars, which I had purchased with locked safes.

Yet, we would carry just about anywhere we traveled because of all the current dangers and shootings our country had been experiencing, in cities, schools, shopping malls, movie theaters, restaurants, etc. Carrying was especially warranted in light of the plight of black men and women seemingly targeted by predominantly white police officers. I soon came to realize that my fear was not unfounded. So, that morning, my mother and I embarked on our road trip to Washington, D.C., and I was armed. Now, during that time, I would read up on which states accepted Ohio CCL and which did not. Yet, I was still strapped, and yes, that mistake of not planning was all on me because I knew Washington, D.C., at the time did not. I had planned to lock my weapon up once we arrived in Maryland, where we would catch the Metro train into DC. It took us six and a half hours from Columbus to Maryland. Yeah, I was moving! Once in Maryland, we rushed to get to the train. My whole plan was to get Mom there, run through the museum, get her over to Martin, go back on the Metro to our parked vehicle, and hit those six and a half hours back home. That was the plan that didn't happen. I forgot to lock my weapon, as I had forgotten it was on my person. Luckily for us, I planned and called relatives who lived in Maryland, just in case it was too late, and I was too tired to drive back to Columbus that evening. That relative was my ex-wife's oldest sister, Phyllis. So, we had a backup plan. Little did I know that we would soon need it. Mom and I caught the Metro from Largo, MD, headed towards the Constitutional Center, where the memorial was located, and started our walk toward the King Memorial. Just before we arrived in the nearby area of the MLK Memorial, we noticed that we would pass the National Museum of African American History and Culture on our way. I hadn't planned on going in and told Mom I would wait for her. I was on a timetable. However, as we walked past the entrance, my mother stopped to inquire about the tickets with one of the employees standing there. We were then informed that I was wearing my veteran's cap, and we could enter the museum for free. We were both excited, and there wasn't a cost; we headed for the main doors. After you entered the doors, there was a walk-through scanner. It hit me, "Damn, I forgot to lock away my weapon!" I forgot to pat myself after getting out of my car. We were inside, and I stopped Mom and told her I forgot to leave my weapon in the vehicle.

I looked outside the double doors and considered going out to plant it in one of the nearby flowerpots, but I would have to remove my belt, which might attract some attention. Plus, there was the thought of someone finding it, possibly a child. No, that was not a good idea. I was at a loss for what to do. It would have taken me over an hour or two to return to the car, which I was willing to do, but I didn't want to leave my mother, nor could she move as fast as I would have had I decided to return to the parking lot where our car was. My mother suggested that I approach one of the security officers, explain my situation, and ask if they had facilities where I could lock it up while I visited. I thought, maybe that'll work. Hell No! That was the worst move I ever made. Once I approached the officer, whose name was Williams, I explained my situation. He asked if I had the weapon on me, and I replied, "Yes, Sir." He then politely asked me to stand by as he left his post at the main desk, and I surmised that he needed further advice. He soon returned along with another officer. They asked me to turn towards the large windowpane and put my hands on it. I did as they asked without question, not giving any cause for them to get rough with me. I've seen all too much in the last few years as to what could have happened had I questioned their authority and why, or made sudden moves. So, I didn't ask why or make sudden moves, following every request of those in charge. One officer placed his hand on my shoulder to hold me in place, and the other asked me where the weapon was located. I told him that it was holstered on my right hip. He removed my weapon, a Glock 43 with a full clip. He then removed the clip from the gun. I turned to my mother, who was now entirely distraught. I told her that it was okay. By that time, their supervisor, Lieutenant Randolf Gadson, a black man, had appeared to say to me that he would have to arrest me for carrying a weapon without an authorized license in Washington, D.C. I quickly asked if I could call my relatives who lived nearby so that they could come and pick up my 81-year-old mother. He did not seem very interested in the fact that I was a veteran there with my 81-year-old mother and that I approached them with "NO INTENT" but to resolve a mistake. They handcuffed me, and Officer Williams escorted me out of sight from the audience that had now become curious as to what was going on with the black man with the veteran's cap, me, to the basement of the museum. Officer Williams, a black man, sat me in a chair in a vacant room. I asked him what I should expect.

He informed me that they were waiting for the Park Police to come and transport me downtown for holding, booking, and jail. And Officer Williams, standing in the doorway of the room where I was sitting handcuffed, could overhear a shocking conversation. The Park Police had arrived, and we could hear the officer ask Lt. Gadson, "What do you want us to do?". The police said, "We work for you." What you want to do is up to you. If you don't want to file charges, we'll just let him go. It's all up to you. Lt. Gadson replied, "I already ran it up the pole." I understood that phase from my military experience, that he spoke to someone higher up, and they made the decision. His hands (Lt. Gadson) were tied, and they (Park Police) had to take me into holding, and there they would book me. And up until that moment, I was a black man without a blemish on either of my civilian or military records. I was and still am a law-abiding citizen; I served my country honorably in both the Navy and the Army, I'm retired 34 years, I served in the Gulf War, I am a decorated veteran (Bronze Star), I have college degrees, graduated from the Department of Equal Opportunity Management Institute, was an EO and EEO Officer, and I could go on. Still, you get the gist of my anger. And white folks always want to label us as "Angry Black Men," hell yes! Those very people in America (non-black) think they must treat us as second-class citizens, while others (non-blacks and whites) stand by and allow it to make us angry. While waiting for the white police officers to collect me, I had an interesting conversation with Officer Williams, who was very sympathetic to my situation. I asked him if he had heard what I just heard from the conversation in the hallway. He told me that he did, and there was no *"Higher Up"* that his lieutenant had to report this (my arrest) to. He was attempting to make some points with someone. I don't know who, but it damn sure wasn't me, and I felt that Officer Williams, although he didn't say it, was not a fond friend of his supervisor. Soon, two white officers came into the room, escorted me back to the first floor, exchanged the museum handcuffs, re-cuffed me, and continued to pip-walk me out the front entrance of the museum into the Park Police cruiser. There was little discussion during the ride. The officers took me to their holding station, where they removed my cap and other personal items from me: my wedding band, college ring, wristband, bracelet, crucifix, necklace, and earring from my left ear.

They also removed my shoelaces, a belt that still had my holster attached to it, and placed me in a small single-man holding cell. After about thirty minutes, I was retrieved for fingerprinting and the famed "Mug Shots." I was officially a suspect of what I did not know. I was there probably for about an hour, and then they transferred me again. I was now headed to jail. That was an experience that I now thank God for as I continue to pray for a good outcome. As I was in the basement at the museum, while being moved by the Park Police, I asked Officer Williams if he believed in prayer, and he replied that he did. I knew there was something good about him. I asked him to do that for me. He nodded his head in the affirmative that he would. As I passed him, I said, "This is not something I'd wish anyone to experience. He said, "Amen." I must admit, the Park Police treated me fairly. After the cruiser arrived at the DC jail and I was in the building before being assigned to cell number twenty-seven, I was told to stand with my back against the wall and then asked if I was hungry. It was about 3:00 pm, and I said, "Yes, I could eat." I watched the employee grab a couple of slices of bologna and slap them between two slices of white bread. He grabbed a handful of cookies, wrapped the sandwiches in cheap brown paper towels, microwaved them for a minute, and handed them to me with a small cup of lukewarm water. I thanked him. I was then instructed to follow the female officer. As I did, I heard someone shout, "Number Twenty-Seven," which would be my home for the night. No one told me I would be spending the night, but it was a "given." I didn't know how long I would be there and was concerned with the person already occupying the eight-by-ten space. I took a quick inventory of my new home. The amenities included one stainless steel toilet connected to the bottom of the sink at the back wall, two stainless steel bunks without pillows or blankets, and a "Cellie." He was huddled on the bottom bunk. As I entered, he rose, removed his belongings, and said, "I'll take the top bunk; you're too old to climb." I didn't take offense, nor did I refuse. I thanked my younger brother and took the bunk. There was a lot of talking and laughter going on in the adjoining cells to our right. It was a party, and they seemed to have known each other from outside or being jailed together, but it wasn't their first rodeo. As the number of arrests increased throughout the day, into the evening, and the night, the inmates were heard calling out each other's names. "Where'd they pick you up at?" "What did they get you for?" "Why are you in here?" etc.

The stories I heard were too many to recall; however, the titles some of the guards labeled by the inmates were so much as to denigrate them, as it was just to be very appropriately funny. I laughed silently, not wanting to join in on the chatter. I was like a party line. You could listen or chime in. I listened. You hear and learn a lot from listening. For instance, it seemed no one wanted to drink the water from the sink right over the toilet, and I agreed. As I listened, I learned that the guards rounded the cells every fifteen minutes, and the inmates were accustomed to the procedures and rules. They would call for water, and a guard, who was both male and female, would carry a gallon jug of water to the cells and fill the white paper cups we all had received when we checked in. During the night, an inmate asked for water and a new cup. The guard told the inmate to use the one he had. The inmate replied, "I would, but my pet roach claimed it as his new home." The whole block laughed out hard and loud. I spit up my water through my nose, trying not to wake up my Cellie or be heard by the other cells. The guard seemed reluctant to give the inmate another cup because now the inmates were confessing that their pets were also looking for new homes in their cups. The laughter kept on, and the roach jokes kept multiplying like roaches. As the guard was walking away after issuing several new cups, I heard an inmate a few cells down say to the guard, "Are you counting the cups you left?" The inmate started laughing, and out loud, he quickly said, "That's Captain Cup". Again, the block broke out, screaming with laughter. Now and then, you could hear someone call out, "Captain Cup, can you bring me a new cup?" Yet, the guard provided excellent customer service and continued to provide the cups. He never let on that it probably got under his skin. However, his response seemed to slow down, and the name-calling soon ceased. I never shouted out for water or a cup. I did keep a good eye on my cup. I didn't want a cellmate, and I sure didn't want a pet. I would wait until the guard was about to pass my cell, and I would stick my cup out and ask the guard for a refill. I thanked them and returned to my cold stainless-steel bunk. I was humble and sorry for not recognizing the situation I put myself, my other wife, and the museum officers in. If it were not for my membership with the United States Concealment and Carrying Association (USCCA) and the law group of Goodman Weber, I would have been found guilty and probably received a five-year prison sentence.

Instead, the gun charge was dropped, and I was released on my recognizance without bail after a night's stay at the cost of the taxpayers of Washington, D.C., and to return for a court date two months later, which never happened. There is another story here. It's about the so-called Justice System Statewide and how it works differently for some folks. I got the inside scoop. I recently heard about how the Public Defenders are overworked and overbooked with cases. Their primary focus was, and is likely still today, to clear their workloads as fast as possible. That meant getting most of their clients, who could not afford decent representation, to take a "Plea" (a deal), in which they were told that they could be facing anywhere from five to ten or ten to twenty years of imprisonment, a scare tactic. My attorney informed me. Yes, I had an attorney. Before I was transferred to the jail, I had my mother call Phyllis, whom I had arranged to stay with the night. Then, I had my mother call Pam and tell her to call

USCCA (United States Concealed Carrying Association) and tell them we needed an attorney. A representative who worked with the association showed up that night before the water, cup, roach, and Captain Cup show. Several months before my mishap, I purchased a membership for Pam and me with the USCCA, which provides legal services that assist you if you find yourself in a situation where you may have to fire your weapon in self-defense. And it was a good thing that I did, not knowing that this would happen, but it did, and I needed an attorney. So, that night, an attorney named David Weber showed up. A guard had come to my cell, and she informed me that I had a visitor. I had forgotten that my mother had called Pam and had her contact USCCA for an attorney. I had a lot of things going through my head at the time. The attorney was not one of them. The guard then yelled out, "Open cell number 27". The gate opened, and I followed her to an open door. Inside was Mr. Weber, a short, stout, breaded gentleman with glasses. He asked me to sit and told the guard to close the door. Mr. Weber introduced himself and told me he had spoken to my wife. I wondered how she was, and he assured me he had spoken to her about what happened, could happen, and should happen once he met me. I felt some relief because she was fully informed and not too worried. Mr. Weber gave me the same upfront information about my charges and the five-year imprisonment I could be sentenced to. Of course, I was a bit in shock but held my composure and listened intensely to his spiel concerning my options.

He informed me that if my insurance (USCCA) did not cover my case, and I decided to take him on as my representative, I was looking at "out of the pocket" ten thousand dollars ($10,000.00) for his firm to represent me. I was over a barrel because no other attorneys knocked on my door, vetting for my business. So, I agreed. Had I not, this might be a different story from inside the walls of a penitentiary. However, Mr.

Weber, after informing me of his credentials, was a veteran, ex-police officer, and a member of the legal team that put away Bernie Madoff. I was a little more confident that I had a fighting chance, yet I was shocked by the attorney's statements concerning my circumstances. He told me I was a different animal (I hadn't taken offense) because I had an attorney, unlike the other inmates. He then followed up to inform me that if I looked around, as he pointed and mentioned the employees (guards), he told me that I was the only one among them who was "Middle Class." Wow! That had never been a thought of mine as to what class of people I belonged to, but it must be something lawyers and other people strive to know and obtain. The way he said it was like I was different from other blacks because I had a job (retired), owned a home, had a college education, had a car, had a bank account, etc. It just struck me as a racist statement or a statement that said, "You got money." I never saw myself as a member of a class other than a black man. Get this: Mr. Weber, my attorney, assured me, whether I approved of him or not, that because Trump (Donald J.) had fired all the prosecuting judges and supported the gun laws, there was a great possibility that no one would touch my case. He hoped to get me off with a misdemeanor. Before my attorney left, he introduced me to the guards by the closed room where we had been discussing my case, and he told them that I was a decorated veteran of 34 years and that we all know that this case was, in his words, "Bullshit!" They all replied, and some nodded in agreement. My attorney and I said our goodbyes. He told me that I would have a representation in the morning in the form of one of his associates, Richard Link, and to ensure that I informed the Public Defender (PD). I thanked him. Little did I know it would be the last time I saw Mr. David Weber. I was escorted back to my new eight-by-ten home. As we walked by the guards and the cells before arriving at my address, twenty-seven, I glanced at their faces, thinking, "Is he middle-class or not?"

I felt ashamed because I was empowered and credited as a member of the Middle Class, basically told I was better than those I was incarcerated with. Okay, let me stop you right here. I did not notice one white face at the facility, be they guards or employees, nor were there any in the cells where I was. We were all of color, mostly my color, black. The following morning, we were herded ten at a time, handcuffed, and ankle-cuffed together. I was always aware of my surroundings, so I noticed we all had the same red waistband with the letter "B" on it. I immediately took it to label myself Black. Hell, why are we labeled? Couldn't they see that we were black? I looked around to take notice of all of the waistbands that I could see. We were Black, Hispanic, Indian, or other, but none were white. Yet, we all were labeled with the "Scarlet Letter B" and considered Black. I mentioned that fact to some folks, and they responded that the population is predominantly back. My reply to such a statement was, "Why isn't the police force in that community predominantly black, and why don't we see predominantly black police officers in predominantly white communities? This is a systemic problem in America. Policing was first started to police black neighborhoods. Look up the history of why and how policing started. The NAACP (National Association for the Advancement of Colored People) states, "The origins of modern-day policing can be traced back to the 'Slave Patrol." The earliest formal slave patrol was created in the Carolinas in the early 1700s with one mission: to establish a system of terror and squash slave uprisings with the capacity to pursue, apprehend, and return runaway slaves to their owners. Tactics included the use of excessive force to control and produce desired slave behavior". Sound familiar? Back to the process of my arraignment. After being escorted from one cage to another, as we all waited to be seen by a court-assigned legal beagle, my number, nine, was called. Two appointed PDs (Public Defenders) called me twice within thirty minutes of each other. As I told the first young man, I had an attorney, and he looked at me as if I were lying. When confronted with the second PD, I told him not to call my number again. As I tried to tell them I had an attorney, they continued asking me if I had a job, owned a home, a car, etc. I believe all they were attempting to discover was if I had any property of worth or value before they proceeded. Neither one of the PDs once asked me my name or if I was innocent. After about an hour or two, I stood inside the courtroom, waiting again for number nine to be called to face the attorney.

When I got closer to being called up, I saw my mother and niece, Karon, my sister-in-law's daughter, and Mr. Link, my attorney, sitting up front, waiting for my name to be called. Mom smiled and waved, and I nodded back at her. I was happy, and I presumed that I was okay. I was called to stand before the judge. This time, not by my number but by my name. As I approached the judge, so did the associate of Mr. Wever, Richard Link. He stood by me, and we both listened as the charges against the District of Washington, D.C. The judge asked me how I pleaded. And before I could speak, Mr. Link said, "Not Guilty, Your Honor." Then he continued to talk to the judge on my behalf, stating my stature in my community and my status as a decorated veteran who had made a mistake. The judge responded, giving me a date to return to court, and released me on my recognizance. I recall the judge jokingly telling me that when I return, I should leave my weapon at home. I replied, "Yes, Your Honor," thank you. I turned towards Mr. Link, thanked him, and hurried to my distraught mother. We returned to the museum to recover the personal belongings they had confiscated from me. Several of the employees there remembered me and said that I had been wronged. I returned to our relatives who had picked my mother up the day before, took a long overdue bath from the roach-infested room where I had slept the night before, and received a great meal, Mom. I left Washington,

D.C., and the district as fast as possible, vowing never to return. Before returning, after several conversations and emails from Richard and David, my case was "DISMISSED." I didn't have to return on June 20th for a trial of the second charge, "Illegal Possession of Ammunition." David informed me during our conversations that once my case was dismissed, we would need to return to the court after 6-8 months to have my record expunged. The USCCA covered 50% of the cost of $10,000 with a grant from the association on my behalf, leaving us to pay $5,000. We spent it gladly. And I then suddenly saw why there were so many black folks in jail or prison. The laws make it a financial burden if you are not of the "Middle Class." That was a slight dig. When I asked about the return of my weapon, David informed me that it might cost more for him to have the gun returned to me than just purchasing another one. Also, it was a practice that police kept weapons from cases they were in, and it might be too late for the serial number to have already been removed. I told him that it was the principal.

I did not want my weapon to end up in the hands of a police officer as a "throwaway." I was later contacted by a security officer from the museum requesting information so they could transfer my weapon to a nearby dealer, where I could pick it up. My gun was returned to the "Bullet Ranch" in Pataskala, Ohio. I have numerous times requested copies of my case file from Goodman Weber Law Group to follow up and seek expungement. However, while doing my research and filing an experiment, I was informed by another law firm in Washington, D.C., that my case was dismissed, and because of the law changes concerning misdemeanors, my record was closed. I never received any positive communication from Goodman Weber to this day. I understand that this ordeal probably could have been avoided, yet I didn't, and my mother and wife were both horrified by the prospect of what could have happened if I hadn't handled it differently.

However, I wish I had been given the opportunity, like many local police or detectives who had forgotten they were carrying their concealed weapons into a location where they had no jurisdiction. When I brought that information to Mr. Weber, he vehemently denied any suggestion of improper conduct concerning my case. After speaking to a few of the hourly employees at the museum who conducted and managed walk-through scanners, I found that it was different, and it was quite possible that the Smithsonian Security Police Officers, under the leadership of Lieutenant Randolf Gadson, had historically overlooked and released others without arrest, mostly officers and civilians, primarily whites. I'd be astonished if an investigation were carried out, and evidence were found that my premonitions concerning the lieutenant's actions were fictitious. He knew my status before arresting me and that I had no intent, and he did not care that I was there with my 86-year-old mother. Would it have been different had it been a white veteran? Yes, but instead, he created a spectacle by parading me out the museum's front doors. A black man, with no prior history, honorably discharged and a highly decorated combat veteran. The real crime was and is the worst kind of crime blacks suffer from in our society. I have met and dealt with folks like Lieutenant Gadson, who have for centuries felt it necessary to appease their "Masters" to show their loyalty to secure their place by degrading their people. That was the act of the Lieutenant, as he had me arrested, to display his authority as *"The HNIC"*.

DR. KING

It was April 4, 1968. I have just turned thirteen. My sisters and brothers and I had settled around the TV to watch one of our regularly scheduled family shows on our floor RCA model television, which was abruptly interrupted with a "This is a Special News Report" announcement by news report Walter Cronkite, saying "Good evening Dr. Martin Luther King the Apostle of nonviolence in the civil rights movement has been shot to death in Memphis Tennessee..." We didn't know who Martin Luther King was until later. As Mr. Cronkite went on in detail about what was being reported to him live, our stepmother started yelling to my brothers and sisters, "You kids, be quiet!" I recall her shouting out the name repeatedly, *"JESUS! JESUS! JESUS!* and she's crying out, "Why"? Our dad just stared at the tube without much emotion. I didn't know then, but that showed he lacked empathy. There was a knock at the door as Walter Cronkite continued to report the event of Dr. King's death. As the eldest son, I exited the floor and opened the front door. There were two young white guys at the door who had no idea as to what had just transpired. They were answering a "For Sale" ad our father had placed on the old black Ford step van that sat, it seemed for years, on the east side of our home. They were interested in buying it. After they asked about the truck, I shut the door and told our father, "There are two guys who wanted to ask you about it." As our father went to the door, I sat in front of the TV. He was always businesslike. I didn't hear if he mentioned anything to the two young men about the fact that Martin Luther King had just been shot (today, I'm sure he didn't). He just shut the door once he was done with his business, returned to the couch he was lying on during the report of Dr. King's death. I wondered why he never mentioned the plight and rights Dr. King and others were fighting for. He never shared any views on civil rights or the politics that governed our lives.

He never gave me "The Talk" about how to react if I were even stopped by the police while driving black, which DWB wasn't a well-known term, but it damn sure had been felt for years before I started driving. So, in our home, we didn't learn about Dr. King's actions and marches until later in my teenage and adult life. It was quiet, and all I remember is our stepmother telling us that a great man, a Black leader, was now dead. "They finally did it, they killed him", she cried.

We all went to bed that night knowing very little else about the importance of Martin Luther King's death, nor, for that matter, his life. I rode with our father in our old white station wagon the following morning. He let me drive, which was rare. The vehicle was a 1954 Ford Country Sedan, which we called "The White Ghost". As we travelled on the freeway, my father noticed another driver who had pulled over, and it looked like he was having some difficulties. The driver was a White man. After the night before, I was a little fearful. But the man had a flat. Dad slowed down and pulled off onto the shoulder of the road. He parked the car. Yep, the driver had a flat tire. Dad wasn't sure how he would be accepted, so he told me to stay put. After about 30 minutes, as I watched, I saw the White man and my Dad shake hands, and Dad returned, started up the white ghost, and pulled off onto the freeway. My father was never much for many words, but he looked over at me and said, "Boy, you'll never know when you'll need help and who'll help." He never mentioned the color of the man's skin. That was our father. However, I never understood why he never educated us about what was going on in our country. There were people in the world who didn't want us here. Why were there so many black people fighting and opposing the justice system and fighting for the right to vote? No, I never learned anything from my father about the civil rights movement, which I would probably be up against as a black man. That was the biggest injustice I suffered at the hands of my father.

Although he seemed to treat everyone equally, he knew that most did not treat us the same. I learned to learn about being a black man alone. I had to learn who the man was who was shot down in cold blood, and why someone thought that we could not have a man leading among us like *"Dr. King"*.

HUMOROUS EXPERIENCE

CHOCOLATE-COVERED ANTS

I love chocolate and milk chocolate, and almost everyone who knows me knows that little fact. Sometimes I get those cravings like a pregnant mother craving her most desired treat, be it the ice cream and pickles or the ice cubes Allison craved in her pregnancy with our firstborn son, Lil' Edwin. On many occasions, I have gone from office to office and desk to desk requesting a good friend for some chocolate they may have hidden away in their possession. They were usually of the same mind when it came to the favor of chocolate melting away on their tongue, and they, too, knew how I might have been feeling when I asked for a piece of that sweet, sweet chocolate. At times, I probably looked like a diabetic seeking a piece of candy, something lovely to fight off the oncoming storm of an overwhelming desire to fill with the taste of milk chocolate. It has always been the milk chocolate that has pleased my taste buds. That want is still the one thing that can interrupt my concentration. I recall several times when I couldn't wait to throw a piece of chocolate into my waiting mouth, and my tongue's taste buds, yet there was one time that I wished that I had not had that curse. I had been deployed to Stannis, Mississippi, during Operation (Hurricane) Katrina in September of 1005 in support of the Air Force as the Property Book Officer. It was my first night, and I hadn't been assigned a working location yet. So, I was put in a tent, mainly swamped and flooded by the storm's aftermath, just days after it hit New Orleans, parts of Mississippi, and along the coast. Before I left home, I packed my duffle bags as usual, and Allison and the kids helped pack some of my favorite snacks. Of course, chocolate. Allison had purchased two of my favorite chocolate bars, Hershey's Chocolate with Almonds. I had four large bars. As I unpacked my duffle bags, now in Mississippi, I set up my area as I always did. I hung a lamp that I brought along with me and opened my footlocker. It was filled with those survival items that most younger soldiers never considered: toilet paper, hot sauce (Tabasco), and other condiments that were enhancements to our MREs (Meals-Ready-To-Eat). And believe me, some of those meals needed enhancement. I think that is why most of the meals had a small Tabasco bottle.

I had packed two pairs of waders for the flooding we had heard about in the areas I had visited at a local sporting goods store. I also heard that there were snakes in the area that the storm may have brought to shore, so I also got a snake bite kit. I even had a mosquito net that came in handy the night I arrived. Well, I completed my ritual setup and laid out for the next morning my change of undergarments, washcloth, towel, toothpaste and brush, shower shoes, robe, etc. Of course, I had wet-pressed a freshly pressed uniform before leaving home. I had enough uniforms to hold me over until a laundry service was set up, supported by the Air Force out of Dayton. I had one set of clothing, a uniform, and underwear left as our first order for laundry went out. It was a two-day turnaround for the service, which wasn't bad. It was wonderful to have my dirty laundry taken away and returned clean. Getting back to my first night. As I said, I had finished setting up and ate a few of the snacks I brought – I didn't feel much like eating the provided MRE because our mess hadn't yet been set up. I was finally in my PJs and stretched out on my cot, which was accompanied by a battery-powered fan that I had the foresight to bring. Military-grade generators had been set up and ran with extensions available as they ran to and from most of our tents. The generators were loud, and I was fortunate that the one that powered the cable to my tent, although I could hear it, was not as close as I had heard it running in the distance. However, I was too tired to go down to the trailer, where I had additional luxuries packed away – an electric fan, to be exact, so I settled with my battery-powered one. It provided the breeze that blew across my body amidst the evening Mississippi heat. The net had added comfort as I slowly fell off into a deep nap. I awoke with a much-needed taste of chocolate, so I reached over to the locker within my cot's reach. I had already turned off my portable battery-powered lamp, and it had gotten darker within minutes after I had closed my eyes, so I had to feel my way around in the locker as I eagerly searched for one of the chocolate bars I had laid out and opened for easy access. I had planned to munch on it that evening, but hadn't thought I'd fall asleep. I found the bar and traced the perforated lines to where I wanted to break off a piece. I quickly broke off the amount I wanted and, with much anticipation and excitement, hurried the candy to my mouth as I opened the net with my free hand. I put three chocolate mini bars into my watery mouth, bit down, and broke them into smaller pieces.

I thought for a moment that I had been chewing pieces of a Nestlé Crunch bar, but I know that I didn't pack any, but maybe one of my loved ones did. Yet, as I pondered it, I continued to feast on my chocolate bar. I realized that my lips had begun to tingle. I slowly reached for my portable lamp and turned it on to find that my prepared chocolate bar had been confiscated and covered by hundreds of tiny hungry black ants. They, too, were devaluing my chocolate as much as I was, their friend who accompanied the pieces of chocolate I had just placed into my mouth and digested. There wasn't much I could do but to continue to chew and swallow what I had started, thinking, what the hell, they're protein, and since they were not red ants, I was good. I could not spit the chocolate out because of a few ants. I brushed off the ones still on my lips and had not yet made it into my mouth. I quickly shook them from my hands and fingers and brushed them from my arms and around my neck. I was lying flat on my back as I began to eat the ant-covered chocolate. But it was dark, and I didn't see them. I quickly took the rest of my bar in the footlocker, brushed off what ants I could, and doused it with water to remove any ants clinging to it.

The cooler was full of ice-filled cold water. I thoroughly wasted the bar off and placed it, after saving it, into a plastic zip-lock baggie. I was not about to throw the chocolate away, as I might not be able to replace it for some days. Sure, I was a bit embarrassed, but no one was around to witness my folly – but I thought I had reacted bravely and smartly. I took another piece of the bar before I placed it into the cooler in its zip-locked baggie. It was still just as sweet, and after ensuring that my bunk was free from the little critters by shaking the blankets I had laid out on it. I briskly brushed off my pajamas of any lingering friends in search of my chocolate. I returned to my bed of rest and smiled at my calamity of fighting a herd of hungry ants over my chocolate. So, if ever asked, I can genuinely say, without hesitation, yes, the most crunchy and chocolatey delicious treat I've eaten by accident was "*C*hocolate-Covered Ants".

HE LOOKED LIKE A SHARK

It was "Swim Call" aboard the ship. I swam and thought that I'd enjoy the beautiful coastal waters of Puerto Rico, where we had just ported hours ago. It wasn't the norm for the crew to be allowed to dive from the ship, but that was precisely what Swim Call was. I had never jumped or driven from the ship's aircraft elevators before and looked forward to doing it. It was where everyone would dive from. The boat had four aircraft elevators, and only one was designated for "Swim Call." The elevators brought the aircraft up from the hangar deck below to the top of the ship and rolled off onto the flight deck, where they would be hooked up and catapulted off the ship's bow. As I mentioned, the Nimitz was the first US nuclear aircraft carrier, carrying approximately six thousand sailors and measuring six football fields in length. She (most ships were addressed as a female) was like a floating city. Most of our aircraft were stored on the hangar deck of the side and brought up during their assigned flying missions that seemed to be run daily, even on some inclement days. The ship carried various jets, some small, others larger. There were F-4 Phantoms, the 3 "Huys" (helicopters), and a Hawkeye, a satellite aircraft used for tracking and spying. I'll let your imagination fill in the possible targets. Our birthing places (where we slept, shit, showered, and shaved) consisted of multiple secured bunk beds in sets of three. I had a middle bunk. Our Birthing Areas (Sleeping Areas) were quite spacious in our department. At the time, I was in the Deck Division as a Boatswain's Mate. Later, I struck (Naval term for applied) for a rate (Job Position) as a Yeoman and an Administrative Clerk. However, because I was a part of the volunteer band, I had participated in playing for the ship as she came into the Puerto Rico shores. The band was flown off in Tropical Whites uniforms by one of the three Huey Helicopters aboard our vessel. We performed military marches – many by John Phillip Sousa and, of course,

"Anchors Aweigh". On board the ship, we were usually given liberty for the rest of the day or weekend, depending on our assigned duties. I overheard the ship's intercom state, "Swim Call" in thirty minutes as we boarded. It intrigued me, and I quickly headed toward my birthing area to remove my sweat-soaked uniform and fit it into my swimming trunks. Each birthing area had a television that doubled as a ship's monitor.

The TV was on, and as the camera panned its way across the ship's bow, I noticed a formation of armed Marines jogging towards the edges of the ship's flight deck. Of course, this aroused my interest and concern. Our division chief was available, and I asked him, "Why are the 'Jar Heads' (Marines) on the flight deck with weapons?" I was in the act of slipping my left leg into my trunks, holding firmly onto the end of my bunk and pulling them up in preparation to put my right foot into the other side of the trunks. As I was just about to pull my trunks up – now with both legs securely in the trunks and my feet flat on the deck- the chief, without much emotion, said, "Oh, they're part of the Shark Watch Team". I removed the trunks I had just struggled putting on without falling to the deck. Chief Layman turned around and saw that I was removing my swim shorts. He asked, "Robbie, what are you doing? I thought you were going to swim call?" I recklessly pulled my trunks off, and just as fast and calculating, several thoughts spun through my head. It's 1975, and black sailors aren't being promoted as fast as white sailors. There aren't many of us in the Navy, and everyone knows that black people don't swim. Yeah – I went there – there would be loaded weapons pointing down towards the water, putting me in one of those Jar Heads' crosshairs. After I snapped out of my trance and with a comedic-like reaction, I said, "Hell no, Chief, I don't want them mistaking me as something they thought they saw after the fact. They've been known to shout "Shark" and start shooting, only to find out that they were killing seaweed. One of them might see me swimming under water, start shouting shark, and firing on my ass. He laughed. I said, "Shit, that ain't funny Chief! I don't want to be shot at and then later the jarheads looking over my body and saying, *"He Looked Like a Shark!"*

HOW I GREETED THE POPE

I enlisted in the United States Navy in 1974, and during one of my many deployments, I took the opportunity to visit Naples, Italy. A shipmate and I, whom I have since forgotten by first name; however, I did remember his initials and surname, which was Italian, Geraldo A. Deltergo, of Massachusetts. He and I were also in the same division of the Deck Department. He had assured me that once we were in the port of Naples, Italy, we could travel by train to visit the Sistine Chapel and the many beauties of his family's home in Rome, Italy. He is Italian, and thinking he spoke the native tongue, I would be introduced to culture firsthand by someone who would teach me as a friend to his people. Once on land, I realized I spoke just about as much Italian as he did when a citizen of Naples approached him, and after they had spoken to Deltergo, he said, "Non capisci," meaning I don't understand. And I knew that. It was 1976, and little did I know that even with our handicap, we would personally meet and greet one of the country's most popular and revered celebrities, Pope Paul VI. However, as an amateur artist, I was set on seeing the sights of Italy and experiencing the local culture. "When in Rome, do as the Romans do", which I had often heard. This would be the first time, though, that it made sense. I attempted to live, no matter how short-lived it would be, since we only had the weekend, and I wanted to pack my experiences with as many memories of Rome as possible. I saw the Sistine Chapel, where Michelangelo painted, the many ruins of Rome, and the Leaning Tower of Pisa. While on the train to Rome, Deltergo informed me about seeing the

Pope, whom I didn't know the first thing about, not to mention the Catholic faith. But I agreed that we'd visit the chapel, which was his greatest aspiration since he was Italian, and this would also be his first time in Italy, his "Mother Land". So, we arrived, walked, and walked until we finally reached our first destination, St. Peter's Fountain Square.

Soon, the pope's guards were all dressed up in the brightest red uniforms I had ever seen, and I believe they were armed. Then the Pope arrived on his balcony of St. Peter's Square. Deltergo, as he attempted to explain, "This is what we call an Audience with the Pope, so when he comes out onto his balcony, he blesses those attending to see him." So, by his standards and other Catholics I have shared this story with, I agree. I was blessed. It was Christmas Eve, December 25, 1976, when Pope Paul VI, who at that time had very little significance to me, nor did I realize the importance of this event to those of the Catholic faith. Here I was, a black man from America, who was a Baptist, yet I thought that we all were Christians. Nevertheless, as a believer in Christ, I was taken aback a bit when I thought about the upcoming event and possibly attending what had been announced as the last televised Catholic Christmas Mass from Rome, Italy. Deltergo and I were fortunate to be among those lucky enough to enter the chapel. Not only were we blessed once, but twice personally by the Pope in one day, and became a part of history. While waiting to go in, as had happened in the other countries we had sailed to, we met someone from our home. This time, it was from my home in Ohio; we proudly called each other "Homey." So, the norm of home conversations took place. We laughed and remembered home and family. The time went by fast, and soon we were ushered into the chapel to see the pope, and we sat together. Here is where it gets a little funny. Once in the chapel, I watched Deltergo as he entered, so I mocked him with intrigue and some humor, not fully understanding the practice. We were soon seated, and the service began. I watched with amazement as the incense smoked as the Cardinals swung the burners with the incense like pendulums, from left to right, walking ahead of the Pope. I believe I heard bells ringing or chimes. The Pope was escorted from pew to pew as those of the faith and visitors like me in the congregation reached out to kiss the Pope's ring and be blessed by him. Like I said earlier, this is where it gets a bit funny. I asked Deltergo, "What are they doing?" he told me they were honoring the Pope and being blessed by him. This was expected. It was a ritual. That was what they did. It was a form of honor. The first thing that came to my mind was that too many lips and germs were wrapped around that ring for me to join in the kissing thing.

So, as the Pope and his crew came closer to our pew, and I was at the end of the pew, Deltergo, an eager guy and more excited than I at the time, asked to switch places, and I did. When the time came, Deltergo, my self-appointed Italian guide and Catholic Representative, leaned over as the Pope extended his hand, Deltergo took hold of it, and kissed his *ring. I watched, and when it looked like everyone was looking at me, I could subconsciously hear them say, "Hurry up". So, I quickly stood up, looked at the Pope, glanced at the Cardinals to his side - I had asked Deltergo about the guys with the incenses in red robes – smiled, and with no disrespect intended, extended my right hand and without pause, the Pope extended right hand, I said, "Praise The Lord," what I was raised saying in our church to other Christians, and with a firm handshake, grasped the Pope's hand, gave him a heartfelt, soulful, handshake that moved from the traditional handshake to the hooking of our thumbs, back to hooking our fingers. Surprisingly enough, there was very little resistance from Pope Paul, as if he allowed me to lead the dance as he followed. He just smiled at me with a nod of his head. After we completed our greeting with my "Giving a Dap" (a soul-felt handshake commonly shared among Blacks within our communities), he did the hand blessing thing between us and said, "Bless you, my son". I saw in his eyes that he realized what I did was a black thing, and he took honor in it as much as I did in his accepting my welcome. As I returned to my seat, my female "Homey" from Ohio said, "Man, you're crazy." And I replied, "Yeah, but I bet'cha Flip Wilson would be proud about, *"How I Greeted the Pope"*.

*NOTE: The Pope's ring, the Fisherman's or Piscatory Ring, is a signet ring presented to the Pope at his papal inauguration. It symbolizes his authority as the successor of St. Peter, a fisherman. People traditionally kiss the Pope's ring as a gesture of respect and obedience, signifying devotion to the Pope and the Church.

Giving a dap is *a friendly greeting, agreement, or solidarity* between two people that has become popular in Western cultures, which was once only "A Black Thing".

HOW SWEET IT IS

I'll let you be the judge, but in my eyes, I believed I was right, and the sweetest justice I ever obtained was when my victims didn't know when it was coming. For example, I attended another required military course at Fort Lee, Virginia. As in most of my advanced training, in which I was mostly on individual orders or TDY (Temporary Duty) from my employed federal position, I would have to register at a local hotel because there were no vacancies in housing or quarters. And that was fine with me. I still got paid either through orders or per diem. On this occasion, I was the most senior of my classmates, who also happened to register at the same hotel as I. This course was three weeks long, and several students arrived a few days early. It was the school's policy that all trainees attend in uniform; however, because we were early, it was Friday, and the class didn't start until Monday, we had the whole weekend, so we wore our civilian clothing. During that time, I acquainted myself with some of my classmates. Knowing their origin, such as state, unit, etc, was nice. It was an especially great opportunity to discover what an SME, Subject Matter Expert, was. This particular time, as I stated, I was again the eldest so far, but I was pretty much accepted into the fold of the young soldiers. I was never one to flex my muscles as an officer, and I didn't see any reason to start. Besides, although I was no longer an enlisted member but an appointed Warrant Officer, I still held to the enlisted creed, since I had been enlisted for over twenty years. And the young enlisted NCOs (Non-Commissioned Officers) felt me as one of them. Thus, they thought that I would fall in line with some of their humor, since I had a since of humor; however, I informed them during our time we were sitting around at one of the restaurants and drink, that I was okay with jokes, but I didn't practice "Your Mama Jokes" and that I did not partake in practical jokes. After our first week, the classmates were getting friendlier and more comfortable, and the jokes began. And I figured that they thought I might be a good target for one of their practical jokes because I was friendly and pretty soft-spoken. But I was not. We were in our last week of the course, and as always, at the end of the day, we would be released to quarters or hotels to study and prepare for our final testing.

Many courses require testing out of the course to receive a Certificate of Completion or DD615, which is the same, but is generally needed for military promotion or career advancement. A couple had asked my classmates to go to chow with them. I did and returned to my hotel room, undressed from my uniform, pulled out my change of clothing for the next day, and prepared to take a shower. Upon opening the door to the restroom, I quickly noticed the toilet lid was up, which I always closed, and as I took a closer look, it was occupied with shit that was not mine. Someone had left a couple of their friends in my toilet. I flushed the toilet and inquired at the front desk. They informed me that, after I explained my problem, someone said they were "Chief Warrant Officer Robinson" and had lost their key to their room. Even the person behind the desk did not ask for ID. I further requested that they send up some disinfectant and air freshener. And they did, along with an apology and a gift card to one of the dining facilities in the area. The following morning, as always, I arrived in the classroom early. There were a few other classmates there, and as the others started entering the room, I paid close attention to conversations and laughter that might be a sign of someone talking about the little joke of Chief Robinson. And sure enough, a classmate who was a bit cocky and full of himself shouted from the back of the room as he entered, along with his underlings. "Hey, Chief, how's it smelling?" Of course, that question was somewhat "On the nose" (pun intended). And the laughter from those he had probably shared his joke with, at old Chief Robinson. I smiled and shut him down just as quickly, "Okay, how about with you?" as though I hadn't a clue what he was alluding to. Again, a few giggles and laughs as the instructor asked us to find our seats. As the day went on, the soldier attempted to give in and acknowledge his joke so he could get a fuller reaction of laughter from his classmates; now, most of the class knew what he was talking about. Yet, I did not let on that there was any problem, and I still didn't know what he was talking about. I could see it in his face as if he had turned as red as he could, that he wanted just to come out and say out loud what he did to me, because his frustration was getting the best of him, in that I would bring it up. I was closer to some older classmates, especially one from Ohio, but not Columbus. He had driven to Virginia and would pick me up for breakfast before class. I told him the night before what I suspected.

He suggested that I confront the soldier and say to him that it was not a joke to impersonate me to get a key to my room and then go into my room, which could be considered a B&E (Break and Entering) felony charge, and then shit in your toilet and not flush it. I told him that I had a better comeback, but I didn't tell him until after I did it. It was mid-July and one of the hottest days of the month, and we headed home. It was the day of departure back to our respective states and homes. There was one last thing we had to do: the graduation ceremony and class photo, which usually took 30 to 45 minutes. Some of us had received permission to leave as soon as we received our certificates. I was one of them, and so was my battle buddy from Ohio. That morning, as we skipped breakfast and headed straight to the building where our class was held, I noticed luggage on the back passenger seats. He told me he offered to drop the Joker off at the downtown bus station. When we pulled up to the parking lot adjacent to our building, where our classroom was held, I told him to go ahead. I'd be there in a few minutes, but I had to make a call. As the three of us received our certificates, we headed out. I had a cab waiting for me. He looked over at me and told me what he had done. I replied with a short laugh, "Oh, that was your shit! Yell, I thought it was maybe one of the workers who cleaned our rooms during the day. My Ohio classmate, I had told him that morning that I was going to get my revenge on that little smart-ass, son-of-a-bitch, but I did not tell him what I had planned to do. We said our goodbyes to each other. I smiled and nodded at the smart-ass as I entered the cab, wondering if the TSA at the airport would ask him to open his suitcase to inspect the small sandwich baggie full of human excrement. Wondering how long it might take before the heat would cause the scent to permeate his package, everyone around him started displaying acts of stinking. My aim was that he would be pulled over and asked about the scent coming from his baggage, and he would be embraced as they held my gift up in plain view for all to see, as his face turned red as he immediately recalled his act of taking a shit in our room and leaving it for me to find. It may not have smelled sweet, but it was a sweet revenge for me. Another time was when I explicitly told a young soldier that I do not "Play the Dozen". Our unit had deployed to the NTC (National Training Center) in Nevada, CA. We had started to settle in for the night, but it was late, and one of my soldiers started to joke around and say something to the effect that he could show me a few things about how to make love to my wife.

I stopped him there. "Listen, Sergeant", I enjoy a joke or two and can hang with the best of them, but there is one thing that I do not partake in: "The Dozen". He asked, "What's that, Chief?". I explained that when I was in school, we would call our friends' parents and talk about family members, and it would get so bad between some kids that fights broke out. Then, I decided not to talk about anyone's family members, mainly once I was "Grown", an adult, and had a family. So, I told him that if he spoke about my parents, wife, or especially my children, we would have a big problem. Once I started on the "Dozens" with you, there would be no "Rules of Engagement," all would be fair in love. And I would not stop until I was satisfied, or someone said, "How Sweet It Is". It's like, "It's not over until the fat lady sings". I continued by telling him that he may feel hurt or bruised by something I might say or do to him. So, if he agreed with that, then the game was on. I had hoped it was, and he would have given it a rest, but he did not. I just about begged him as I suggested that he not "Go down the rabbit hole" with me because I could dig deep. It got quiet, and he must have taken my warning as a challenge, and before long, he got brave, and it was on. After a few jokes landed on me, and then he and the tent started to get loud, our senior officer in the tent insisted that we stop and get some sleep. We did, but not before I got the last dig in. I said goodnight to the younger sergeant and told him I'd see him in the morning, and that I liked my eggs. There were a few laughs and silence. Several soldiers, amused by our back-and-forth bantering, gave a few "Ooooo" before all the lights went out. The following morning, a few hours after breakfast, I was ready to put the young man down. I could hardly sleep thinking of how to get my message to the young buck sergeant. We were setting up a portable satellite, and I called the soldier over and asked him, as I pulled out my right back pocket, "Can you hold onto this for a minute?" Without asking why, he took hold of the inside part of my back pocket I had pulled out. He looked at me funny. I told him to hold on to it tightly, and he had to hold on. I began walking around the portable satellite, and there were a few senior soldiers who knew what that act implied and started laughing. The soldier immediately let go and asked, "What?"

He was soon informed that it was a known prison practice that informed other inmates that the person holding onto their back pocket was their property, as you walked behind him in submission. Then another soldier, jokingly shouted, "Dude, the Chief just made you his b^!#h, he owns your ass." I didn't hear a fat lady singing, but the humiliated voice of my subordinate softly saying, *"How Sweet It Is!"*

I GET THE BROWN ONES

I must tell you about my now adult son, Ilyas, and daughter, Ayrika. Because I am their daddy and cause I can. And those of you with grown ass children, you know what I mean, because they don't tell us everything. Even those children with whom we think we have a closer relationship than their other siblings. Of course, I'm talking to parents with more than one child. A single child doesn't have someone they can confide in and know that they will take with them to their graves. Well, most of them say they will, but we know by now, when they are no longer kids, but grown, and find that most of it was just funny, so now it all starts to come out. Yep, as my two began to share tidbits of what they were up to when we weren't around, they were about their dirty deeds. Wow, I thought my son and daughter were "Ride or Die" until little tales about some of their "Together Adventures" were starting to be shared with "Daddy", "Pops", the old man, they probably call me behind my back. Allow me to share what loyalty looks like with my kids. Lil' Edwin did something he was too young to do and knew he was wrong, then involved his 3-year-old sister to cover for him. She said that she did not know where he was. When confronted with his whereabouts, Ayrika held her guns. Once we had our son home, we inquired why he didn't tell his sister where he was. He said, "I told Bird where I was". If you could have seen Ayrika's face and heard her as she said, "Ooooo Bubby, you promised". Suppose her eyes could have hit her brother right in the eye. She would have. And because of his betrayal, he received the same punishment as her "Bubby"; if you're a black parent, you know. Another time, Bubby spilled the beans again and told me about the candy store robbery he and his little sister had pulled off. when they stole candy from a German candy store. The plot, so I was told, was that Lil' Edwin spoke German fluently. He said he would go in and mesmerize the tenant with his ability, while "Bird" was to go and get the candy. She was to get as much as she could in her coat. It was wintertime. Ilyas, today (Lil' Edwin then) tells me that once his sister got what she thought was enough, she headed toward the exit while yelling, "Bubby, come on, come on".

She quickly headed out the door while her brother was still talking to the store tenant. When he got outside the door, he said his sister was almost half a block from him with a trail of candy behind her. He said, "She was hugging her coat and walking very fast but never looking back." My son told me that once they got home, they spread the candy out and that they didn't like any of it. It was all for not. So, yep, I asked my grown daughter about their adventure and asked if you could have heard her again, "Ooooo, Bubby told you that?" She held the secrets close to her chest while her "Bubby" had become an open door to the safe. It is mostly always the one who tries to stay loyal. In this case, it was and probably still is faithful to her "Bubby". Like I said, we know our kids (you know yours). Like Sly said, "One you love, the other, you'd just love to burn", but blood is thicker than mud. My kids are different, but they will "Ride or Die. I recall taking my daughter with me to the store to pick up something. As I always did, if I saw a coin on the ground, depending on the child with me at that time, I'd tell them to pick it up. "It's yours." Since Ayrika was with me, she hit the jackpot. She was about 4 or 5 years old. I saw a dime in the parking lot as we were headed to the vehicle. I told her, 'Bird, ' it's a dime. She picked it up, looked at it, and said, "This one is for Bubby". I said, "Why?". And she said, "Bubby, get the silver ones, and *"I Get the Brown Ones"*.

IT DOESN'T SMELL RIGHT

For years, I have told those close to me that I smell everything, and it's been like that for as long as I can remember. I believe there's a curse that comes with having such a keen sense of smell. Like the famed quote from the TV series, "Monk," "It's a gift and a curse." The gift is that I can smell it before I step in it, and the curse is that whatever I inhale, it always seems to manifest itself through my flatulence as a gastric gift, a good old fart. There were many times that the various scents I experienced, some good, others pretty bad, cursed my sensitive palate and invaded my stomach walls, forcing me to share those scents with innocent bystanders. I would try not to offend folks by slipping away into a secluded area where no one would know how funky I could be. Also, if I had to release the curse silently, I quickly relocated – yell, you know what I mean, you've all done it too! If you're honest, you know you don't like sitting on the fragrance you just expelled. So, I did as most of you have done or attempted to do. You got away, excused yourself by going outside or to a nearby bathroom, and got some relief from the built-up pressure or rumbling warning that you needed to release the beast soon. Yell, I know this is quite personal, but we all have gas; it's a natural human function, but it's rarely discussed openly. I share this embarrassing yet somewhat humorous experience that surprised me more than it did my wife, Pam. Critters are abundant in our area, as we live in a condo backed by a few acres of forest. Several of its wild critters frequently visit our backyard from the tree line. We have deer, wild turkeys, rabbits, and various birds and rodents, like squirrels, chipmunks, possums, and skunks. Once, we were woken by a coyote. So, early in the morning during a hot summer night, Pam and I were abruptly awakened to what we thought was coming from outside: a strong presence of what could only have been that of a skunk. We quickly closed our open windows, but it was so strong that I began looking around our room, under the bed, crib down our stairs to our living area, checking the kitchen, and then going down to the landing area towards our garage. I opened the garage door, hoping there was a skunk so that it might run away. The scent was so strong that I thought maybe a skunk had found its way into our home when the back patio door was opened during the day. When I say the scent was strong, I mean it was pungent.

I returned to our bedroom; Pam was wide awake now, and we both knew it had to be close. But, nope, it wasn't. Yep, you got it. It was me. Evidently, during my rest, my body allowed a silent killer out. As I explained earlier, I probably must have inhaled the scent from a road-killed skunk earlier that day. Inevitably, that gift visited my nasals, and when the bacteria that had fermented the carbohydrates and did not digest in my small intestines, they married, and the perfect storm slid deep into my colon, the large intestines, visiting me and my sleeping wife that night. We realized that the stink was coming from me. We attempted to fumigate our home with healthy fresh air, turned on an essential oil diffuser, and lit a few candles. We laughed and soon fell back to sleep. It was the craziest conversation the following morning. Pam is convinced that I have a keen sense of smell, and she will never again doubt me when I tell her, *"It Doesn't Smell Right."*

MY SEVENTIETH

I don't know how long this "Sting" I was about to experience had gone on, but my wife, Pam, amongst her family, had always been known to pull off a prank or practical joke on them. I hadn't yet been on the end of one of her well-planned schemes until recently, but I soon found it out on a personal scale. And I will get to it soon. I had been privy to some of Pam's hilarious antics in the past with a few of her family members, who shared them with me during our visits. Pam's most significant time performing her acting was on the first of July, "April Fool's". Besides her family members, many of her close friends have been the victims of her laughable crimes. Some of them, however, have left many to swear off answering their phones on that day in fear that one of Pam's practical jokes would be on the other end. Her daughter, Tamra, stopped answering the phone on that day. I even tried calling so that she would not see her mother's name on her phone before answering, and she wouldn't even answer my call for fear that her mother would talk me up to be her accomplice. Pam's jokes were fearfully funny and weren't just her jokes. She loved catching you off guard, unsuspecting. It is most definitely her "Will House." Let me give you a taste of who you may think this Pamela Sue is, because her plots to get a laugh come from a profound and sometimes disturbing place of humor. I honestly believe it runs in the family. Her brother Robert, who is fondly called "Bobby," a lifelong minister and pastor, always had a laugh just waiting to get out during any conversations I had with him. He loved to laugh, and it was contagious. So, we were coming up on what might have been my third or fourth time experiencing Pam's April Fools' Day pranks. And I could tell how she struggled to outdo her last one, but she pulled through, and it went like this. Tamra and her husband, Chris, had moved into their new home several months before April. Pam was determined to get her joke into their home one way or another. She had been told that no one at their home would answer the phone on April 1st, and they also would not allow her to visit them until the following day. They feared being pulled into one of her mother's super funny, practical jokes that typically made Pam laugh the hardest, like her brother Bobby. Man, they love to laugh. Of course, I was in it before I was in it.

Pam had typed up a bogus letter of notice, supposedly from the Homeowners Association (HOA), that informed the Gates (Chris and Tamra) that several neighbors had complained about their walking their dog, Sonny, and not picking up after her. Chris and Tamra had also recently put up a privacy fence. Pam wrote in the letter that the height of their fence was not per the HOA rule book, in that it was too high, and they would have the adjustment within two months, or they would have to pay a heavy fine for the violations of the HOA codes. I found the HOA's logo, posted it on the letterhead, and typed the address on a letter-size manila envelope with the bold "URGENT NOTICE." Then, Pam and I drove to their home so I could put it inside their door without them noticing me. I parked our car a block from their home, sneaked over to their front door, placed the envelope into it, rang their doorbell, and hurried away like a thief, fearing being caught, and I was. Because during that time, our cultural environment was sick with white people calling the police on people of color for the slightest things. If they thought we were either not supposed to be in a particular area, neighborhood, etc., or appeared to be doing something they perceived as illegal, the police were called. Sorry, I had to go there because that sort of thing was getting out of hand. Well, I'm sure I looked like one of those guys that day. We returned home, laughing about our caper and speculating how they probably would react upon receiving it, seeing the outrageous fines, and finally, after reading the last paragraph. Believe me, the notice looked perfect right down to the official seal. Pam even quoted the citations and regulations from their HOA Owner's Manual. The letter's ending, though, read, "April Fools, You filthy Animals!" in small print. Of course, that is a well-known line from the Christmas movie, "Home Alone," and the Gates knew it was from Pam. We soon received the long-awaited call to share the laughter. However, as we spoke over the phone, Tamra was surprisingly laughing but had to explain how very concerned and quite upset her husband, Chris, was at first while reading the complaint and saying he was refusing to pay a fine for an unfounded truth because they always picked up after Sonny and would not take down the fence they just installed. But when they got to the "filthy animals," they knew they had again been outmaneuvered by thinking they would not be a part of Pam's April Fool's practical joke. Yet, they were hit by a smooth criminal and operator. Don't let her sweet demeanor fool you.

Okay, back to how she got a big one on me. I tell you, if my doctor had taken my blood pressure that day, she would have rushed me straight away to the emergency room. And it was high up to, during, and a little after the event. So, a few weeks before the event, Pam had returned from one of the three days she worked for the VFW Charities in downtown Columbus. She informed me that her office was planning a departmental party on the 21st of March at 6 pm, and one of her friends asked if I could make my famous BBQ Baked Pork & Beans. Of course, I was honored because Pam asked me to. I said yes, of course. Then she added, "And could you do me another favor?" She had me at "Of Course". It seems I can never say no to her. I've made the beans, greens, and my famous French Banana Pudding for her office function. I asked about how many people were attending. She told me that she wasn't sure because it was VFW folk; she wasn't sure who would be attending, but she threw out the number, "possibly fifty." She then told me that some of her work associates were bringing fried chicken and wanted to know how much they should order. I told her fifty to seventy-five. The day of the event had arrived, and Pam had laid out the clothes we would be wearing. Anyone who knows us knows we matched most of the time. So, she asked me if I wanted to wear my yellow shirt and told me how good I looked in it. Do you think I'd say no to that? Right, I said, "Ok, Babe." Pam informed me the night before that she had to go into the office to help set up and return to pick me up. So, the following day, I loaded up the food and everything she had purchased for the party. I asked her if she needed me to go in with her. She said that there would be enough help there. I was good with that. It gave me time to continue proofreading and revising parts of this book. She left home at about three o'clock and assured me she'd return for the party. Well, 6 p.m. rolled around, and she was not home. I called and couldn't reach her. She was on her way home when she finally answered my second or third call. That was when my blood pressure started to rise. We were late, and I had forgotten earlier to put the greens in the car when she went in at three o'clock to set up the food, so we had to get them to the event. I was a bit upset. She pulled up the driveway, opened our garage door, and ran into the house. I didn't ask. I was ready with the greens in hand, and they were about as hot as I was, having just taken them out of the oven. I jumped into the driver's side of the car and waited for her to return from the house.

When she got in the car, now on the passenger's side, and I was about to back the car out, Pam said, "Wait, I have one little favor to ask." I said, "What is it, Pam?" and was not too pleasant. She said, "Can you bring your tenor saxophone?" She loves the tenor. I asked her why, and she told me that they had hired a band, and some of the employees who knew me knew I played saxophone and wanted me to play with the band. I told Pam that I probably didn't know the musicians, and even if I did, I didn't feel comfortable going in on someone's gig without being asked. Then I asked her if anyone had asked the band if it was okay. She said, "Yes, they're okay with you playing with them, they know you play saxophone". I reluctantly said "Okay", ran back into the house, and grabbed my sax. We finally were headed to our destination, and Pam said, "Oh, I have to make just one stop." Was I mad? Yes! I was getting there fast. I slowly said, "Where?". She said, "At the Post." I said, "For what?" She said, "Chairs." Yes, the conversation was going on like that. I told her we don't have any folding chairs at the post, and our chairs are too big to fit in the Equinox. At most, we might get four chairs. I can turn around and get the folding chairs we have at home. It would be faster, and we wouldn't have to go out of our way on our way to your office. She insisted, and I caved. The madder I got, the faster I drove, and the longer the trip felt. She was humming to the radio and tapping her hand on her door, and I was getting increasingly irritated by the minute. I later told my cousin Jason that I was almost "Wild Bill Mad." He may have choked on his drink in his attempt not to laugh out loud. Pam and I arrived at the post; I quickly backed up the SUV to open the back hatch to load the possible two to three chairs. I quickly jumped out to go to the post for the chairs. I hear music playing, open the door, and I see Mel Stewart, a bass player I've performed with over the past twenty years. I hurried towards him and said, "Man, you know I'm a member here; why didn't you guys let me know you were playing here?". Mel smiled and looked toward the drummer, Smooth, whom I had also played with for over twenty years. Again, I asked, "Smooth, why didn't you guys tell me you were playing here?" he told me, "You're here now; you got your horn. It's your birthday." I replied, "Yes, I got my horn; my birthday is next week. Pam and I just stopped in to pick up some chairs; I've got to play at her office party. Yes, it was all flying over my head. I hadn't a clue as to what was happening.

Then Pam tapped me on my shoulder, and as I turned around, she said, "Happy Birthday, it's your party, this is YOUR party, Happy Birthday." I looked at her and said, "Wow! Damit Pam, you got me, baby, thanks." I was so upset that I was upset at her. When I barged into the post, I didn't notice anyone but the bass player. I didn't see all of my family and good friends there, the balloons, and what should have been very familiar, like the small café table lamps and signs Pam had ordered. I had asked about them earlier when she ordered them, and she told me she had mistakenly ordered them and sent them back. They were set up on all the tables at the post. I felt like a fool, and I was in shock. But I can genuinely say that this was the best birthday party ever because my beautiful woman, my wife, Pam, had pulled off the ultimate surprise party for *"My Seventieth."*

PISSED

It was another field training exercise in "Wild Chicken" (Wildflecken, Germany), I was stationed in Hanau, Germany, in a Field Artillery Battalion. I was now a 13 "Bravo" (13B Cannoneer), called "Gunner". Because I had been promoted to E5 (Sergeant in the army), I was immediately put in charge of a section of about 9 to 12 soldiers, who were more experienced with the M109 Self-Propelled Howitzer, which I was now the chief of. I had just reclassified and trained on 102 – 178 tow cannons in Fort Sill, Oklahoma, and shipped directly to Germany. After addressing my section and counseling the two sergeants in our section, who were outranked in time and grade by me, I had to assure them that I would be taking advice and supporting them as I learned my job as their Section Chief and Gunner Chief in the field. Although I had been book-trained and was a fast learner, I had no artillery field experience, and everyone in the field knows that books don't teach you how to interact in the field. It is much like a person who can read music but never learned how to adlib and is suddenly thrown into a gig and expected to take a ride the first time without ever having played the tune without a chart. You must have that experience. I was like a fish out of water. So, here I was in the field and only had the knowledge I had gained through exams and minimal hands-on experience in a live environment. I informed my sergeants away from the other soldiers that I was only school taught and would depend on their knowledge and experiences and if I ever stepped on my dick in front of the soldiers, that they did not correct me in front of the soldiers, but to pull me aside to tell me what or where I went wrong or was not right and I would respect their suggestions and corrections. Soon, I was back in the water. We grew to become a great section. A few months passed, and we were scheduled to convoy to a nearby exercise location, specifically for howitzer firing of projectiles. It was "Showtime", and I was up to prove to the other section chiefs that I was ready, a musician who is now a gunner. It was as bad as (a joke) calling someone a bookworm, in that the hard-core soldier didn't think anyone well-read had what it took to be in the field and could hack it. They didn't know that I was a Robinson! I attacked the field with vigor and the task as a section chief with a welcoming attitude.

I had a team that respected my leadership, and I had two sergeants who had my back. Before getting to the field, my Gunner, who led the team for the most part and had several years on the "Gun" (the howitzer), informed the team to follow his lead, and we would get through the training, which was also a test for me. All the sections were tested on teamwork and getting the fire mission correction; the consistency of correct rounds (155mm High-Explosive projectiles (HE)), the number of powder bags used (white or green), accurate deflection, the azimuth of the tube, and hitting the assigned targets. It was all a timing issue and counted on the teamwork of your team and the Gunner getting the correct combination into the breach and pulling the lanyard (rope) when directed by me, your chief, after receiving directions from the Fire Mission Command. That weekend, I *"Cut My Teeth"* (began learning my craft as a Gunner Chief) in leading our team to success. My team was always the first section to fire our rounds down range towards our targets and hit them. And we were never the last team to fire. That gained me some credit from the other chiefs who doubted my grit because I was a musician. The night ended, and it was time to turn in. We were all tired because it was about noon, and after shooting the breeze, most everyone congratulated me on having a good night. Someone brought up the subject of my snoring. "Yeah, Chief, you've got to get something done about your snoring. You sound like a freight train is coming up here." An Army Large GP (18X52) tent housed about twenty men. I had heard all the jokes about my snoring and jokingly informed everyone to bring earplugs. And a lot of them did heed my warning. It was the third night, and some soldiers were fired up about wanting to get a good night's sleep, knowing we had a fire mission. I told them that I would do my best not to snore, knowing that was not something I had control over. The snow started falling hard, and the wind blew just as hard. And that is where Wildflecken got its name. It was known for being cold in that field during wintertime, and it was November, just a month away from being deployed into the war zone. Of course, we didn't know that then, but we had an idea that something was a brew. It started quieting down, and we all climbed into our all-weather sleeping bags, rolled up on our army heavy-duty folding cots made of canvas and aluminum folding legs. I climbed into my bag fully clothed with the zipper pulled not quite up. And I waited until everyone was asleep so they could get some sleep before I dozed off.

It didn't happen. I had fallen asleep and must have zipped my bag all the way up because I woke up and was sweating profusely. I immediately removed my clothes. It was the norm because it would usually be cold when we got into our bags. Most of us would climb in with our uniforms on, and once our body heat warmed up the bags, which got good and toasty, we'd come out of our outfits and sometimes into our birthday suits to keep them from getting too wet from the sweat. Well, at least I did. I don't know for sure about anyone else. I didn't care. But I wanted dry clothes to put on in the morning. After I had removed all my clothes, I quietly fell back to sleep. Everyone was sleeping well cause I hadn't heard anyone shouting or yelling, "Hey Chief, you're snoring, turn the fuck over". I thought, well, it's going to be a good night. I soon fell back to sleep. It wasn't long, but I woke up and had to take-a-leak. I tried to wait until it was time to get up, as I constantly tried, but my bladder had a mind of its own. I finally gave in and quietly put on my uniform. I first put on my pants and the top. I intended to get out, put my boots on, and step outside the tent to relieve myself. To my surprise, as I unzipped my bag, I received a face full of fresh, cold snow. I had been moved outside the tent. My soldiers had picked my cot up with me sound asleep and placed me outside the tent. I looked outside my bag, up towards the sky, and it was still dark, the sky full of stars. Then I looked over my shoulder towards our tent, noticing it was buttoned up. I was pissed, but even more, I was not going to attempt to move my cot back into it in all the snow that had accumulated. I zipped my bag down just enough to roll over and once done, quickly zipped it up and over my head, and yes, here comes the pun, I was thoroughly *"Pissed."*

STRIKES, NOT STRIPES

It was another summer coming up, and we were out of school. I had to find something to get into to keep me busy and away from home. My best childhood friends, the Peppers, were bowlers. And when I say bowlers, they bowled. Their father, "Mr. Peppers," was an Air Force veteran, like many fathers in our neighborhood. He and Mrs. Peppers were bowlers. This would be the choice of entertainment for their family of four children, Richard, Jr., David, Nancy, and the youngest, James. His family called him "Jamie," and so did the neighborhood. The two oldest, Richard and David, were about my age. We practically grew up together from grade school through high school. The three of us were in the marching and stage bands together. Richard was my best man at my wedding in 1976. We hung out together most of the summers at the local swimming pool and played street football and basketball at our elementary school grounds, except when our families vacationed. Yet, that was old-school play back then for the kids today who don't understand what playing outside means. I don't recall who decided that we should form a bowling alley, but I know it wasn't me. I didn't have a bowling ball, as did all the Peppers. They had their bowling balls, bowling ball bags, bowling shoes, and probably bowling ball socks. They had those special wristbands, powder, the bowling ball rags and towels, and their family team bowling ball shirts when their family bowled together. They were bowlers in every sense of the sport, and they were good! Now, I know it wasn't me who came up with the idea of forming a summer Saturday team to bowl at the Piketon, but I was all for it, even though, as I said, I didn't have a bowling ball. I had nothing that even said that I knew anything about bowling. But I did my research by watching "Bowling for Dollars." I learned a lot from our TV. There were ten pins; you had to knock down as many as possible in two attempts, and the highest scorer won. Richard and

David were good scorers, and they were very competitive in everything they did, especially Richard, who today probably owns about 3 or 4 of those ungodly bowling rings you obtain for bowling a close to or perfect game. I still don't know that much about the score. Our third member was Paris Gore.

He was dating the Peppers' sister, Nancy, so he was a shoo-in because the Pepper boys kept him close, and I understood that, as most of the guys of our age understood, because Nancy was a beautiful girl. However, in defense of Paris being on the team, he was also a good bowler. He probably picked up some tips from the Peppers, as he spent a lot of time with Nancy and her brothers. Paris was also a band member. He, David, and I played the saxophone, and Richard played the trumpet, which was our common interest. Their common interest was with Paris because he was dating their sister, Nancy, and they were forever the protective brothers. As you can imagine, I made up the fourth team member and was the weak link on the team. I soon realized that I was their handicap, literally. As the summer went on and we started to gain a little momentum and notoriety as a formidable winning team, I became a fair bowler, still using the loaner balls at the alley. One Saturday during one of the tournaments, I bowled a "Turkey," scoring the same score three times in a row. Of course, up to that point, I didn't know about the turkey. The Peppers told me if I bowled the same score on our last game, I'd win a patch for bowling a "Turkey." I came up one pin short, and my buddies scored me that "Turkey," so I didn't even bowl that "Turkey," but I got it. After announcing my accomplishment over the intercom, I was so proud of the patch they presented me with that I decided I was a bowler and would get my bowling ball. I had already purchased some bowling memorabilia, a couple of wrist bands, and powder bags to dry the palms of my hands, and I brought a white hand towel from home to keep my borrowed bowling ball dry. Now it just so happened that I had decided to be sharp and prepared the following week after my "Turkey" win, before our upcoming Saturday match, in which we were up against one of the better opponents. A yard sale was held by a neighbor who was a retired policeman. And you guessed it, he had a bowling ball for sale. It was black and without a bag, but it was a bowling ball, and he didn't want much for it. I think I gave him 3 dollars for it - a dollar for each hole. As I said, it was black but lacked its luster, and I knew I had some work to get it cleaned up and shine again. Although I tried everything under the sun to get that ball to shine, nothing worked. But I was very creative. I think creativity ran in our family. Our father, who is very handy with his hands, especially as a mechanic, could tear down an engine and put it back together again.

He built the second addition to our home, a garage and a shed. The shed housed some of our gardening tools, shovels, rakes, a lawn mower, and several cans of spray paint in various colors. Yep, I found the shade of paint that would look good on my bowling ball, semi-glossy black. Of course, I had to clean off my newfound friend with turpentine to remove the various polishes I had tried to bring out its luster, to introduce it to its new coat of fast-drying black spray paint. Boy, I'm telling ya, after a couple of coats, my baby made a grand entrance that Saturday morning as I presented her to the lanes. It was Saturday, and it was time to bowl. I walked down to the Peppers' home, as I did most often, because Richard was the oldest of us and the first of us to drive and have a car, a light blue 1969 Chevy Corvair. It was our ride. I wrapped my ball in a towel because I didn't want to get it dirty before the games. But I showed it to Richard and David, bragging about how good it looked, and they agreed. At least, at the time, I thought they did. I really couldn't notice because I didn't care. I had a beautiful black beauty of a bowling ball, and she was mine, all mine, and together, we were going to rack up some pins that day. As the fellows and I walked into the alley, I walked right past the loaners, not looking in their direction, yet I felt their three socket-like eyeballs staring me down in a sarcastic way, as if to be casting me as a trader, a cheater. Although I was and still am 5'7", I walked tall, right past all the loaners to my place, where our team met with our opposing team. That morning, I felt and looked at the part of a person about the game, bowling, and I dressed the part and moved throughout the lane areas as though I owned the place. I had removed my ball from its home towel and laid it by my seat, so no one noticed I hadn't had a bowling bag. As Richard, David, and Paris pulled their bowling balls from their bags and placed them on the rails, so did I. "Wow," I heard someone say, "Man, that's some shiny ball, Edwin." I thanked 'em but made light of it as if it wasn't a big deal. But it was a big deal. Not what you think. It was a big deal because, just after a few threw down the lanes, a lane attendant approached our area to inquire about the several black stripes that showed up on their lanes as he pointed them out to us. "Whose ball made those stripes on those lanes?". No one said a word, as I had just thrown my black beauty down the lane, which, just by chance, got hung up in the return pin carriage and didn't return as it should have. I immediately disappeared as the attendant continued his inquiry.

I disappeared and ran to the loan rack I had abandoned. I grabbed a loaner without checking to see if it even fit my hand and fingers. I placed it on the bowling lane rack as the attendant looked away. When he turned around, I told him, "I don't know, this is my ball right here," pointing to the ball I had just laid down. The attendant reset the pins, and the black beauty did not return home. The attendant departed; there were a few seconds of silence, then laughter. As we continued our game, someone asked me, "Hey man, aren't you going to get your ball?" I said, "Hell no, what makes you think that's my ball?" I told rhetorically as I denied the truth and proudly boasted, *"I Throw Strikes, Not Stripes"*.

THE DARNDEST THING

The late Art Linkletter said it best, in his famed Family TV Show, "Kids Say the Darndest Things", and later repeated a second time by Bill Cosby. And my granddaughter, Jerniah, has said the darndest things. You know, some kids, especially the very young ones, somehow always have a little more insight into any given or particular situation. I have just recently received quite a dose of some of those personal observations, unsolicited opinions, and thought-provoking comments from one of those little people we call grandchildren, which, in my case, are a bit different from our children. As a child, I was taught that you spoke when spoken to and stayed in your place. But we all know that times have changed, and like me, some of you have become your mother or father. My father spoiled my kids, his grandkids, and I followed that path and found myself indoctrinated and bombarded by the intellect of one of my granddaughters, Jerniah, whom we lovingly call Ni-Ni. Ni-Ni if you would, close your eyes. Now, imagine the cartoon character that was a little chicken with glasses. That was Egghead Jr., and he was always given Foghorn Leghorn a hard time because of his intellect. Well, that's my Ni-Ni. Unlike Egghead, Jr., Ni-Ni was and still today is a thinker and a talker, and I'm sorry to say, I don't think she got that from me. I'd love to claim it, but I can claim she has adapted my sense of humor, and it drives her Mama Allison crazy, and our daughter loves it. However, Ni-Ni's humor could be somewhat questionable at times. For instance, one Saturday morning as I was on my back, up under our kitchen sink, attempting to replace a faulty faucet, - and yes, I was like Dr. Huxtable or Rock from the tv shows "Bill Cosby" and "Rock" who felt they could save a penny doing the work themselves. And sometimes I did. So, with little light and elbow room, I was interrupted to be interrogated by Ni-Ni, the youngest of her two sisters, at the age of four or five, going on seventy-five. Now, at her age, she had good diction except for pronouncing my name. Everyone else was okay with it. But she called me Papa Eg-Win. She didn't see a great need to correct it if I answered. Like Pavlov's theory, I respond every time. Yet, her vocabulary is that of a 5th Grader. And no, I am not smarter than a 5th Grader, but I'd put money on Ni-Ni.

So, she bends over and looks into the confined place and ask, "Papa Egwin", and of course, I know that's my name, so I reply yes Ni-Ni – this being only about her 57th question thus far - she's only been awake for about 5 minutes – gonna be a long day, and she asks, "What are you doing?" I told her that I was fixing the faucet, and she replied by parroting my statement to let me know she was listening and understood me. And I say, "Yes, Niah", with a bit of patience. She returns to an upright position and says, Umm…and pauses. Next, she asked, "Papa Egwin", and we danced again. And her final statement was, "Do you know what you're doing? Immediately, I raised my hand, bumped my head in reaction to her question, and assumed that my wife had put her up to asking me that question. She denies it and laughs as if to say, "She knows you don't." Kids don't just say the darndest things; they make statements of garnered truth. They don't think about whether or not they are politically correct; they know that something needs to be said or asked, and they need the answer to understand their newest unexplained experience. Well, I've realized I also need to watch what I say around Ni-Ni because she is always listening. When Ni-Ni is acting up, I might say, Ni-Ni, you want a butte whooping? Of course, she'd nod in the negative and smile at me as if to say, "Pa-Pa Egwin, you ain't gonna do that", as if saying, I'm your little partner in crime". Little did I know she understood what I asked about the butte whooping and learned how to say it. As we did quite often, while lying on the living room couch, my haven of comfort, Ni-Ni, would climb onto my belly and lay her head on my chest. I would hum the Lullaby song I sang to my grandchildren, and she'd soon doze off to sleep. One evening, Ni-Ni climbed up onto my belly as she would do now and then. She said, "Papa Egwin, I love you." Before I could respond that I loved her too, she quickly lifted her head and said, "But I'm tired of getting my butt whooped", as if she was attempting to open up a conversation for negotiations. Well, you can imagine how surprised I was at that encounter. Of course, I told her, now Ni-Ni, you can't say the word butte, and she nodded and smiled and said, "Papa Egwin, but I am". I searched to tell her in words that she understood and would ease her little concerns and resolve her anxiety, and assured her that I understood her request. I told her Now you know Ni-Ni, that all you have to do is obey and do what Mama Allison and Papa Egwin ask you to, and you won't get any butt whopped.

She smiled and shook her head as if to say she accepted what would probably be a challenge, but she understood our resolution. She climbed onto my belly, lay her head back on my chest, and calmly fell asleep. From that day on, she's never received any punishment from me. Today, Jerniah is a mother of a beautiful son, making me a great-grandfather for the first time. She has decided to study law to become an attorney. Ain't that *"The Darndest Thing?"*

THE WHISTLER

As a teenager, I was probably known by everyone in our neighborhood as one of the Robinson boys, since we had six boys and two girls. It wasn't unusual for families back then to have a large family. Yet, they eventually got to know me as their neighborhood Columbus Dispatch Carrier, and if I have to say so, I was a good "paperboy", as we called them back then. Some called me the "Whistler" because I whistled the whole route as I threw my papers. There were some homes where I'd have to open their gates and walk into their yards to get the paper to their porches. I was pretty good and took pride in getting the newspapers onto their porches. If I missed, I'd take the time to walk up, pick the paper up, and place it on their porch or inside the screen door. In inclement weather, I would put the papers in plastic bags, and if I didn't have the bags for protection, I'd walk up to my customers' doors and place them inside their screen doors. I received various comments about my services and took pride in keeping my customers happy. Those happy smiles meant good tips for the collection week, especially around the holidays. I looked forward to Christmas mostly. And I'd whistle all the Christmas songs I knew. I've continued to whistle because it is one of my ways of feeling good. My customers back then would complement my whistling by saying, "We knew that was you coming up the street by your whistling, and it was collection week," or "We could hear you whistling way over on the other street". It was true that I loved to whistle, but it could have been even truer that I loved collection week, and I guess it was evident in my whistling because collection day was payday for me. A percentage went to the Columbus Dispatch, and I kept the rest. I don't recall what it was, but I'm sure I didn't get what I was worth because I provided quality customer service, which we hardly receive today. And there is no whistling. Today, I continue to whistle and sometimes have to catch myself because I may be at my workplace, but

I don't want to annoy anyone. Sometimes, I may shop at one of our local grocery stores or department stores, and I find myself whistling away, usually along with the song being aired over their intercom.

Once, I was so engrossed in myself and just whistled aloud with such confidence that I was interrupted by another shopper, saying, "You know, that's something you don't hear much of anymore". I thought that I was bothering the elderly man and apologized. And he said, "Oh no, it sounds great!" I thanked the kind gentleman for his compliment and continued whistling, now vigorously. As I shopped, I thought, "Why aren't more folks whistling?" I thought there were more of us, but it's becoming a lost art. And I felt it was funny to imagine my wife attempting to whistle a noticeable song. No way, but amusing. And it is weird when a person really can't whistle a tune. They may be able to whistle, but a tune noticeable by someone else is another tune – pun intended. I consider myself a reasonably good whistler, and it was brought back to my attention recently during a not-so-happy occasion, the funeral of a neighborhood friend. As some of the friends I grew up with from the old neighborhood had returned from the burial site to the church where they held the repass, we sat and talked about the old days. The subject came up about nicknames, certain events in the neighborhood, or situations we shared, and my instinctive whistling when I was the paperboy. "Yeah, Edwin, we could hear you whistling as you circled the block from Clarfield to Moundview and then to Augmont, especially when you were coming around to collect the newspaper bills due". I responded, "Yeah, it was payday, but I never knew that there was a difference in my whistling on collection week; however, you'd be happy too if you knew you were about to Get Paid?" And someone said, "Yep! That's why some of your customers would say, "Here comes Edwin the Whistler, collecting his bill." Everyone at the table broke out into laughter. Afterward, the repass ended, and we bid our goodbyes and departed the venue. As we headed towards our vehicles, and I strolled whistling the last song I heard, someone from the parking lot shouted, *"I Hear the Whistler"*.

TWISTED

It was summer and time for our annual training week in the Guard Band. Every year, we would travel to Ohio and perform in various parades, at several senior citizen communities, local fairgrounds such as Kings Island or Cedar Point, and Put-In-Bay. As usual, the band provided its transportation and drivers. It was my turn to drive. I was responsible for signing out a 48-passenger bus and ensuring the maintenance was up to par. After signing out the vehicle, I'd pull the bus up to the band location at Rickenbacker, and the band members would load their instruments and personal belongings before the commander. He would usually be the last to enter, give a quick safety briefing, and provide the driver the nod to move out to our first destination. Before travelling, the commander would inform us where we were headed for our first scheduled performance. All the information in the two weeks would have been posted on the unit bulletin board, and I was responsible for ensuring I had the proper information and directions. So, once I got the nod to head out, "Let's Go Robbie", the commander said, I said, "Yes, Sir," and closed the double doors, rechecked the mirrors, and looked toward the rear through my rearview mirror to ensure everyone was seated. Most of the travel time was no more than two to three hours. That morning, we were headed to Port Clinton and over to Put-In-Bay. We were to be there for the weekend. It was Friday, we would unpack and sleep that evening, set up the following Saturday morning to perform, and head for our next performance on Sunday. That is at least how I remember it. It could have been a shorter stay. It always varies. While travelling, of course, we had scheduled stops for gas and meals. About halfway towards Marion, Ohio, we had a planned stop for gas. And when we did that, the members got off to "hit the head" (military term for restroom), take a piss, or grab some snacks. After I had topped off the tank, I walked into the station's store to pick up something to drink. I had seen a TV commercial concerning a new beverage, and it was a hot Friday, so I thought it was a good time to try out that new drink. I hurried to the beverage section because most band members had already shopped and returned to the bus by then. The commander and I were the last at the clerk's stand to purchase our products. I was in front of the commander, holding what I was dying to try.

I picked some in the refrigerated section, so they were good and cold. When the store employee asked, 'Who next?", I moved up. Then, behind me, I heard the commander ask me, "Robbie, you're not about to buy that, are you?" I said, "Yes, sir, I've wanted to try this out since I saw the commercial." He looked at me and said, 'You know that has alcohol in it, right?" I looked down and read it out loud, "Twisted Lemonade, 5% Alcohol by Volume." I looked at the commander; he was laughing at me. I headed back to the refrigerator to return my beverages and said, "Damn, Chief, that's twisted". Before I could board the bus completely, I could hear the laughter of the band members, and the rest of the trip was long and filled with jokes on my behalf to Put-In-Bay, and some of them were pretty *"Twisted."*

WOODY

I grew up not liking cats because we never owned one. The only cats we saw were the feral cats that came from the field next to our home, and they weren't very friendly animals. I won't tell you what "people" used to do with cats they could catch. Let's say I've repeatedly asked for forgiveness for my acts in our "Catch and Release" Cat Program. We did have a dog or two as children. But as I got older, there wasn't much room for a dog, and I had never been one for cats. I didn't care for a cat until I re-enlisted in the army, married, and had children. I was stationed and assigned to Fort Lee, Virginia's 392nd Army Band. My family followed a few months later. So, we were befriended by a fellow bandsman, BJ, and his wife, Barbara Johnson. They did not have children, but they did have two cats, and on occasion, Barbara would babysit our children while their mother and I were at work. After about a year, the Johnsons received orders to deploy to Germany, and since our children had grown attached to their cats, they asked us if our kids would like to have them. They both loved one of the cats. Our son favored the B&W and our daughter, the Calico. After fighting back, I gave in. I did not care for cats. But I quickly found out that they had their own personalities. The gray and white Calico was a real female dog. Her given name by the Johnsons was Misty, but that name did not fit her temperament, just as Mittens was certainly not fitting for the B&W cat. So, we decided to wait until they grew into a name that we thought was appropriate for each. Well, it wasn't long before the Calico's character reared its ugly head when it snapped at me. She scared me, gave me a few goose bumps, which made me pause. But I had to let her know who the boss was. Angered a bit, I snatched her up by the back of her neck, held her high in the air, face to face, and yelled, "Listen, Karla, you don't rule anything here". We then had an understanding; she left me alone, and I left her alone. She became Karla from that day on. I hadn't considered calling her that, but I enjoyed the TV series "Cheers". Those who know of the show understand. Now, we still hadn't found a good name for the B&W until one evening, something happened. Afterwards, the kids had run their bath water in preparation to take their bath after dinner, which they had routinely done for weeks. This time, though, they forgot to close the door and had left it open with the lights off.

The B&W would find his fun all day while the kids were at school by jumping in and out of the dry tub. That particular evening, he found out quickly that it was not dry. Suddenly, we heard a wild commotion from upstairs, where the bathroom was located. It was water splashing and the wildest sounds you've ever heard from a cat. We turned to look toward the stairs where the cat sounds were still coming. And there he was, soaking wet from having dived into a tub full of water. He had scurried quickly down to the bottom landing of the stairs and paused, frozen there, looking in our direction as if he had something of importance on his mind, something he desperately wanted to say. Of course, we laughed hard because he looked cute, sad, yet distraught. If we could have placed captions over his head, it might have read what his eyes were already saying: "Which one of you Son-of-a-B*t*hes put water in my tub?" Laughing at him, the kids grabbed a few towels to dry him off. I think I was laughing the hardest because he and I had become friends by now. Yep, he turned me into a cat lover, which I thought would never happen. As I helped the kids dry him off, I called him a real knucklehead. He was a lovable knucklehead, just like the character on "Cheers", but he was our *"Woody."*

YOU'RE NOT MICHAEL JACKSON

It was the beginning of 1987, and I had just re-enlisted in the United States Army, leaving my dear family, wife, son, and daughter behind until Uncle Sam could provide housing for us. Our son, Edwin II, was 8 years old, and his sister, Ayrika, whom we pronounced "Erica", was just 5 years old, and boy, did she already have her personality. Ayrika was a 2-month premature baby. My wife, Allison, whose doctor, Dr. Alfred Thomas, delivered our son, calculated Ayrika's due date to February 14, 1981 (Valentine's Day). However, Ayrika did not have it, and Santa Claus dropped her off the day after Christmas, December 26, 1980. Ayrika Daniece Robinson weighed 4 pounds, five ounces, and was 19 inches long. After being prepped and probed by the nurses and doctors, a nurse passed her to my left hand. My baby daughter's head full of dark black hair lay softly between my index and ring fingers. Her butt rested just on the heel of my palm, and her legs stretched with all ten toes just past my wrist. She was crying from the needle probing, and I was doing my best to console her. She was beautiful and she was strong. Yet, she had some complications. Our doctor informed us that Ayrika would have to go into an incubator that would help her breathe. She had asthma, and her lungs were not strong enough for her to go home, plus it was the hospital's procedure that all babies should be at least 5 pounds before being released into the parents' care. A couple of weeks passed, and Ayrika never gained any additional weight, but her health improved, and the doctors agreed that she was strong enough and allowed her to come with us. Of course, Allison and I prayed, as our family and church members did during that time. Our pastor, Bishop Sherman Watkins of Greater Emmanuel, now Higher Grounds, visited and prayed with us over our daughter, still in the incubator.

Years later, when Ayrika began to speak, we noticed her having difficulty pronouncing certain vowels and had some concerns. Yet, our son, Edwin II, understood every word his sister said and became our interrupter many times. Later, we found that Ayrika needed her adenoids removed, which was the cause of most of her speaking difficulties. Yet, as she was attempting to learn to speak with the freedom that the operation had provided, we thought it was best that she be enrolled in Speech Therapy to assist her in overcoming some of her speech habits caused by her previous medical condition. Soon, she excelled – as she has in many other things since - so that not too soon afterwards, she didn't require the training as she spoke with force and clarity. She was always a fast learner, and although small in stature, she was strong, as many people discovered after shaking her hand. Yet, Ayrika's sense of humor fell a bit short. There would be times when she would find her brother and mother, and I laughing out loud about a particular thing or situation on the television, and Ayrika, while sitting right in front of the TV, not more than 3 feet from the screen, would turn around and ask, "What's so funny?" She didn't get it, but was in love with Lucille Ball. Ayrika would sit in front of the TV and watch the "I LOVE LUCY" sitcom from the beginning to the end, and laugh so hard that it made us laugh, and Jerry Lewis laugh the same. Ayrika's humor was all about the physical part of humor. And Lucy and Jerry were physical comedians, with the face gestures, falls, and awkward moments when Lucy was working on the candy assembly line and couldn't keep up with all the chocolate drops that needed to be packaged. Ayrika relates to that type of humor. To this day, I can't recall anything else that made her laugh harder than her big brother, Edwin II, whom she affectionately called "Bubby". He could make us all laugh as he easily mimicked various comedians or actors and recited their memorable or funny lines. He's natural. He and Ayrika share a special brother-sister bond. Yet she is special in that she's my baby-girl, her mother's daughter, and of course, Bubby's little sister and partner in crime. I'll explain later. Oh, there was one thing about Ayrika. She could always let you know when she was upset. There were times when we would look up late in the evening, and before my wife and I could tell the kids it was time for bed, Ayrika would have already gone to her room and shut her door. And had we made too much noise outside her door, maybe laughing at the TV, she would stroll out and say, "Can you keep it down, I'm trying to sleep".

She did that at an early age until she left home. On one special occasion, Ayrika let on how she felt about a situation when she and her cousin, Yon Daryl Armstrong, who we called "Yonnie," were in a commercial with a very special visitor. Yonnie, at the time, was the Children's Hospital Poster child for Sickle Cell. Unfortunately, he lost that battle he so bravely fought for thirty years. In 1985, Rev. Jesse Jackson was campaigning in Columbus. Rev. Jackson was an adopted child and had agreed to do a few commercials in Columbus, Ohio, during his bid for the office of President of the United States. And my sister-in-law, Deborah "Debbie" Horn-Armstrong, Yonnie's mom, headed up the Foster and Adoption Programs for Franklin County Children's Service. She contacted Rev. Jackson's administration to request his acceptance to do the commercials. She thought having Rev. Jackson speak on Fostering and Adoption would be a good idea since he had personal experience. Our children, Yonnie and Ayrika, will be used as models in the ads. I had just re-enlisted and was in Virginia when Allison told me the story. Allison started preparing Ayrika for the shot when they learned about the commercial. She told Ayrika who she would meet and what they would do during the filming. I was filmed; I believe in a local church. The producers were preparing Ayrika by having her sit on Rev. Jackson's lap and having her cousin behind the chair on which the two were seated. They produced two videos that day, and they aired soon after. What caught everyone off guard was when Allison and Ayrika got to the church that morning. They were informed again about the event, what she would be doing, why she would be doing it, and who she would be meeting and performing the commercial with. Ayrika was finally about to meet Rev. Jackson. As he entered the waiting room to visit Ayrika and Yonnie, Rev. Jackson bent over to introduce himself by extending his right hand to shake Ayrika's. He said, "Hello, little girl, what is your name?" And without hesitation, our 5-year-old daughter looked straight into Rev. Jackson's face and shouted, *"You're not Michael Jackson"*.

LIFE EXPERIENCES

DEAR EDWIN

She was gorgeous, and she enchanted me. We sat beside each other in all the classes except for Biology. She smiled at me, probably at one of my jokes or smart-ass statements about something our teacher might have said, but she smiled at me. Of course, it was after a couple of weeks that we were in class, and we got to know each other's names at least. I had a thought about her, and I wanted to share it with her, but I didn't know how to tell her that she had a beautiful smile, which mesmerized me. Soon, the thought got the best of my nerves, and I pounced on the next time she glanced my way with the smile I eagerly awaited. When our eyes met, I unintentionally but gently took hold of her hand, stared directly into her now surprised mahogany eyes, and said, "Has anyone ever told you that you have a beautiful smile?" I hit gold! I could have sworn that she blushed if it wasn't for her small, coco-brown complexion. I'm almost sure she did as she lowered her head and slowly turned her face away. Yet, she did not retract her hand, and I could still see her smiling, somewhat embarrassed or shy. I was never that bold when it came to girls. I was shy myself. She continued to allow me to hold her hand through the class as she finally returned and said thanks. She and I became good friends and soon an item. I was working a part-time job and had a car. I was a sophomore, and she was a Junior at our High School, but I did not have as many classes as she did. I had taken additional courses the summer before graduating early. I would finish my last class, go to work, and return to pick her up to take her home. I was a romanticist and sometimes purchased bread and lunch meat, a couple of sodas, and some fruit or a couple of cupcakes or donuts, and suggested we stop at the local park for lunch. She was soft-spoken and up for an adventure. She was a sweet person. We had a fast-paced relationship, and I'm not sure what went wrong, but I believe I could have been the problem. One night, I was invited to her home, and I had already met her family, mother, brothers, and sisters. She didn't have a father. And my visits became regular. Then one night, when my car was in the shop, I had a friend drop me off. I told him I'd call him when I was ready to go home. Time passed. Her family had all gone to bed, and she and I were alone.

One thing led to another, and before I knew it, we had made out. It was way past 11:00, and I had to get home. Not thinking of the time, I called my friend, and his father answered and told me that his son was asleep and could not come out to pick me up. I told her about my problem, and she offered to pay for a cab to get me home. I usually had cash on me, but that night, I didn't have enough for a cab, which was over ten dollars. Although I had become a man that night, I still thought like a boy. I saw her the next day in class, took her hand, and asked her if she was okay. She smiled that wonderful smile she knew I loved and said, "Yes, I'm fine". And I remember telling her, "Yes, you are". So, it may be corny for some, but she was "Fine" to me. We continued our relationship until she attended a college-prep course the summer I graduated. I recall visiting her with my uncle Calvin and my cousin, who was a female. When I arrived, I caught some vibes from her friends that they didn't think Robin was my cousin. I talked to her, and she was very distant from me. I remember talking to her about my going into the service, and she was pretty much against it, asking me not to leave her, but I enlisted a few months later. Now, in the United States Naval Boot Camp, I would write and call her, and our phone conversations were very short, and she very seldom replied to my love letters. Finally, I got hold of her on the phone and caught that vibe again that something wasn't quite right. I asked her if everything was okay, and she said yes. That soft voice kept me until I got home to her. But I had a feeling that our relationship was going south, if it hadn't already gotten there, and I soon would find out. After I graduated from camp, I returned home, quickly cleaned up, cleaned up the car, and drove with some anticipation and hesitation, remembering our last phone call. I parked in front of their home and headed toward their front door. Her brother was on the porch and called to tell her I was there. She opened the door; I reached out to hug her and found out then that there was a problem. I sat down and asked her what was wrong; she was slow to answer. I handed her a copy of my graduation photo in my tropical whites. She held the photo and said she didn't think we should keep seeing each other. I was in denial because I should have known I had received my "Dear John" over our last phone call while still in boot camp. It was over. Upset, I marched toward their front door without a word, jumped in my car, and left a trail of gravel and dust behind me. I got home a lot faster than it took me to drive to her home. I may have been speeding.

When I got home, looking like a fool, I noticed that my sister and our stepmother were silent as they glanced at each other. I asked my sister if she knew. And she told me she had been seeing another guy for some time. Yep, I was the standing fool. I stood for some time looking at both, and they knew that I wanted to ask them why someone didn't tell me. But I didn't and turned, marched to my bedroom, and slammed the door. It was the first time that I was truly hurt. I don't know which was worse, not being told that it was over by those who knew it was over, or that I couldn't accept that she had sent me signals my eyes saw but my ears refused to hear of the incoming messages carrying departing news for me in the form of a *"Dear Edwin"*.

GETTING PAID

Talk about getting paid for my musical talents. I had always wanted to be a professional musician. Not the kind that was famous and world-renowned. I just wanted to get to the point that someone would pay me for playing. That day finally came as I belonged to yet another local band after playing for and with several groups, ranging from gospel, Funk, R&B, Pop, Jazz, and marching bands to school and military bands. I even played with a country group. But there was a place that I thought back then was the epitome of "Arrival." You've made it, and folks wanted to hear your music. It was "My Brother's Place", owned by "Bubbles Holiday", a big promoter of musicians and featured artists on tour and traveling through Columbus. It was on Long Street, and there were others that our band booked on Mt. Vernon, like Mr. P's and Ivory's clubs, which Dave Humphrey owned, and many of the local musicians performed at these very same clubs and bars. There was the famed Hank Marr, Rusty Bryant (Personal Lessons), Gene Walker, Bobby Floyd, Bobby Austin, Cornell Wiley (Bass Instructor), Joe Yates, Greg Pearce, Kenny Weaver, James "Smooth" Elliott, The Hamptons; David, Chucky, and Mark (distance relatives of the late Lionel Hampton), Rock Hall of Famer, Melvin Stewart, Rodger Parish, Arnett Howard and my life-long running friends and partners, Melissa Redman, Joyce Robinson-Agbaymabiasa, and James "Smooth" Elliott. Other one-time known clubs to visit were "The Up and Down Lounge" and "The Valley Dale Ball Room". Artists like Nancy Wilson and Otis Redding played these. I was fortunate to perform with most of them throughout my career. But it was, I thought, back around 1983-85, that our band was booked for "My Brother's Place". I thought, "We've made it." Our careers were on the right track. But lo and behold, as we finished breaking down the set and packing our gear to return home, I was pulled to the side by our bass player, Mark

Hampton, our acting manager. He handed me eight single one-dollar bills. If it wasn't for the fact that I was currently then the Choir Director at our church and I had to get home and prepare for service, I might have acted a fool, argued, and cursed Mark out after he gave me the excuse that we had to share the door – split the "Cover Charge" with the management. The band consisted of seven members.

I said, "Hell, Mark, it was a packed house, and you mean to tell me that the band made $63.00? Man, my mother and her friends came to hear us play, and they paid $10.00 each. That was 40 bucks! I threw my padded saxophone case into the passenger door of my van, which I had opened to load my equipment stands and microphones. Without saying anything to him, I slammed the door shut after loading my equipment, jumped into my van, started it up, and left with a bad taste. It was the norm to split my pay with Allison. So, she woke up and asked me how we did. I said, "Okay", pulling out two twenties and a ten-dollar bill from my wallet, folding them together, placing my pocket money on her nightstand, and telling her I made a hundred bucks as usual. She said it was nice, rolled over, and returned to sleep. I had played at "The Up & Down Lounge" and "Valley Dale Ballroom" before, and it wasn't my first time playing at "My Brother's Place". It's not like I was a challenged musician. I played in a band and performed most of my life. I later enrolled as a Music Major at Ohio State University in 1978 after a stint in the United States Navy. I volunteered to perform in the USS Nimitz Ship Band, where I was stationed. Although we had primary duties, our command supported the band as we toured Europe and showed off the Navy's first nuclear-powered aircraft carrier. So, most of our time was spent rehearsing to perform in the countries we visited: Germany, England, Scotland, Spain, Morocco, Tunisia, Italy, and Puerto Rico. It became our primary duty. During that time, we played in concerts and performed military tunes and marches. On May 5, 1975, we performed for President

Gerald Ford during the ship's commissioning. In July 1977, I honored my 3-year contract with Uncle Sam and returned to Columbus, Ohio. I soon joined a community gospel group. One of our members, Melissa Redman, started on trumpet and switched to playing the electric bass guitar. The group's director was a Music director in the Columbus Public School System, Joyce Robinson (no relation). Melissa was also a student at OSU and a member of the "Jazz Rock" Band along with Bobby Floyd, who was on keyboards. Melissa encouraged me to join the band. Later, Dr. Sullivan had booked us to play "My Brother's Place"; even though it wasn't a paid gig, it was "My Brother's Place". I had dreamed of becoming a returning booked performer shortly after that night. I should have been dreaming about getting paid handsomely for performing at "My Brother's Place".

However, my military obligation is not over. My 3-year contract was a 6-year contract: 3 years of active duty and 3 years of reserve duty. So, I enlisted in the US Naval Reserves on Yearling Road, Columbus, Ohio. So I was informed that there was a military band in Columbus, the 338th Army Reserve Band. In 1978, I requested a transfer and enlisted in the Army Band. Yet, it wasn't until I had performed at my Brother's Place that I realized I was a professional musician and was paid well to play my saxophone. And I was getting paid when I was in the Navy for all those overseas gigs Since then, I have been satisfied with chasing the paid gigs. I later enlisted in an active Army Band at Fort Lee, VA. The pay was good, and I could "Woodshed" my skills. I did 3 years with the 392nd Army Band and ventured into other Military Occupational Skills. I deployed to Saudi Arabia in 1990 during the Gulf War and took my horn. I was Alan S. Webster #153's Minister of Music in Hanau, Germany. During my deployment in Iraq, Iran, and Kuwait, I provided spiritual accompaniment at religious services that we rendered. We returned to Germany after our deployment, and our mission was over. My family and I received orders to ship to Fort

Hood, Texas, where we joined The Christian House of Prayer in Copper's Cove, TX. I soon joined the Worship Band and acted as the Horn Section Leader. That was a great gig. I was honorably discharged on March 10, 1995, and immediately enlisted in the Ohio Army National Guard 122nd Army Band. I served with them for 5 years and continued to perform in the church as a Minister of Music and member of a Worship Band. And if asked about which gig is paid or pays more, without hesitation, I'd say, "Playing for the Lord" is the most rewarding gig because even when I am not playing, I'm *"Getting Paid"*.

HOUSTON, WE HAVE A PROBLEM

Ronald Houston was one of my Naval "Running Buddies". Edward "Poncho" Harper was the other. We volunteered to play in the ship's band, USS NIMITZ CVAN-68. Being the only African Americans in the band, we naturally gravitated toward each other, and it didn't hurt that we were all in the same department, the Deck Department. We were what they called "Deck Apes", basically the ship's janitors and labor workers. So, wherever you saw one of us, you saw at least one of the others. Harper and I trained in Boot Camp together in Great Lakes, IL. I don't recall where Houston trained, but he was on the ship and a boatswain's mate in our division. Boatswain mates scraped and painted the boat, mainly the outside, where we removed the barnacles and returned the ship to its color of Ship's Grey. We moored the boat to the docks and drove the liberty launches that carried our sailors into the docks of Germany, England, Scotland, Italy, and Spain. However, because we were members of the USS NIMITZ Ship's Band, we saw little of the hard life. The Nimitz was the Navy's first nuclear-power aircraft carrier, and the United States toured her throughout Europe to show our muscles. And so, the band was to announce our arrival, and the band would perform on the pier as the ship cruised into the country's port. And band members, dressed in either Dress Blue or Tropical Whites "Cracker Jacks", would be flown from the ship's deck in one of her two CH-46E Sea Knight helicopters to the country's port. The band in formation would perform all the well-known naval marches and tunes as the ship pulled in with sailors "Manning the Rails", docked, and moored by our fellow Boatswain mates. And once we had completed our duty as bandsmen, we were released to enjoy the country and its customs. This event took place at every port we visited and at stateside ports. One occasion I recall was when we ported to Fort Jacksonville, Florida, where an announcement was made that most of the local hotels offered all sailors a discount if we stayed at their establishment. It was the weekend in Houston, and I had decided to take up the offer and spend that weekend enjoying the beach and Florida sunshine as civilians. I don't know what plans Harper had. Still, he did not run with us that weekend, so it was just Houston and me.

Houston was a few years older than Harper and me, and he had more worldly experience and ideas on simulating certain situations and environments. Houston was well-read and very intelligent concerning many things. He always had some literature in the back pocket of his dark blue dungarees and was found somewhere on the ship, nestled in a corner, reading a book or magazine. Houston was more adventurous than most, and that appealed to me. Because of it, we would find ourselves in intense situations and predicaments. Well, this time was no different from some of our other outings. I followed along and assessed the areas we would venture into, and on that day, the weather was perfect. The hotel that Houston persuaded me to stay at was very nice. It looked expensive. Covetable Mercedes and other relatively costly imports and sports cars surrounded the hotel parking area. As guys were exiting their vehicles and handing their keys to the valets, they either walked toward the double brass doors being held open by a set of doormen or around the building toward the outside pool that was visibly seen from across the street, which was a four-lane fairway that housed several palm trees. Houston and I followed the two guys who were headed toward the pool. We wanted to check out the area where we were immediately addressed by a gentleman in swimming shorts and a long terry-cloth robe that was open. He introduced himself as Michael and welcomed us to the hotel. The way he started in on how great the place was, Houston and I, at least I did, thought Michael worked there. But he didn't; Houston was aware of that fact. Michael, who reminded me of my brother Michael, maybe it was the striking similarity and way he carried himself, yet I paid little attention to it. Michael told us about the discount, walked us up to the counter inside the building, and offered to show us the area later if we were interested. Everything was easily accessible from the poolside. To this day, I still can't believe that the cost was only $10.00 each, $20.00 for one room. We hurriedly paid for the room and headed to a store to purchase some swimming shorts, carrying a change of clothes in a small laundry bag. Michael escorted us to our room and wished us a good stay. He was very accommodating. Later, we found out that he was wealthy and lived there. Once Houston and I changed into our shorts, we headed out, waved at Michael, who was now outside by the pool, talking to what could have been friends or guests like us. We stopped to inquire about local restaurants, the best locations on the beach, etc.

We were looking for a transportation rental. Fort Jackson was a prominent place. We also asked when their pub, located downstairs, was available. After we hit the beach and stopped at a suggested restaurant, where we could sit in our bathing suits, we returned to the hotel. We didn't get a rental because Houston was very tight on spending his money. I suggested we didn't need the car since everything was within walking distance. I agreed. So, back at the hotel, we stopped in the pub for a drink or two. It was located on the sidewalk opposite the hotel. Houston and I took a stool at the bar parallel to and facing the sidewalk windows of the pub. Behind the bar was a panoramic mirror, and as I received my 7 & 7 and took my first sip, I glanced into the mirror and quickly said, *"Houston, we have a problem"*. He said, "I know Rob, it's not a problem". The hotel was gay! Owned and operated. We hadn't noticed it when we registered. That is, I didn't. We had walked twice by the pool, and I hadn't seen the lack of women. Houston, a little bit less than me, probably did, but never said anything about it. And that's when it hit me. My brother is gay, and it was Michael's mannerisms that reminded me of my brother. I should have noticed, but I had never been homophobic or against gay people, so maybe that was why I was not that tuned into the atmosphere. However, we were sailors, and we already had a bad name. I didn't want to be caught up in rumors about Houston and me living it up at a Gay Hotel. I was young and hadn't yet realized that it was okay. Besides, it was the 70s, and people still hadn't been accepting of the gay community, although I had always been accepting of my brother. So, after Houston said it wasn't a problem, I told him I wanted to find another location; however, it was late, and we probably wouldn't find a place as cheap as ours. So, I was disturbed by being there, just very cautious, and hoped no one from the ship would see me. Houston couldn't care less. It was 1976, and I was still young and uneducated about the culture, so I was hesitant to stay until our appointed host, Michael, approached us to see if we were getting around okay. I explained my concern about the establishment, that we didn't know it was for gays, but he assured me that they weren't exclusive and that we were not in any danger, nor would we be approached unless we wanted to be. Then he tapped my shoulder and laughed. It took little convincing, and Houston's convincing was that it only cost him ten American dollar bills; he was happy to pay, gay or not. We stayed two nights that weekend.

It was an educational experience for me back then, and I had the opportunity to speak with Michael, who was, as I said, kind and forthcoming. As I asked, we shared our background. I told him he and my brother shared the same name and mannerisms. He right away understood that I was telling him that he was gay, and our conversation seemed lighter on the topic of homosexuality. Houston was not much interested in our talk and was more interested in getting "hammered". Michael was buying. The weekend was great; it was time to return to our ship. We thanked Michael for making our stay pleasant, for his friendship, and his candor about his life. Once back on our boat, I did not share our experience with our shipmates for fear of the backlash from those less educated about homosexuality. Since my naval stint in the 70s, I have been more accepting of all people and their cultures. Today, the community is LGBTQ (Lesbian, Gay, Bisexual, Transgender, and Queer). And I've thought many times, why are black people so hard on the Gay Communities when we've been so segregated and ostracized for being different? And we haven't been the only people who have experienced the prejudiced acts of those who see us as different. The Asians, Jews, Irish, Catholics, Christians, Jews, Democrats, Republicans, blue eyes vs brown eyes (research it), and so on. There is no end to those who seek out others who are different from another group of people. We are all different. This is probably too much "On the nose", but "Why can't we all get along?" Thank you, Mr. Rodney King. I have learned that gay folks, both men and women, are first human beings, like I am first black, then a man. Okay, I'll get off my soapbox. But I have no right to judge anyone's way of life. I spent my whole career defending the rights of others, and no one told me that "Others" was not inclusive. So I fought for all Americans' protection, freedom, and rights. So, when Houston profoundly said to me that it was not a problem, there was not one, when I immaturely said, *"Houston, We Have A Problem"*.

Note: "Ship's grey," often called "haze gray" in the US Navy, is a paint color scheme used on warships to reduce their visibility by minimizing contrast with the horizon and vertical patterns, making them harder to spot.

I AM

Another short story. I was a member of a local Columbus Jazz band, led by bassist Mark Hampton, a distant cousin of the late Lionel Hampton. he and his brother Chucky, a guitarist, were great musicians and formed the group. Our keyboardist was Dr. Fred Armstrong (no relation to Allison), and the singers were Al Taylor and Tammy Perakis. I forgot the drummer's name. We're performing at the Crazy Horse Lounge in Columbus. As we performed on the stage, I noticed a familiar face in the audience, a classmate from our high school, a friend from the neighborhood, Bret Rayford. I nodded at him, and he acknowledged me with a nod. I took it so that he would remember me. It had been at least twenty to twenty-five years since we had seen each other. He looked the same as when we ran the hood, and as we all know, "Black Don't Crack." We finished the set, and I rested my sax on its stand. I walked over to the table where Bret was seated, and we embraced each other as we all did when we saw a friend after a long time in the neighborhood or school. I sat down with Bret and took another glance at him. Bret was a handsome guy. He was conservatively dressed in a dark two-piece suit with a smart-looking shirt and tie combination. I told him, "Man, you're dressed like a doctor or something." He smiled and said, "Well, Edwin, I am." You can imagine I was shocked, not at Bret being a doctor, but that I had *"hit the nail on the head"*. I laughed, and he smiled along with me. Without much of a pause, I stopped laughing. I took another stab at him, jokingly stating, "Hell, man, as crazy as you were back in the day, you could only be a psychiatrist or psychologist", and I continued laughing because I thought my saying that was funny. I looked for Bret's response; he wasn't laughing; he just smiled, and in typical fashion of psychiatry form, seemingly in a deep frame of Freudian thought, quietly said, "Well Edwin, *"I Am."*

Today, Dr. Bret Rayford is one of the nation's most sought-after Clinical Psychologists with a master's degree in counseling from the University of Cincinnati, a Doctorate in Clinical Psychology from Wright State University, and an MBA/Healthcare Administration from the University of Hartford. His appointments: Assistant Professor (Yale University School of Medicine), Director of Health, Mental Health and Addiction Services (CT Department of Correction), Superintendent (Connecticut Juvenile Training), Bureau Chief, Juvenile and Adolescent Services (CT Department of Children and Families), and Superintendent (Solnit Psychiatric Residential Treatment Center).

I OWE A FEW WRITERS

I can honestly say that in 1978, while a student at Ohio State University, a keynote speaker was invited to speak to students at the Union Hall on the main campus. The speaker was the famed playwright and author, whom I knew little about at the time, but had heard his name, James Baldwin. This small figure of a man sat before about a hundred or more students, who seemed to know of his accomplishments, surrounded to listen to his thoughts about life, racism, and his involvement through his stories. I was more interested in the layout of ripe and sweet fruits prepared and available to all. I remember the whole freshly sliced pineapples and the juice that ran from my mouth over my lips and down my chin from every bite. So, I did not gain much from Mr. Baldwin's presence, but I remember his high-pitched voice that lingered after each sentence. I recall him talking about two books, "Amen Corner" and "Go Tell It on the Mountain." Now, life and my experiences in it, or opportunities to experience life, are hilarious because it was later in the 80s that I found myself as a hired stage musician for a local community actor's theater group called "Columbus Centre Stage," directed by Janeanne Sesson, whom I believe was the founder of the organization. The black project was the foundation and the start of some of Columbus's local black actors and actresses. Two of the plays that I performed, get this, were the "Amen Corner" and "Go Tell It on the Mountain." I thought reading both books after the plays were closed was only prudent. It was "Amen Corner" that stirred my heart at the death of the character portrayed as he lay on his deathbed towards the end of the show. We were directed to play the tune "Amen." Joyce Robinson, the music director, with whom I have told folks that we are not related, but over the past 40 years, she and the bass player, Melissa Redman, have become a family to me. I learned about James Baldwin's writings during those two plays and eagerly began to read more. Then there were Paul Lawrence Dunbar and Langston Hughes. Although I must admit, I read others like Edgar Allen Poe and Shakespeare. Then I met Dick Gregory. I had purchased his book titled "Nigger" years ago, and I saw it in a Used Books Store. When the opportunity came about, I finally searched my library to read it. He was an accomplished author and comedian who changed how white audiences thought about him as a black man.

More so than that, though, he was like many of our great black writers; he was an activist. After reading the book's title, I found that the book was more of an autobiography than one might expect. As Mr. Gregory left his publisher, the printer asked, "What is the book's title?" before he exited the door. Mr. Gregory turned and told him to just put "Nigger" on it, and he did, all in lower case. I don't recall when I realized the power of the pen or the power of the written and spoken word, but I knew I had a flair for it. It mainly came after reading about some of the writers I mentioned. My parents didn't inform me of who these people were. And that they were trying to bring about changes concerning the rules of how black people were or should be treated. I remember hearing Cassius Clay, now known as "Muhammad Ali", speak confidently about himself and his opponents, especially to Howard Cosell, a sports announcer and Ali's adversary, when they began a conversation. They were both great wordsmiths. I was amazed at the poise and strength that Ali displayed. And there was no doubt that Cosell was just as impressed as he continuously attempted to cross Ali up with a new word. I heard that they were best friends. Let's skip to yet another interesting person, the late Dr. Rev. Martin Luther King, Jr. It wasn't until the night of his murder that I knew of him. Until then, I hadn't heard anything about him at home. And it was especially true that there was rarely anything positive said about black people in history books. Let alone at school or at home. I can say that no one had ever spoken about him to me, be it in my house as a child, at our grandparents' home, or especially not at my grade school. I was 9 years old when Dr. King was assassinated. We know he was killed on April 4, 1968, murdered in cold blood by a white racist man named James Earl Ray. I guess my siblings and I were sheltered from the activist movements of Dr. King and other outspoken leaders for equal rights, which was shared with me by Dick Gregory. So, over the next 50 years, I'd have to educate myself on our plights for equal rights: equal pay, the right to vote (thank you, Medgar Evers), and as human beings and as Americans. I've been blessed to see the after-math of the fights that have been fought and the battles that took place in the request of equal opportunities by people like Harriet Tubman, W.E.B. DuBois, Dr. Martin Luther King, Malcolm X, Mother Theresa, Gandhi, Nelson Mandela, Harry Belafonte, Sidney Poitier, Angela Davis, Louis Farrakhan, and today, our late but very still a phenomenal woman of our times; the writer, artist, actress, and activist, Maya Angelou.

Her must-read book of poems is "I Know Why the Caged Bird Sings," which is insightful. Of course, there were many others I hope to read soon and research in-depth. I urge people to get involved and share our and your family history with your children, as I did and continue to do. Because of what I've done, our children are teaching their children - our grandchildren - about their heritage, our history, and the sacrifices we've endured so they can live a much better life as an American, not just a black person in America. As a younger kid, I had heard about comedians like Bill Cosby and Flip Wilson. Still, it wasn't until I was older and allowed to listen to the uncut versions of comedians like Moms Mabley, Slappy White, Redd Foxx, Dewey "Pigmeat" Markham, Rudy Ray Moore (The Signifying Monkey), and Richard Pryor. I was a teenager when I found Dick Gregory's "Light Side", Dark Side LP Album, which belonged to my mother. I didn't know at the time, but it was only one of a two-set album, but I kept it and re-discovered it years later as I reorganized my collection of LPs, mostly "borrowed" from my mother's collection. I guess I'll have to return it because I shared that with Mr. Gregory, and he quickly said, "You know what that's called?" And he didn't give me a chance to reply. I guess it was rhetorical, as he said, "That's called stealing". We both laughed, he signed the album label, and he told me, "Now what you do is, you record this and return it to your mother". I said that I would. Then we sat as I thanked him for his contributions, comedic works, courage, life struggles, and family sacrifices. I told him it was his, and Sidney Poitier inspired me to write my life stories. And it was an honor to have had that time to speak with him. I believe Mr. Gregory will be listed in the history books as one of the "GOATS" (Greatest of All Time), in his career, who made a significant change(s) in our society. We now reap from his and others' sacrifices that opened doors of opportunity for us, my children, and theirs. As I shook Mr. Gregory's hand and thanked him, in comedic form, while pointing at the album, he said, "You give the album (pointing at it in my hand) back to your Mama and don't steal another thing from her. Put that in your book," and smiled. I thought he would complete with, *"and smoke it"*. But he didn't; however, he did say, insisting, *"You owe me"*. So, I smiled and shook his hand again, saying, "Yes, Sir." I knew then that *"I Owe a Few Writers"*.

LOOKING FOR FAULT

After years of verbal punishment for past faults, indiscretions, disappointments, and inability to be the perfect mate within our marriage, I realized I was passive-aggressive in our relationship. I was raised in a home of violence, and I apologize up front because, as sad as it is, it was a recurring drama, and so it will be with the confines of many of my shared experiences. Our father was a womanizer, a beater, and a bully. It was his way and no other, much like what my life had narrowed down to in the last ten years of my marriage to my wife, and she, too, was an aggressor. I was more like my mother, as my father had often reminded me, as if it were a bad thing. I had decided that the best thing I could do was to appease my wife and give her what she seemed to want, a life where she chose all the outcomes in our home. And that was the mistake. Now, I know why there is domestic abuse. But, like my mom, I guess I was always the peacekeeper, the passive aggressive. I always attempted to see the best in everyone, especially those in the family. Outside the family, I wasn't so passive, especially regarding family. Allison had told me many times over the years that I was the cause of her illness. But I wasn't. Besides, she was never sick. She was, however, never diagnosed as a dedicated hypochondriac. Whether we should have ever married had become very questionable over the last ten years of our forty-year marriage. Before the marriage went awry, there were signs that most of our family members saw but I didn't. I took the brunt of the fault. What you are probably thinking happened, happened. And it sure would have happened to an even better man had he been in my predicament. And yes, over time, it came to light. As we all know, "What goes on in the dark, comes out in the light", sooner or later. In my case, it was later. I had sought comfort, conversation, companionship, and compassion, which were not found at home.

Yes, those are excuses, and there shouldn't have been any. But there you are. When confronted with the bare facts. I was caught literally "Red Handed". I sent roses to the woman on Valentine's Day. And several days later, the flower company sent a letter thanking me for the purchase. You guessed it, Allison intercepted the letter. Yep, a rookie move, but it was never really in me to go out and cheat. I never thought that was right. I had always confessed and practiced being a woman man. Okay, I was wrong, and I admitted it to my wife.

I openly confessed to my indiscretion, asked for forgiveness, prayed for forgiveness, did a couple of "Hell Merrys", and did whatever I thought would ease the situation, mine and Allison's, of course. But yeah, I was caught. And yes, that's what it is when "The jig is up. Yet, this act came on the cusp of a perfect storm of circumstances we were dealing with. Now it was no secret that Allison had her issues, the hypochondriac thing, but this time she was going through some mental things, as we both were. We nearly lost our son to a drive-by shooting. He was shot twice in the back and left dead just down the street from our home as he was on his way to the bus stop to work. Our daughter was headed off and joined the army, and then our son, soon after his recovery, was arrested and incarcerated in the state correctional institute. I was under career pressure. I was still in the Ohio Army National Guard, and my chain of command, especially my commander, was starting to treat me differently because of our son's guilty verdict and his imprisonment. One of my superior officers once asked, "Chief, did your son do it?" I looked at him and calmly asked, " Why would you ask me that question? It isn't any of your damn business, and you don't have that right to ask me anything of my family, SIR!" He backed off and probably wanted to write me up for being insubordinate. Still, he quietly walked away without a word. Everyone was on eggshells around me, and I knew that the officer more than likely shared my statement with his "Good ole-Boys". Most of the guard members were from Newark, Ohio. No one else ever confronted me again concerning my family. It was evident and apparent in my demeanor that I was feeling hurt, knowing our son had just been sentenced to prison. I'll say no more. But that was what I was already dealing with. Yes, a lot was going through my head. It was a bad time for both Allison and me. But the thing that popped the cork and brought it to a head came later in the year. The storm was still brewing at our home, and then my little brother, Tunney, took his life by shooting himself in the head with a .22 pistol. What I experienced during that week with my wife concerning my brother's death was horrific. Since my return from combat, Tunney and I had just rekindled our relationship as brothers. When I first enlisted in the Navy, he was just a baby, and I had been away from home for at least twenty years. A lot of time was missed, and we were trying to make up for it.

What I experienced from my supposedly helpmate was more than heartbreaking in that I felt "set up" by Allison for more than just the opportunity to inform me of my brother's death. She thought it was the perfect opportunity to point out personal pain, or maybe it was her vendetta against me, her chance to let me know how it felt to have a loved one die. Perhaps to watch me die. She would tell me all the time, "You don't know what it is to lose a close family member to death." But I did, I lost my aunt, who I grew up with almost like a sister. I grieved her death and that of my stepbrother, Duane. He was my brother. He grew up with us and his mother, our stepmother. So, maybe Allison thought I took her feelings about the deaths in her family lightly. I did not. When her mother passed, and shortly after, her two older brothers died. I was there for her. I was the architect who planned and set up the memorial service for her oldest brother, Robert, who was found dead alone in his home. And he and I did not get along at all. I once had to tell him and his little sister, my wife, that if I ever came home from work and found him sitting with his feet under our dinner table and wasn't invited in the first place and having my wife, his sister cooking for him, he and I were going to have a problem, mostly him. I had even helped care for her father in our home for five years since he was diagnosed with Alzheimer's, and during hospice as he was made comfortable with his bout with stage four cancer. I transported him to and from the adult-care facility in Bexley at the Wexler's Jewish Center for Alzheimer's patients. When he passed, I DID know what it felt like to lose a close relative. He was a great father to me. I still hurt when I think about his passing. But I guess Allison thought that her family was not my family. Up until that time, though, I hadn't yet lost my parents to death, and maybe she didn't see my stepbrother as family. I did. And I loved my in-laws, Mr. and Mrs. Armstrong, and their whole family. They accepted me and I was one of them. I called her "Mother" and him, "Dad". Like I said, he might have been a frame of a man, but he was a great father-in-law. Allison asked him if he knew who she was in his last moments with us. He replied, "Yes, Bee, I know who you are". Bee was short for Elizabeth, Allison's mom, and that was what he called her. Of course, you could see the hurt on Allison's face, especially when she asked him if he knew who I was. And he quickly responded, "Oh yeah, that's my pal Edwin". He rarely called me by that name. It was either Edmond or Ervin. What he said were his last words before he fell asleep.

It was raining hard that evening. The hospice personnel did their best to comfort him and us. It seemed that right as Dad acknowledged who I was, the thunder sounded, the lightning cracked the sky almost simultaneously, and the rain stopped. Dad was gone. During that time, my position as a Military Technician required traveling for business, training obligations, and professional networking. On my return from one of those scheduled trips came the blindside. Allison picked me up from Port Columbus Airport on that occasion. I entered the passenger side of our car, and gospel music was playing. I started to change stations to hear the current news, as I always did, but Allison asked if we could keep the music on. I agreed. I asked about the current news, and the conversation was converted to her telling me we had to make a short stop by our pastor's home. Again, I agreed. Upon arriving at the pastor's house and entering, to my surprise, many of our church members were present. They brought food, snacks, cookies, cake, chips, and beverages. Of course, I asked what was going on and was told immediately that it was just a fellowship, and I took it as such. Later in the evening, as I was sitting across from the pastor, my wife approached me and said, "Honey, the reason we're all here and you are here is to tell you that your brother killed himself yesterday". I don't know how long it took before I caught my breath, and a sound finally came from my cry, but when it did, it was the worst pain I had ever felt in my chest. Once it arrived, all I could hear was silence, not my voice, not even the pastor, who was sitting right in front of me, and not any of the members from the church. I was looking at him, and he was looking at me. His lips were moving, but I heard nothing. In that silence, I looked at the faces of everyone who seemed to be wanting to console me, and they, too, were saying something. Still, I did not hear a sound until I finally caught my breath, and whatever that sound was that came from my mouth was horrifying, full of pain and hurt as if I was trying to catch my breath but couldn't. Still strongly hurting from the news of my little brother's death, my wife leaned over towards me as if she had a secret to tell me and quietly whispered, "Now you know how it feels. Imagine my stare towards her morphing into a pair of hands and physically grasping her throat, trying to choke her out. That was the rage I felt from her statement. She struck me like a cold-hearted, venomous cobra, hitting her target, my jugular, with precise accuracy.

She probably thought that it was a perfect time to strike out at me, in that I was feeling what pain she had been harvesting from the passing of her loved ones. Her act, though, did not create what she probably intended. Instead, it pushed me further away. I never thought that event would lead me to what I shared with you earlier, but it did. However, it was not planned. Yet, I hurt the core. I used to try telling myself that it did not just happen but also happened. Again, any sin done in the dark will soon come out in the light. I felt guilty about it and attempted to mend it by seeking biblical and professional help. I asked for her forgiveness, and I even got a vasectomy, which she demanded I do. I took on my responsibilities and did whatever I thought would mend our marriage, but she was not having it. She had played the long game, and I felt that she just wanted me to suffer the rest of my life. I continued to seek help from our church, the VA Clinic, her sister, a minister, and marriage counseling. But she did not want to participate. However, it was too late. Fifty percent of our relationship, she did not desire to mend or assist in any attempts to mend it together. It seemed that the harder I tried to heal our marriage, the harder she attempted to dishonor my name through social media, emails, messaging, and Facebook. I tried to explain the events that led up to and surrounded how or why it happened. But in the back of my mind, those words rang louder and louder, "Now You Know How It Feels!" Yes, it still should not have happened. but it did. Yet, some would say they understood why. For the record, this other lady was hurting from the death of her husband and found comfort in me, a hurting man. I accepted the blame for my shame and admitted I could have chosen another avenue. Yet, at times, I felt I was, to put it in a golfing analogy, "Laid Up", for someone else to get me to the hole. Listen to Betty Wright's "Clean Up Woman", which might have served me well had I been *"Looking for Fault"*.

MY CYCLE CHASE

Our father had purchased a motorcycle for us. I was about 12 or 13 years old, and none of my brothers or sisters had ever ridden a motorbike before, let alone ridden on the back seat with someone who could. The bike was a small 70 cc motorcycle, and we, mainly the boys, attempted to mount the new toy. We were the envy of the neighborhood because no one else on the block had one. Our family was better off than most families during that generation, although I was too young to know it, and our father was too busy working to share our status and income. To illustrate, we were the first family on our block to have a color TV and extend our home, which our father built with some of his close working friends. Lots of them either worked for the city or at the Anheuser-Busch brewery, where he worked. And it wasn't a surprise for our father to come home with something used or something that needed repair. One day, he came home with a small motorcycle and told us we could. He took it for a lap down our street to show us what we had to do and how to control it. I remember jumping onto the bike. It took some time before I understood how to switch the gears in the left foot pedal and learn the acceleration and braking system. Well, I finally got the combinations together after a few days and spills – they weren't serious – I came to master the bike. I got so good that I could muster up the courage to pick up some speed to see how fast I could master the 70ccs. Once I became comfortable hopping on the bike and taking her for a spin, I would travel around the three streets that we all were familiar with and knew - Clarfield, Augmont, and our street, Moundview Avenue. The three streets ran parallel, and Moundview Avenue was the center street. I was familiar with all three because I was the neighborhood paperboy, and everyone knew me. I even rode up to our local grocery store and pharmacy to pick up items for our stepmother, Nathelene, who often had me make weekly trips for her favorites, canned shrimp and Kools cigarettes. She knew the motorcycle was not roadworthy, nor legally licensed. We had been warned by our father not to take the bike on the main roads, but we had to cross the main roads to get to the local elementary school grounds, the church parking lot, which made it a great place to ride, and several fields that had some awesome hills. There was one location that we called "Suicide Hill" and the "Camel Hump". What memories!

The names tell it all. One Saturday, I had just ridden from the hills and around the blocks in our neighborhood and noticed a police cruiser coming up behind me as I was only half a block from my home. I thought, what the hell? I didn't know they had seen me, so I floored the 70cc and clutched it as fast as possible, attempting to get the most out of the little engine to get me to our home. Still thinking, "If they catch me, they're going first to beat me before they cart my ass to jail." But I was not thinking; I was scared. Sure enough, and sure enough, the police cruiser lit up its lights and sirens and pursued me as I headed home. I got to our backyard as the cruiser pulled into our driveway. Our father came out, and I don't know what they discussed, but I remember one of the officers telling me that the bike was illegal, and they were giving me a warning. After the police left, my dad gave me a "talking to", but I didn't get a beating. The next day, I was a hero and legend for that summer with my run-in with the "Cops" during *"My Cycle Chase"*.

MY EGO WALL

Always intrigued by the settings of one's office or workplace, I usually would comment on a family photo or an award that would be readily visible. Well, this time, as I recall, it was about 1983. I was a federal employee, and I had scheduled an appointment with the EEO office. I knocked on the door and was asked to enter. There sat behind his desk the manager, whom I had seen but did not know, but he reminded me of Frederick Douglass, a Civil Rights Activist, because he sported a large salt & pepper afro with a matching mustache and beard. After shaking hands, he asked that I excuse him for a minute and left the room. As usual, while waiting to be seen, I noticed that this office wall behind the large officer's military-type office desk, which was made of dark cherry wood and topped with a glass desk cover, was backdropped. From wall-to-wall with perfectly aligned, spaced, wooden-framed awards, certificates, and accomplishments. I was immediately impressed. Returning to the room, he addressed me by my first name as he handed me one of the 2 cups of coffee he had returned with. We had already met, speaking to each other on numerous occasions as we occasionally passed in hallways and the employees' cafeteria, but we had never been officially introduced. So, I mentioned his wall and how impressed I was with it. He then replied that it was his eagle wall. I was a little confused because my immediate thought went quickly to that of the prey. He saw that I was wrestling with the term and repeated by explaining that he was speaking of his id, as in ego. So, his ego wall reminded him of his accomplishments, that he could conquer whatever he attempted to do. What an excellent way to enhance your self-esteem and motivation, by reassuring yourself of your worth. After meeting with the EEO Manager, I left with several notes I had taken from his replies to my questions concerning EEO and EO, which I was interested in and contemplating taking a course on EEO/EO at the time. However, the one thing that has stayed with me to this day is his "EGO WALL". Before I arrived home, I stopped by the neighborhood store and purchased several frames. I was so excited about the ingenious thought of the ego wall that I ran into the home, spoke to my wife, asked her for our children's awards, and began framing them. Once framed, I posted them on both of our children's walls.

They hadn't gotten home from school at the time, and I wanted to surprise them with their ego walls and what they represented. I wanted to show them that no matter what anyone says or tells them about being successful, they would always have the ego wall that reminded them of the truth. They have completed what they started, achieved success, have many accomplishments, and are winners! Their mother and I were proud of them and what they had accomplished in such a short period. They were in grade school at the time. There came a time, though, that I had to address our children that no matter what they accomplished in life, there would be people attempting to demean their success. That time was when a young female friend defamed our son's Ego Wall during one of her visits. She had taken a permanent marker and drawn big, bold "Fs" across all his certificates on his bedroom wall. Of course, we contacted the parent to address their daughter's actions. However, that was a great time to reinforce what I had already embedded in our children, especially our son. Although his certificates were destroyed, he had achieved and accomplished those tasks, and nothing could ever remove or take that from him. The certificates were only paper. Later, as our children got older and advanced to and through middle and high school, their ego walls turned into ego binders. It is good to know where you've been, where you came from, what you've done, and know that you can achieve what you've attempted to do. You have to decide what you want to do and do it. And once you've done it, move on to your next endeavor because you can achieve something new daily. It is not the size or type of the accomplishment that matters. It's the accomplishment alone that matters. I can honestly say that our children have achieved and accomplished their life endeavors. They have been great mentors to their children, and I have no doubt they will be the same as my great-grandchildren and theirs. These days, with all of our new and wondrous social media and its fast-growing technology, I can easily see my grandchildren's ego binders converted to ego spreadsheets on an electronic ego media device and no longer being used. However, being of the "Old School", I prefer *"My Ego Wall"*.

MY FIRST DATE

It was the sixth grade at Clarfield Elementary School, and I was interested in Eileen Smith. She was fair-skinned; some back then would have said Yellow. Others would have called her a "Red Bone." I don't know where all these names came from, but as you know, black folks had a lot of names based on the color of our skin. Nevertheless, I thought she was beautiful, not just in her looks but also in her personality, and her smile smote me, and I guess we flirted. I know I did. Then, I took it too far. While we were at what the school called a recess, which was about a forty-five-minute break when we were released to play on the playground, I pinched Eileen on the butt. Then, it wasn't as blatantly a sexual crime as it is today, but it was reported to our teacher, Mrs. Harris, whom I was also smitten with. Remember, I told you, Mrs. Harris was a beautiful "Red Bone" too, and I was her pet because she loved saxophone players. I don't know who ratted me out, but it wasn't Eileen. I found that out when Mrs. Harris called Eileen and me outside the classroom door. She asked me as if I were a grown man, "Mr. Robinson, why did you pinch Ms. Smith's rear?" I know why, but I said, "I don't know". She then asked me if I liked Ms. Smith. I looked at Eileen and said, "Yes, Ma'am." I think Eileen blushed as she smiled. "Do you like Mr. Robinson, Ms. Smith?" she asked Eileen. Eileen looked at me, still smiling, and nodded in the affirmative. I smiled back. Then the teacher told me I should have just told Ms. Smith instead of pinching her on the rear. She sent Eileen back into the classroom, and suddenly, I noticed the old familiar wooden paddle come out from behind Mrs. Harris, which she had been holding during the whole interrogation. I was then informed with a firm warning that I was not pinching any girl on the rear again. I braced, expecting the paddle to strike my butte; however, their incoming blows were lighter swings than I had anticipated. Yep, I believe I was her pet, and she was still my favorite teacher,

and I was still deep like her. I re-entered the room, and the class clowns had their time with my pain from the paddling. But they didn't know that it was more of a show. Mrs. Harris couldn't just let my indiscretion go without addressing it and applying a little corporal punishment to the culprit, me.
Of course, I portrayed a student in pain and shame after a good swatting. Once the laughter on my behalf subsided, I soon took a peek at Eileen in hopes of catching her smile, and when I did, it was all worth it.

It was likely that a week had gone by, and I had finally found the nerve to ask Eileen if she would "Go With" me (be my girlfriend). Again, it was at recess, and as always, I was with my friends, and she was with a few of her girlfriends. It was a known secret that we both liked each other, and our friends knew it. When my friends weren't noticing me. I turned toward Eileen and called her name. She was already looking my way. We both walked toward each other. I took what seemed to be an enormous amount of time and, with some strength, blurred out, "Will you go with me?" To my surprise, she smiled, nodded, and said, "Yes." I was excited and elated. Without a word, we quickly turned away from each other, almost in a military about-face fashion, and returned to our corners with our friends. Mine hadn't missed me, nor did they know I had left the herd, but as I looked over at where Eileen had returned with her girlfriends, I knew she had told them that I had asked the question because they were all giggling. That was the buzz and conversation among our classmates after recess. A few days had passed, and Eileen and I hadn't talked much; we were both new to this "Dating Thing," so we just looked at each other and smiled now and then, mostly once in class. During one of those class days, that "Dating Thing" became a real thing because, at the end of one of the days, Eileen handed me a note and quickly headed away. I opened the note, which read, "My father wants to meet you this evening". I was scared. I had a paper route, and while delivering my papers, I was planning as a sixth grader what I was going to say once I met Mr. Smith. I was thinking about how I should introduce myself. All that stuff was running through my head, especially what I thought he would say to me. Once I finished my route, I headed to the Smiths' residence. Eileen lived not too far from my home, but it still would have been a longer walk if I hadn't been riding a bike, which I did, and it still was a long, slow ride. I wasn't in any big hurry, but I was, and I didn't want to be late either. Before I knew it, I approached their home, rolling onto their driveway. I slowly and carefully dismounted my bike, quietly (not in a whistling mood), slowly walked up to the door, and knocked.

Eileen's brother Edward answered, turned around, and yelled into their home, "He's here." Mr. Smith came to the door, opened it, reached out his hand to shake mine, and said, "Hello, Mr. Robinson, come in, we've been expecting you", or something to that effect. It was over seventy years ago. I was on pins and needles thinking about what I had gotten into. He welcomed me to sit on the living room couch next to Eileen, who smiled at me and said, "Hi, Edwin." I looked at her and said "Hi" back to her. Mr. Smith yelled into their kitchen, where Mrs. Smith was cooking, and said, "Mother, come and meet Mr. Robinson." She did. Mrs. Smith was white, and it was no surprise because it was known that Eileen's father was black, and her mother was white. Yes, interracial marriages were probably still a new thing in the '60s, but I was cool with it. My parents had an interracial married couple who were good friends, and they visited our home many times. I guess you could say I was used to it. Anyway, Mrs. Smith said it was nice to meet me and quickly returned to what she was doing in the kitchen, and the interrogation began. It was all so formal, and I was very uncomfortable, not knowing what would happen at this meeting. The most I can recall from the ordeal was that Mr. Smith noticed I had given his daughter a ring and asked me, "What are your intentions?" I do remember telling him I had none. I told him he had gone to the fair and wanted to give her something nice that I had won because I liked her. The rest of that evening was a blur to this day. I don't remember if I was asked to stay for dinner. The food smelled good, and I am sure he enjoyed it because he was very nice. However, I was probably so nervous that I just wanted to get it over and out and on my way back home as soon as I could. I remember being so relieved to leave as I rode my bike faster than usual, getting back home. I never shared that with anyone until years later. I was always a "Kiss and No Tell" kind of guy. Boy, talk about awkwardness in class the next day. Eileen and I smiled at each other, and she thanked me for coming over. Her dad said that I was a real gentleman, and her mom liked me. I don't know if Mr. Smith wanted me to date his daughter, but it was a good report. Well, the niceties were over because it was no more than a day or two later that our "Dating Thing" ended abruptly. I remember it was Friday, and at the end of that school day, when the school bell rang to go home, Eileen handed me another note as she quickly walked past me. That time, the note read something like, "I'm breaking up with you because you draw better than I."

I don't think we were ever in competition as artists. I surely wasn't. But it probably was her easiest way out of her commitment as my girlfriend, and letting me down easily. I wasn't heartbroken any more than I was surprised. The following Monday in class, whenever I could catch Eileen's stare, I would smile at her, and she would return that beautiful smile with her eyes. It was like a gentle kiss that said we were still good friends. I will remember Eileen Smith not as my first break-up but as *"My First Date."*

MY FIRST HANGOVER

It was Christmas Eve in 1974 when I experienced one moment of drunkenness. That same year, I left home early on Tuesday morning, July 22nd. It was a rebellious and cowardly move because, just minutes after hearing my father leave for work, I called the Naval recruiter and left the comfort of home. No one knew that I was going to leave home. I hadn't mentioned it to my closest friends. Months later, and realizing the mistake I had made joining the Navy, I returned home on my second 2-week furlough to attend the funeral of my Uncle Joe, who served in the Navy for over 30 years and died just months after his retirement, from a heart attack. My father and I never spoke of how or why I left home, but I believe he knew he was a big part of it. Uncle Joe was my grandfather's brother. I think Uncle Joe's death was from his sudden stop from his once busy life as a Sailor. After the funeral, I returned to my duty station in Norfolk, VA. I was 19 years old and ready to prove I was a grown man on my terms and old enough for the choices I would make in life. Drinking alcohol at that time seemed to be my "Rite of Passage" into manhood, among other things. Getting drunk was my goal, and I knew exactly what I wanted to drink, but I was ready to drink what I wanted to drink this particular night. I was prepared to celebrate my first Christmas away from home. I was "Free" of parental rules, from sibling brothers and sisters, and guidance and protection from myself. It was time to sow my "Wild Oats", and getting drunk was part of my hazing. However, I didn't know what effects drinking tap/draft beer all night might have on such a young non-drinker as I was. Woo......the last thing I remember was I was dancing with a great-looking woman; she was into me, and I sure was into her. That was it for Christmas Eve of '74 for me. The rest of that night was and still is a blur. The following morning, Christmas day, my head thumped like two stereos "Boom-Boxes." I could feel my brain swelling in and out as if someone had smashed one of my big toes with a sledgehammer - imagine how your toe would think after something like that, or you just hit it hard on the corner of your steel bed leg. "Hot Damn, Oh Mighty," my dad would have said. Well, my head felt just like that.

So, I woke that morning, Christmas morning, around 0900, forced my way to sit up on the side of my bunk, and slowly raised my head from up under the pillow I had at or about 1100 - without washing up and brushing the ivories, yet in time for chow just a few steps across the street from the Nimitz Hall where my dorm was located. But it took every bit of 30 minutes for me, once at the curb crossing, to the cafeteria as others passed me by. Once in the doors and I was to acclimate myself, keeping my balance, I hurried to the line and supported myself as I drug myself along the tray railings, holding both ends of my tray as if I were driving, and slid the tray along the rails to the end of the counter and register, loaded up as I went along. I don't even remember what I was getting; I grabbed the food I saw. I sat down at the nearest table to eat. I sat there for about 5 minutes - maybe 15, drooling at the thought of eating anything. I got up, got two cups of coffee (black), drank them slowly, took another 45 minutes to get back to my resting place at the dorm, called the family back home, wished them Merry Christmas in short statements, quickly got back into my bunk - with clothes and boots, and I woke up 1200 noon the next day. To this day, I still don't know how I got 2 of the scars on my body, but I was told by my good comrades (then buddies) that Christmas Eve night, I won the fistfight hands down with one of the visiting Royal Navy sailors, but he walked with the girl. My father told me, "Boy, never fight over a woman." What I don't know, and I might have been better served had he informed me, but he didn't, that if I was ever going to get shitfaced, there was nothing worse than a beer *"Hangover"*.

MY FIRST SAX

Chris Powell was "The Saxophonist" in high school. I looked up to and wanted to emulate. He graduated the year I became a freshman, so I took on the challenge of becoming the next "Chris Powell." I quickly enrolled in the Jazz Band and joined a local band. Our band would visit Chris's rehearsals, which were held in his family's basement. I was so impressed when I watched Chris put on an LP (Long Playing) Album, play a particular part so he could hear the horn or sax part, remove the needle from the record player, and immediately play what he had heard. At an early age, I was enchanted with the brass horn resembling an upside-down question mark, the saxophone. I was only a child when I heard someone personally play the saxophone. Then, like buying a brand-new car, you don't think many people have purchased one yet, and then suddenly, everywhere you look, you see the very same car you just bought. Well, it was like that for me. I saw the saxophone being played on TV and saw it in pictures or advertisements on the billboards. Once I could recognize the saxophone's sultry sound, I would pick it out from listening to and hearing it on the radio and the stereo player my father had purchased. I recall sneaking into our family living room when our parents weren't home to put on their albums of Junior Walker and The All-Stars, Eddie Harris, the innovator of the electric saxophone, and Charlie Parker, among so many others. As I got older and old enough to hold a sax and produce a sound, I signed up for saxophone lessons at my elementary school, Clarfield. In the fifth grade, the school started a music program for volunteers. You just had to have your instrument or rent one. I didn't have a horn, but I quickly signed up. I informed my father about the school's music and instrument rental program. He didn't want to rent me one, but some time afterward, he had brought home an alto saxophone, which he had borrowed from his brother, my Uncle Bruce. The music teacher was a student from Ohio State University. His name was Mr. Bob Ore, my very first music teacher, and the lessons were free. Another classmate, Vaughn Stephenson, and I were the only saxophone players.

When Vaughn and I graduated to the sixth grade, our new teacher was Mrs. Susan Harris, a fair-skinned black woman with freckles. When she found out that Vaughn and I played the saxophone, she immediately, without any shame, told the class in so many words that we were pets because she loved the saxophone and saxophone players. She was beautiful, and I was a very young, impressionable boy who played the saxophone. I think our homework has become much easier. Maybe not, but being her pet wasn't a bad thing. Then, I knew I was on to something and wanted to be a saxophone player. I played with my uncle's sax until I got one. I was proud to have an instrument and cared for it as if it were my own. It was my first saxophone, but it wasn't my saxophone. It was a loner until I either decided I didn't want to play it any longer or got one of my own. Some time had passed, but one evening, when I returned home from school, there was a prominent case in my bedroom. I knew it was a saxophone. Our father, at that time, worked for the City of Sanitation, and he found the horn on his route. Someone had thrown a saxophone away, and he threw it in his truck and brought it home for me. He worked in the white suburbs, places like Bexley, Gahanna, Upper Arlington, Whitehall, and Worthington. In the '60s, there were very few blacks living in those areas. Most realtors were practicing "*Red Lining," and the apartment owners never had vacancies when black applicants applied for a vacant apartment. I know because it was 1977 when Allison and I called an Apartment Community in Whitehall, and they said they had several vacancies until we showed up. I admit Allison sounded like she was white over the phone. But that's only when she isn't mad. Then you find out quickly that she's a full-blooded African American, a black woman, and some of this and that. It was 1969, and as I told you, our father brought a horn home. White folks threw away lightly used or no longer wanted items, and someone thought this horn needed a new owner. I was the owner. Someone had put a King Tenor Saxophone on the curb for pickup and disposal. My father brought it home. Finally, I had my very own instrument, and right away, after opening the case, I cleaned it up. The case smelled of mildew and mothballs. The horn needed cleaning and oiling. I wasn't very knowledgeable in caring for a saxophone other than cleaning the mouthpiece and the goose-like neck, so I did that.

I had received lessons in grade school on the alto saxophone and had not yet played the tenor; however, the fingers were the same, but the tenor was in Bb, where the alto was in Eb. I was just happy to have it and thanked my father for it. So, it was a saxophone, and I would give it my best shot. I've been playing one ever since. That saxophone was very tarnished and somewhat of an eyesore. I took a bottle of Brasso and an old family towel – hoping no one would notice it missing – and polished it out. The pads were worn, but we couldn't afford to replace them, so I made pads for the missing keys and glued in the loose ones. I also washed one reed in a glass with warm water and soap. I did the same for the mouthpiece and neck, knowing that someone's spit was once in both. I was amazed, but I was about to get a halfway decent sound out of it. I was in Junior High at that time, and when I got to the band with my horn, opened the case, and pulled out my baby after I shined and oiled her up, I noticed she wasn't the prettiest, but she was the shiniest sax in the band. And oh boy, when I started to play that baby, I let the others know that I was a saxophone player, and after rehearsal, there weren't any comments on how bad she looked or smelled from the motor oil I had used to oil the springs.

She held up to the task that day. She wasn't a Selmar by far or anything close to the name brands. However, the players weren't Ed Robinson, and I worked hard to be the next Chris Powell. Chris had made a name in the neighborhood in their local band as a great saxophonist. He later signed with Motown with his band, "The Cannibals." I soon obtained some notoriety in the Junior High School Band. I was later acknowledged when I was selected for the All-Ohio Boys' Band at Ohio State University, where we performed during the State Fair. My goal later, as I graduated from George C. Beery Junior High, was to attend Marion-Franklin Senior. Soon, I was a rising star and easily took the First Tenor Chair in the jazz band. In our local band, I picked up the horn parts by ear from songs such as Earth, Wind & Fire, Mandrill, Tower of Power, Chicago, etc. It wasn't long until I realized I had arrived as a player in a band, as my Uncle Bruce had. Years later, I excelled to the point that I performed professionally in the military, both in the Navy and Army Bands, for four sitting presidents, and local and national gospel performers like Rev. James Cleveland and Shirley Caesar.

And musicians like Rusty Bryant, Gene Walker, Bobby Floyd, and Mary McClendon. Yes, I had a career as a musician. That would have never happened had it not been for my Uncle Bruce allowing me to borrow his alto saxophone. Thank you, Uncle Bruce, for *"My First Sax"*

MY FIRST GRANDSON

Who has not heard the phrase, "God's Gifts," about grandchildren? Or the fact that they are such a gift in that you can always send or give them back to their parents, your children, whom you now smile at, they are getting back what they give us, their parents, when they were our little ones? Yeah, some of them were Hellions, and some were Angels, but we loved them just the same. I have so many laughable memories of raising our grandchildren. You see, our son's boy, Wahli, was our first, my first grandchild, my first grandson, and our daughter gave birth to three lovely little stair-step girls. Their grandmother, Mama Allison, and I were blessed to assist in raising them as their parents served our country in combat in the US Army. Wahli, born out of wedlock, lived with his mother. Our relationship was not a keen one, as Wahli's grandmother and his mother did not see eye-to-eye. We faced challenges in getting visits, which we had to involve the courts to resolve. Wahli, at a very early age, was brilliant in that he practically taught himself to read way before the acceptable learning curve. At three years of age, he had learned to navigate and operate the smart TV to open captions on the screen, and he would read the captions along with the characters on the screen. One of his TV teachers was "Searching for Nemo". Between times of disagreements with grandmother and mom, they would visit and straight to the TV, Wahli would dart towards and without asking, change the tube to his favorite TV show, select the caption, and sit right in front and begin to enjoy his ritual of listening and reading along with the selected show. As grandparents, we recall all the things our grandchildren made us laugh about, and Wahli always left a fantastic impression on us during his visits. Once at the grocery store, he was walking with his grandmother, Mama Allison. As they neared the meat section, Wahli felt it necessary to inform his grandmother by saying, "Mama Allison, you know I'm a carnivore", meaning he loved meat, and maybe she might want to stop to purchase some. Wahli was always full of wonderment. Our son, Ilyas, reminded me that once, while he was feeding Wahli pieces of watermelon, Wahli, almost two years old, started to cry out as he pointed at the seeds in the watermelon, shouting, "Nice, Nice, Knee!" Ilyas asked me, "Pops, what is he saying?" I told him that I think he is saying "Nasty." He believes the seeds are roaches.

After Ilyas told Wahli, "No baby, those are seeds, let Papa Edwin remove them for you". And once I had removed the seeds, Wahli ate away at the melon. Another time I distinctly remember was one Saturday morning when Wahli was staying with us. I thought that I would teach him how to use the toilet, so after explaining how little boys and men use the toilet, I let him walk into the bathroom with me, opened the toilet seat, and began to relieve myself. Wahli stood patiently by my side and watched. He looked several times back and forth at me and down at the toilet, and before I knew what was in his little mind, his curiosity had him reaching his hand directly into my stream. Of course, I stopped all operations, telling Wahli as calmly as I could that he doesn't do that. But I knew my grandson, and the science in his mind was working, and I didn't want to make him feel he had done something very wrong, but that he didn't have to do it again now that he knew what it was and where it came from. I had him wash his hands, stand at the toilet, and do what I did. We had success, and no, I did not reach my hand into his stream, for those of you thinking it. Today, Wahli graduated from the Ohio Media School and is looking forward to following in the military careers of his grandfather, me, and his Aunt Ayrika by enlisting in the US Air or Space Force. I am proud of our grandchildren, all of them, which now includes Pam's grandchildren, who are all doing very well and seeking higher education and careers as contributing members of their communities, wherever they end up. But there is a particular pride that comes with saying, *"My First Grandson"*.

FROM FOSTER TO ADOPTION

Had I listened carefully to Allison when we were on and off dating, I might have taken some of the things we discussed about being married, having a family, and how many children she said she wanted. Notice that I did not say how many we or I wanted. But, years after the fact, and it was way too late, I was all in. I was talked into fostering. At that time, our family was affiliated with the military and stationed in Killeen, Texas, at Fort Hood, the largest installation of the United States Army. So, I reluctantly signed up and attended the classes and took the courses, and before long, I was a qualified Foster Parent. We soon had two little ones come to us, David and Krystal, ages 6 and 7. Their parents were separated, Dad was a soldier in some trouble, and Mom had never worked and needed a restart. Allison and I took on their children so mom could be trained and obtain a job that would support her and the two "kiddos" (that's a term I just came to learn). Remember I mentioned how they, children, say the darndest things. Well, the first came from David, who was very picky about what he ate. One evening, Allison made meatloaf and mashed potatoes, an easy and most liked dish, right? David wasn't having it and said "I ain't eat no meatloaf before, I don't want none, and ain't eating it". Well, if you knew Allison, he was about to be schooled in telling an adult what he was going to or not do. After receiving those choice words from what they all called her, Mama Allison, David sat at the table and, reluctantly and slowly, dug his fork into the meatloaf as if he were targeting it or someone he had in mind. I carefully looked out of the corner of my eyes, as did our son and daughter, especially after David had voiced his opinion to their mother. I must admit, Allison made a mean meatloaf, and we all loved it. And don't you know, David shouts out as in a declaration, "Mama Allison,

I'm gonna want some more of this". We all broke out in laughter, and Mama Allison gladly heaped a larger piece of meatloaf onto David's plate, and he scuffed it down. His sister, Krystal, was like our daughter, Ayrika, and grandson, Wahli. They were and still are, to this day, carnivores. Krystal had a mind of her own, literally, and she knew it. I say that because she and her brother, David, had got into a bit of disagreement, and out of the blue, we heard a loud cry. It was David. He came into the living room and told us that Krystal bit his big toe.

Of course, Mama Allison called Krystal from her bedroom, which she was sharing with our daughter, Ayrika. Allison asked David, "Why did she bite your big toe?" And he replied, "I don't know." Of course, she had a reason. People don't just go around biting people's big toes. Edwin and Ayrika snickered, and I laughed as well. I jumped in and asked Krystal once I stopped laughing. "Krystal, why did you bite your brother's toe?" She looked dead at me and said, "Because my mind told me to". We all tried not to laugh out loud, but it couldn't be helped, and David laughed right along with us. I asked our son recently if he remembered the incident, and as usual, with such a great memory, told me, "Yeah, Pops, I remember also once Krystal told you that her mind told her to, you said, "Well, did your mind tell you that you were going to get an ass-whopping?" He continued saying, "Pops, that was crazy, and Bird (he called his sister) and I looked at each other and laughed, cause you always had a saying like that, and it was only some time that you were going to use one of your sayings on them like you did on us". David and Krystal reunited with their mother the following year, and it was a sad day for us all. I recall going into our son's room, where he had shared with David. He was asleep, holding a photo of David on his chest. Then there were Johnathan and Javon, the same ages as David and Krystal, who came to us. We quickly could tell who was in charge,

Javon. She was 5 or 6 years old, and Johnathan was 6 or 7. They had been "In the System" for some time, and Javon knew that she could do no wrong. Well, until she came to our home. The other homes that they were in were white, and their case worker told us that they could not control Javon, and when the case worker would visit their home, Javon would sit up and listen to their conversation. Well, we weren't raised like that. We did not sit up in grown-folk conversations. Javon found that out soon enough. When the case worker asked where Javon was during her visit to our home, we told her that she was in the bedroom. The case worker was shocked because she, too, was used to children sitting up in their business. Allison, whom I now recall as Navi, told me, "We don't let children run around here." She seemed impressed and shocked at the same time. Johnathan was a quiet and kind kid, and he loved basketball. One evening, as he and the neighborhood boys played a pickup game, I saw Johnathan, now 7 or 8, and his mannerisms as he played reminded me of Michael Jordan. It wasn't until almost twenty years later that I found Johnathan and the other children on Facebook. Johnathan was playing basketball for a California College, and guess whose tongue was hanging out as he seemed to be headed for the basket? Yes! Johnathan was in all his glory playing the game he loved. And since I was checking in on him, I decided to see where the others were and what they were up to. David had joined the US Navy and had a son. His sister, Krystal, was working for a legal firm, and she had a daughter. Johnathan's sister Javon was also working and in a relationship. We were about to accept the adoption of Johnathan and Javon after being authorized to take them home with us on vacation to introduce them to their new families. Yet, their grandmother, at the very end, after saying that she would not, changed her mind and said that she would take them in. We again were heartbroken. A couple of years went by, and I had been discharged from the army and again was talked into re-enlisting in the State of

Ohio Foster Care Program. It wasn't long until Corey and Shawn needed a home, and we were the home that said yes. Both were with some disabilities; however, they were soon found to be highly functional. Corey, the oldest, was eight, and Shawn was seven. There was this thing the organization called, "The Honeymoon Period", where we had thirty days to get to know each other, to see if we could deal with each other, the boys (we began to call them), and us. As you would know, if you asked any of my children, I joked a lot with them, maybe sometimes too much. I don't think so. But, you know, kids. So, one day, coming in from work, the boys were at the island about to eat. They were still a little nervous being in a new environment, so I entered slowly and gradually looked around them and spoke to them, asking how everyone was. Then I started saying to Shawn, "I see you got a little piece of meat on your plate, and I got a big piece." Then I said, "You got a large amount of vegetables, and I got a small amount." Shawn looked at me, smiling, and soon he pointed at my forehead and announced, "Little brain, big brain", pointing back at his forehead. I then knew we had a smart kid on our hands, and I congratulated him on his checkmate. It was nothing but God who has placed us in the throes of helping others less fortunate than us and allowed us to love them and see them succeed in their place as contributing adults. I don't believe that I would change a thing as far as what we were blessed to do and be, caring Christians.

Today, our sons, Corey and Shawn, are living stress-free in a group home on their own, traveling, working, and making adult decisions. Along with Pam and I, our families, good friends, our Christian Church friends, VFW partners, and organizations like Nehemiah House of Refuge, Gentle Hands, Adult Non-Medical Center, and others, we have been more than blessed in assisting the guys to a stable lifestyle. We could never say thank you enough for helping us provide a loving atmosphere for Corey and Shawn. They are our sons and permanent members of our families, Pam's and mine. I guess you could say that we are more than a blended family. And the answer is "No" if you're wondering if it was hard to love God's children from *"Foster to Adoption"*.

MY LITTLE RED BUGGY

Let me first put it right. The 1969 red automatic shift Volkswagen "Bug" belonged to my father, and my stepmother and I used it until my dad purchased another car for "Tony", which our parents' friends and relatives called our stepmother, whose full name was Nathelene Morris-Threatt-Robinson. And when she had her vehicle, the Volkswagen was mine. I don't remember it being put in my name, and it probably wasn't. Dad was good at saving a dime, and I was, at that time, pretty much ignorant of the Department of Motor Vehicles policies, and insurance was not a state requirement. It had not become a law. I was sixteen and worked part-time jobs when I could get them. I took some pride in the bug by washing, waxing, and detailing it to bring out its rosy-red color. And I'd clean it inside and out, as well as the engine located at the back, where most cars had trunks, and the trunk, of course, was in the front, where I first thought it was for the engine. Again, another area I had very little knowledge about. At the time, I knew I could look at a car from a distance and tell you if it were a Volkswagen, Ford, Chevy, Buick, or Cadillac. But I didn't know much about what was under their hoods, but our father did. He was a mechanic and had, on the side, bought and repaired used vehicles and resold them for profit. During that time, I recall driving a red 1955 2-door convertible Thunderbird. After the repairs, which might have only been body repair, a new fender, some dents removed, etc., the cars never lasted too long before being sold. Dad was good with his hands. I didn't find out that he worked as an automotive mechanic until I started researching my family's history and realized that my birth certificate documented my father's occupation as a mechanic. Although I already knew that he was great at repairing cars. Just this past year, while he and I were going through our history and my ideas for inventions, he shared his idea for an electric starter for the automobile. He came up with it back in the 50s. He still has his original drawing. However, he never submitted it for a patent, and as most know today, the electric starter switch was developed.

He always came up with something when working on one of his vehicles. For instance, he added a fuel tank to his truck in preparation for our road trip to Canada in 1974. I don't know when he purchased the Volkswagen, but there it was, on our driveway, and I was just fit to be tied, thinking it was for me. Several months had passed, and I had obtained a job working as a "Busboy" at the Marriott Inn Hotel, where three of my best friends also worked, Richard and David Peppers, and Joe Robinson - no relations. As teenagers, we spent a lot of time in the back of the restaurant, where we washed dishes and stocked some products, like catsup, mustard, and wine. One evening, Joe called me from the back of the kitchen to offer me a sip of the cooking sherry. I took the bottle and raised it straight up to swallow what I thought would be a taste of the sweet nectar of red grapes. Just as quickly as I took a mouthful of the liquid, I spat it out just as fast, maybe faster, as I sprayed Joe and everything in my range. Oh, Joe got a big laugh out of that, and so did the Peppers, which Joe couldn't wait to tell them. To this day, thanks to Joe, I know that cooking sherry is not for drinking. We all pulled some practical jokes on each other and tested each other. Richard was always the challenger, and as I recalled, one night before we all punched out on the time clocks, he decided to follow each other out. We all had our vehicles and lived in the same neighborhood. We knew we were no match for Joe's Pontiac G.T.O. "Goat". He had juiced his muscle car, and as long as I can remember, Joe was always into racing. So, it was basically between the Peppers and me. I didn't have a ghost of a chance, in that I had the Volkswagen, Richard had a Chevy Corvair, and his brother, David, had a 1966 blue Chevy Impala. Their father was a "Chevy Man," and my father, for the most part, was a "Ford Man". Had I driven my father's pickup, I knew I could have blown their doors off, but I thought I could shift the bug to give me a little edge as we travelled through the back end of the Eastland Mall. By that time, around 9 or 10 o'clock, most of the mall customers' cars were gone, and the parking lot was empty. I raced through the back lot heading toward Refugee Road, but I hadn't seen the curb around the trees that had been planted. All I heard was glass breaking around me as my bug rolled over and came to a stop. I knew that all of the windows were either broken or cracked.

But as Richard, David, and Joe stopped and helped me out of the car, there were no immediate signs of damage. With their help, we flipped my red buggy over and noticed that the front driver's side axle was broken, and we all realized that I was in big trouble. I asked my friends to stop by my home and inform my father that I was in an accident. Oh, I was very worried about his being upset. Knowing he was probably asleep, had to get up, come pick me up, and get the car towed. I was in big trouble. That night was the longest night I ever experienced as I waited for my father to show up, and he did. Dad didn't say much after he asked me how fast I was going. I said, "About 60", and he knew that I had to have been going faster than that. Yet, I knew he was upset, but probably too tired to fuss with a scared, lying teenager. That night was a quiet one and one of my longest rides home. I would save up enough money to purchase my very own car, a pretty 1964 Canary Yellow Ford Galaxy 500 with a black Soft-top, which, like most teenagers, I couldn't get fast enough to replace *"My Little Red Buggy"*.

NINE STITCHES

I was nine, but my age has nothing to do with the nine surgical stitches. I had already been introduced to Christ by my grandmother, "Grandma Gregory", who was what most people called back then, in the sixties, very religious. My brothers and sisters and I attended the Shaffer AME Church in Macintyre, Ohio, which was in Jefferson County. We lived in Cadiz, Ohio, at that time, where we were living without our mother. So, let me get to my reason for the title. Years later, my brothers, sisters, and I were back in Columbus, Ohio, living with our father and stepmother. It's a long story, and most of them are with me. However, that afternoon, we – the neighbor boys and I - were playing a game of hardball and baseball in an adjoining field to our home. We also played football on the same field. And when the weeds were high and no one had come to cut the field down, it was a great hiding place for Hide-and-Seek. Kids don't play those games anymore; they play them inside. Well, as I said, we were playing a game of hardball, and our side of the opposing team just got an "Out," and the other team was up to bat. I had been chosen to sit out and allow one of our substitutes to play. I sat on the sidelines watching the other team bat and anxiously waited to get them out so I could be reinstated into the game. The batter that was up was Derryl Turnbo. At the time, I thought of Derryl as a bully. I didn't know he and I were friends, but that changed years later. Yet, as I eagerly watched him up at the plate awaiting the pitch, all I could think of was that we needed him to strike out so we could get up to bat. It was a tied game; we were last up in the previous inning. Suddenly, the ball was thrown, Derryl swung, hit it, and his bat flew – the top of the bat first – straight towards my forehead, just above my left eye. BAM! I was knocked out, straight to the ground, and all I could recall at the time was the warmth of the blood running down my face.

With one eye open that hadn't been covered with blood, I could barely see Derryl as he ran towards his home. The game stopped as my friends yelled for help from my mother and father, and someone shouted, "Somebody call 911 for an emergency". I don't remember the emergency squad ever showing up. However, my father did. He picked me up and put me in our all-white Ford Country Sedan Station Wagon, which our family lovingly called "The White Ghost"

My father rushed me to Grant Hospital, where I received nine stitches on my forehead just above my left eye. So, you ask, where's the connection to Christ? Well, back in the late 60s and early 70s, there were terms used to describe those folks who were fanatics about "The Word", being "Saved", and my friend Derryl was one of those folks that we called a "Bible Thumper", "Holy Roller", or "Jesus Freak". And they would run you down to share their experience in being "Saved". My friend Daryl was one of them. I remember him chasing me down in our Junior High school hallway, telling me I needed to be saved. Although he knew I was in church and had started playing saxophone at my church, Corinthian Baptist, he felt compelled in his conscience that I had not yet accepted Christ as he had. He truly believed that I needed Jesus. Derryl was playing bass guitar at his church, Bible Way Baptist Church. And I had visited Bible Way a few times. The same guy who hit me in the head with a baseball bat, hit me with the bible, and it wasn't long before I accepted Christ into my life. People like Derryl Turnbo shared their experiences and the word of Christ with me. It wasn't until many years later that I could thank Derryl for his insistence on helping me see that I needed to repent of my sins, ask Christ for forgiveness, and accept Him as my Lord and Savior. Now, a Deacon, Derryl Turnbo, resides in Cincinnati, Ohio, and we have reconnected to be good friends. I credit him with cultivating the seed of hope my grandmother from Cadiz planted in her prayers that I would accept Christ.

Who'd think that those nine stitches caused by one person would lead to my being saved by listening to that person's words about his transformation to a "Saved" person? I currently play saxophone and bass guitar at our church, and Derryl Turnbo performs bass at his church in Cincinnati, Ohio. I spoke with Derryl concerning that unfortunate accident and asked his permission to write about the incident. He agreed, but only if I informed you he did not intentionally knock me in the head with his bat, I mean, out cold! "LOL", (I had to get one in). I assured him that I would. Yes, it was an accident, and over sixty years later, we share God's grace, knowing He does work in mysterious ways. Today, Derryl and I serve in various capacities in our communities and prospective churches. Maybe the bat softened my head enough to accept God's grace sooner. It was all in his plan, as were the *"Nine Stitches"*.

OH, HAPPY DAY

Edwin D. Robinson, Sr.   **Robert L. Burford, Sr**

It was a time for vacation, travel, and spending time with family and friends. Still a member of the 392nd Army Band, we had become close friends with another army band family, Robert "Bob" and Brenda Burford, and their two young boys, Little Bobby Jr. and "Sam" Samuel. Their kids became friends with our two kids, Little Edwin and Ayrika. Our upcoming friendship could be attributed to the band having only a few African American members. Bob and I, among the other blacks, gravitated toward each other. And at the time, there were only about half a dozen forty-four members. As I recall, three were married and had children, one was married without children, and two were single black band members. Bob was a seasoned musician, and I sought his knowledge and experience as a fellow musician. Plus, his wife was very personable and probably a good match for my wife, as well as for friends who have things in common, such as our kids. As it was, Bob and I were opposites when it came to expressing feelings. He was very subdued, a quiet and composed person. He knew how politically difficult being a band member was, especially being Black. However, he didn't voice his opinions as I did. I also appreciated Bob's restraint and how he dealt with it. Yet, as I said, I was a bit outspoken, "The Angry Black Man", the elephant in the room, so to speak. The fact that only so few African

Americans were in the band kept me at odds with my counterparts, especially when I knew there were many more talented musicians than we had. However, most of my complaints were not without good reason, yet I believe I was labeled just the same. Bob kept me sane, and we could talk about some things I saw as unfair, which I continued to address throughout my military career. Those special times with Bob and his family probably got me through the other stuff.

For example, when we performed at the downtown St. Petersburg Amtrak Station, it might have been the gig that paid the most in our musical careers. I started off saying it was a vacation from our full-time job as musicians. A time to spend with our families. It was Saturday morning, and the night before, I was approached and asked by the bar owner of the pub located in the Old Towne Farmer's Market area in downtown St. Petersburg, Virginia, if I could get a few band members to come to the station in the morning and play for his best friends who had just married. The important part was that he would pay us for our time. Of course, I was in. I had to convince others to join on their day off from playing all week. He requested us to play "Happy Days Are Here Again" as the married couple departed from the train. I assured the owner that I would take the information back to the band and attempt to gather a few members. I returned to the base and called several members, yet no one accepted the gig. Bob and I had scheduled to leave the base by noon to travel to Busch Gardens with our families. But I was able to convince Bob to play. We both had to inform our families that we would have to pack our vehicles and quickly stop by the railroad station for a short performance for pay. The pay part helped me convince my wife and get her to agree with it. I don't know what Bob's conversation with Brenda was about, but I'm sure Bob wouldn't have a problem. Now Bob was a French horn player, and I was a saxophone player –

yep! Somewhat of an awkward duet, but it worked. And I had always thought myself to be pretty good at applying harmony. So, once Bob started the melody and we played it a couple of times, I occasionally provided harmony for color. Music filled the air as onlookers listened. We showed up, and although the owner was somewhat disappointed in our number, he agreed, and Bob and I warmed up our instruments and ran over the tune that the bar owner desired, "Happy Days Are Here Again." After several times over the melody, Bob and I waited for the train to arrive and the newlyweds to depart. It wasn't long before we heard the train whistle at the station, and Bob and I prepared our instruments for our performance. By then, we had an audience that seemed perplexed about what we were about to do or why we were present. The owner came out to greet his friends, and as they came to the steps to depart the train, Bob and I began the melody with vigor.

Neither of us knew the entire song, so we continued to play the verse until the couple passed us with smiles of amazement and appreciation as they mouthed the words, "Thank you." The owner smiled and gave Bob and me an affirmation that he was pleased and that we had surpassed his expectations of a good performance. We had completed our duet, and it was time to get paid, which was usually a sensitive area, especially since neither the owner nor I had agreed upon a fee for our talents. I approached the owner, and he said that he was very grateful for our presence and that he and his friends truly enjoyed our playing. He never mentioned that all he heard us play was the song's beginning. And I didn't let on that we didn't know the whole tune. He reached into the rear right pocket of his pants and pulled out a hundred-dollar bill. Of course, we probably could have devised some change for the hundred-dollar bill he held. He intended to pay us twenty-five dollars each, which still would have been a deal for the fifteen minutes Bob and I were there. Yet, I said, "I don't have any change," and he said, "Hey, just take it; it was worth the money." I quickly took the bill and returned to the parking lot, where Bob had returned and packed up our horns. I told him we had just been paid the largest fee for the shortest gig we would ever receive for playing. We played for about five minutes after arriving at the station. Talk about making our wives happy for that day, *"Oh, Happy Day"*.

PEOPLE I'VE MET

Richard Bird is a great friend, one of my white brothers from another mother. He hired me when Walmart had no black managers managing their Lube &Express Shops in Ohio. He has published a book called "Famous with 12 People". Richard is one of the famous people. After meeting and working with Richard, who also introduced me to reading and seeking "How To" literature and sharing good vibes, I was blessed to become good friends with some interesting people. I don't know if I'm famous with twelve people yet, but I know I'm close. Yet, it seems that my path in life has led me to meet some fascinating people who are often considered famous. Judge Greg Mathis was one I had the privilege of hosting here in Columbus during a Black Expo. He was very kind and open to conversation, just about anything, and attentive during our talks, which we had a few since he was here for the day. When the HBO Movie sparked my interest in the Tuskegee Airmen, I met and got to know a few real-life Tuskegee Airmen personally: Mr. Robert "Bob" Peeples, Major Don Cummings, Captain Alex Boudreaux, Robert Brooks, Harold E. Sawyer, Col. C.I. Williams, and the only Tuskegee Airman Ace Pilot, LTC Major Lee Archer.

But I got to meet and know many of these heroes as friends, and they encouraged me to apply for the Warrant Officer's Corps. My association with the Tuskegee Airmen introduced me to Warren Mott of Mott's Military Museum, Mayor Michael Coleman (Dem. OH), Governor Bob Taft, Senator Jay Rockefeller, and our first Black American President, Obama. I was blessed twice by Pope Paul VI in Rome, Italy, on December 25, 1976. I met the late Mr. Jefferson Thomas, one of the nine students, the "Little Rock Nine," who integrated Central High School in Little Rock, Arkansas, and were a catalyst in changing school segregation laws. I invited Mr. Thomas to speak at the Ohio National Guard's Black History Program at Beightler Armory. I asked Ohio State's first Black Athletic Director, Gene Smith, the following year. I also performed for his predecessor, Ross Bjork. I had a few minutes to speak with Coach Jim Tessel when he was at Ohio State, when he was a visiting speaker at DSCC. Cornell Wiley was my Bass guitar instructor, and he performed with Nancy Wilson, Rusty Bryant, Hank Marr, Gen Walker, and many other great musicians. Professor West was another Cornell with whom I was allowed to sit and discuss racism. Not only did I have the pleasure of attending Rusty Bryant's home lessons, who lived only a few blocks from our home, but I also met and performed with the late Gene Walker, another saxophonist who toured with the Beatles. My life has afforded me opportunities to meet and sit with significant figures, like Pope Paul VI, and Dick Gregory, who was the keynote speaker at the Impact's 3rd Annual Ripple's Award Luncheon at the River Boat Restaurant, Columbus, Ohio, May 29, 2014. I wasn't surprised when he called me out for stealing my mother's album to get his autograph. The man didn't pull any punches in life. I didn't expect him to be with me when I told him how I came about his album. Some others who have shaped my life were Mr. and Mrs. Samuel Bantustan of Texas, with whom I attended their training conference for EEO, EO, and Mentorship Program Training. It was an eye-opener. The First African American, Major General Richard William Alexander, was the Adjutant General of the Ohio Army National Guard. He dubbed me his favorite Saxophonist in the Guard Band.

PLACES I'VE PERFORMED

With various bands and groups, I have been blessed to perform as a musician in many countries, states, cities, towns, fairs, amusement parks, conventions, venues, clubs, etc. I'm sure that most of my adventures have been covered in one or two of my stories, but as I'd said, they all may overflow depending on the time of the experience. However, just to put them all in one place, I was told that maybe I should. I'm sure I'd miss a few, but here it goes. Of course, I began in church, played in local bands, junior and high school, and was selected as a talent for the All-Ohio Boys Band in 1977. I performed on live TV, the late Eddie Saunders' Gospel Hour, and on stage with gospel greats like the late Rev. James Cleveland, Shirley Caesar, Dottie Peoples, Martha Abbott, and the Mighty Clouds. I performed at the Chicago Blues Festival as a backup musician for Tiny Tucker. I never had the opportunity to play with the late B.B. King, but I played at his club, Beale Street in Memphis, and I also performed "Beale Street Blues" on Beale Street in New Orleans. I played at King's Island, Cedar Point, and Put-In-Bay. I did Cincinnati, Clippers, Cooper, and OSU stadiums. I have recorded professionally. I played on several cruise ships and in the Bahamas, St. Martin, and Puerto Rico, where I met a Dominican Republic Street musician. We could not speak each other's language, but our instruments spoke the same. He played his alto harmoniously, and I played my soprano, as we performed "Girl from Ipanema." It was never my desire to have the life of a celebrity. Music was the one gift that I thought God gave me to find peace in my life. Yes, I had some fantastic musical opportunities, yet I stayed grounded in church and worship. I loved to play and settled into being a professional. Being paid as a musician in the military did that for me. In 1988, our Army Band performed with a visiting Russian Band at the Military School of Music. They joined with us, musicians from our armed forces branches: the Army, Air Force, Marines, and Navy, as we collectively performed at The SCOPE Theatre in Norfolk, VA. We performed as a full orchestra for "The Phantom of the Opera". I also performed at the White House, the Kennedy Center, and other venues for four sitting US Presidents: Ford, Reagan (Nancy Reagan at her "Just Say No" speech), Carter, and Bush Sr. I'm satisfied. God allowed me to play music with many artists, and I have enjoyed the *"Places I've Performed."*

SAVE THE WIN

It was another summer that had come around, and as in our previous summers, we, the neighborhood kids, the Gustus, Halls, Jones, Robinsons, and the Peppers, started planning and looking for things to get into, I mean, do. And as school let out, most of us found out what we wanted to do. The Peppers, Richard, David, Nancy, and Jamie - in that order of the oldest to youngest - were my best friends, and we lived a few homes between us, just down the road from our local school, Clarfield Elementary. Early that Saturday following our Summer Break from school, I walked down to the Peppers' home as always. And as always, everyone was still sleeping, getting up, or eating breakfast. I was always eager to get into something. So, I just hung around until they came out individually, first Richard, the oldest, then David, and finally Jamie, the youngest. We always had something to do if it wasn't just playing in the dirt. Of course, that was when we were much younger. We grew up together through grade school, Junior High, and High School. I can't remember when we first met as friends, but we were and have been, to the present day, as adults, and now with grandchildren, it seems that I've known them all my life. And they probably would say the same if asked. We plan to play other neighbors (Southfield vs Them, etc.) in football, baseball, or basketball. And we'd meet at one of our school grounds or an agreed-upon location like the empty field we once had right next to our home. I recall it so well because my father occasionally told me to cut it down when it was my turn to mow our lawn. It was then that I hated that field. Other times, I loved it because it provided lots of uses. For instance, when we were younger, it was a great location with its tall weeds that hid us while playing "Hide and Seek." We played dodgeball or tag football in the streets when the fields were wet from an earlier rain, or I hadn't been cut down that week. That field had been emptied for years before being covered with two "pre-Fabs", prefabricated homes built at a factory, transported and assembled on site, replacing our field. It was a sad time and a happy time. Hey, I didn't have to pick up the trash collected from the neighborhood, and I no longer had to cut down the weeds because they had gotten so tall and were spreading into our adjoining yard. It was a sight to watch those trucks travel down our road with their beds loaded with just half a home.

And before you knew it, two homes were set upon the foundations that had been dug that morning, stapled together within hours, and completed with electrical and plumbing by sunset. All in one day's work, the outsiders replaced our designated home field, which we had used for years for visiting football or baseball teams. But that didn't deter us from finding ways to enjoy our summers. There was the Marion-Franklin Recreation Center and Swimming Pool. The Peppers could all swim; I had just learned the prior summer. So, I was new to the art of diving but a fast learner and willing to attempt some of the dives that my friends had already perfected: the Cut-Away, Half-Nelson, and the Two-and-a-Half. It was always a competition among us, but a friendly one. It was great to see their faces as I courageously climbed up the high dive ladder after proposing to perform a feat none of us had tried or conquered, like the two-and-a-half cut-away or the Half-Pike. Among our group, Richard was usually the one who challenged us. Although we all became quite good at our diving skills, we would fall into place one at a time to convince and support each other as divers in our commitment to excel. Soon, someone would amp up the challenges with something new, and often, I thought the challenge was on me. Of course, most of the challenges were never spoken but felt and understood. And we had difficulties playing in the fields, playground courts, racing down the street to the next telephone pole, or at the pool, especially from the high dive. Competition was the glue to our friendship, so it was at the pool, and that summer we decided to get into the Center's Swimming Team sponsored by the local Recreation Centers. Our center was the Marion-Franklin Recreation Center. And our competitors were the other city rec centers. We quickly formed our Medley Relay Team, which consisted of Richard as our Backstroke Swimmer, me as their Breaststroke Swimmer, Michael as our Butterfly Swimmer, and David as our Freestyle Swimmer. Richard was our lead man in the race, and his brother, David, was the team's anchorman, who always brought home the win with his fast Free-Style Stroke, or what is also called the "American Crawl". We were a team to be reckoned with, especially when we were guests at the white centers because, as the myth went, "Blacks don't or can't swim", and we were far from not being able to swim. Our team had skills far beyond swimming, as I stated earlier, we were also great divers.

I knew from my experiences as a musician in the Columbus Public School System that our schools were less supported and we had less to work with, and it was not different when it came to neighborhood recreation centers. The black centers had little support, and the white schools and centers had all the accolades. They would show up with team uniforms with warm-up suits, towels that bore their center's names, and all the other amateurs who said they were winners; logo-marked water jugs, banners, and sometimes even a pep team with cheerleaders. We had none of that, but we had endurance, confidence, and a spirit of teamwork. I believe I once showed up wearing a pair of old, worn-out shorts because I didn't have a pair of swimming shorts. Even with our confidence, I was taken aback when we arrived at our competitor's location for a meeting, and I saw how much bigger and older some of them looked, and they probably were older than us. The centers knew who we were and our potential at our meets, but they couldn't outswim us, the Marion-Franklin Swim Team. We made the most of every opportunity that we had in Southend. We were proud of our neighborhood. I also don't recall any former training, but someone had to have mentored us during that season. I don't remember their name. Yet, because our competitors thought we were awkward and untrained, our white counterparts initially didn't take us very seriously. When we showed up in our array of psychedelic colors in the 70s, they did take us seriously once they found out, but it was too late. The meet was over, and they usually were headed home without a win against "Those Black Boys," I recall being described as. We usually had to wear our street clothes and undress at the poolside because they wouldn't allow us to undress in their locker rooms. So, with our afros, maybe one or two of us still with the pick still in it, peeled off our platform-heeled shoes and dressed as we had just left the club, take our time to look around at the audience and our opponents, which again, were primarily white and some even looked at us as if they had never seen one – a black person, in person. We would hardly have many present at the meets to cheer and root us on, except for our coach and occasionally the Peppers' parents and sister, Nancy. They were always very supportive of their family's participation in sports, and a couple of friends who were capable of traveling to the locations that were usually on the other side of town and known to be out of our (Blacks') territory.

The taboo places were Bexley, Gahanna, Whitehall, Reynoldsburg, Upper Arlington, and Worthington. You did not want to be caught after dark by the police, even if you were driving through. They would pull you over to ask why you were in their community, which underlined their thought that you don't belong there. Yes, Driving While Black didn't just happen in this century. Yes, we were stereotyped - all the time. As usual, one of us - more likely me - was late for this event, and our center's name was being called up for the next heat, the 400-meter Relay. We hurried and removed our dress clothes. We always looked good, if nothing else. Richard was up first. He prepared for his Backstroke by jumping into the cold water near the wall and gutter of the pool, placing his feet up against the wall, and bringing his knees up to his chest and his back arched to get the most out of his push from the wall as he held onto the gutter, awaiting the signal of the gun. Richard was strong in his event and always gave our team a good start and lead, especially for Michael, who had the Butterfly event as a challenge. Mike also kept our lead, or was close to a win. As he returned and touched the wall, it was up to me to either keep our lead, gain it, or bring it back, at the very least, close enough to David to finish strong, and he always did. We always went into the water expecting a good show, if not a win. We were among the best of teams, and as I said, the four of us were fast swimmers; however, in the Free Style, David was the quickest when it came. That was why he was our anchor. During this relay, the starter pistol fired, and Richard sprang backward from his position in perfect form into his lane. He easily left his competition in his wake. When he touched the wall, I slipped into the gutter while diving into the pool and fell into the water. Without coming up for a breath or getting out of the water to re-dive, I faced the direction I needed to swim, pushed as hard as I could from the wall, and when I came up with my strokes cutting through the water as if I was performing karate chops and then pushed the water away from my chest the hardest I had ever done. I swam like hell to catch up. I was so upset about losing our lead that I didn't open my eyes until I hit the wall. And although I was in pain from twisting my ankle in the gutter, I still did not want to lose the race for our team. I was determined to, at the very least, catch the group and allow Michael to redeem my mishap.

As I hit the wall from my first lap and made my underwater turn after my first leap, I took a chance, lifted my head, and opened my eyes to look to my right and left, and saw that we were in front of the rest. I closed my eyes, pushed harder, and kicked just as hard. I don't believe I took another breath or lifted my head from the water. It was the fastest I had ever swum, and I probably could have beaten David's freestyle with my breaststroke that day. When I hit the wall, I saw that I had caught the other swimmers. As I exited the pool and stood somewhat stunted, I could hear my team yelling and echoing, saying they're still swimming, man; you left their asses, Edwin. I had regained our team's lead. Michael didn't have to work very hard. As I touched the gutter, Mike leaped from his starting position into the water and came up with both his arms as he began his 50-meter journey, doing what he did best: beating his foe and bringing the lead lap to David. So, as he did, David posed on the pool's edge – they didn't have a platform. Once Michael hit the wall and raised his hand, not knowing if he had caught up with our competitors to give us the needed lead. But he had caught up and passed the other swimmers. Halfway across the pool, we had taken the lead by at least one swimmer on his return to hand off to our anchor. David was a strong swimmer, and the win was in sight. It was all over once Michael tagged the wall, and David dove over him into the pool. David's entry was perfect, with just the minimum of water splashing and covering his back. He kicked into his noteworthy freestyle strokes and rhythm. Watching him swim his laps was like watching a work of art. As David returned with our competitors lagging, still heading toward their first wall, David kept our lead and increased it by more than eight strokes. We had won, and it was our favorite win for that summer. We had a nice win, and I had an even nicer knot on my head. To this day, whenever I hear someone recite a verse from the famed comedian, singer, and actor Rudy Ray Moore, better known as the character "Dolemite," "Shine, Shine, you're stoking might fine, but if you miss one stroke, "Your black ass is mine." It was in that very moment when I dared not miss a single breaststroke, it was my time to shine (pun intended) and *"Save the Win"*.

SIGNIFICANT LIFE EXPERIENCES

To my family and good friends. Life has been good for me because I have experienced many things that most of you may or may not know. So, this is my attempt to share those few things, places, and blessed experiences with you. Among all these experiences, though, are the love experiences I have had. Those who loved me and I loved deeply. Of course, when we are young, do we understand what love means and what should be incorporated to endure life's arrows? No. But I tried to be the best I could in all my relationships. As I matured into the man I hoped to become, I stumbled upon the secret to love, how to and what to accept in being loved, and that was putting God first and then loving yourself. Again, you may have already read or heard of some of my exploits. Still, within these paragraphs, I will attempt to share all I can recall, starting with my first experience finding my "Sea legs" when I boarded the first nuclear-power aircraft carrier, the Nimitz, as we sailed the seven seas. Never having been on a ship before, let alone a boat, I never got seasick like many shipmates. I've swum in the forbidden Hoover Dam, the Ohio River, Lake Margrethe in Grayland, Michigan, the Florida Gulf, parts of the Mediterranean Sea, sections of the Atlantic and Pacific Oceans, and several ponds, one of which was in Canada. During my stint in the Navy and later the Army, I was introduced to various cultures and their traditions. I learned to appreciate different cuisines. In Europe, I loved eggplant parmesan in Italy. I accepted the warm beers and welcome of the women in Germany. I was shocked to realize that Morocco, Africa, was not the "Motherland" but mostly Arabic. Maybe I should have paid more attention in my Geography class. In Tunisia, I attempted to eat pastries that I later found out were saturated with camel fat. I joined the natives in Spain as they enjoyed teaching me the game of Bocce Ball. I improved my game by playing darts at several pubs while stationed in

Portsmouth, England. For the first time, I rode a double-decker bus (on the top). I called home from one of the red telephone booths on a street in England and learned that when asking to use the restroom, it was called the Loo or Water Closet. Once in Edinburgh, Scotland, I listened respectfully to several stories told to me about the Loch Ness Monster by elders who seemed to own a permanent seat at their local pubs.

They called the bathrooms there the "bog". I had to get used to calling it the "Head" in the military. As our ship sailed, I saw many incredible sights. I saw whales, sea turtles, porpoises, and dolphins. I saw Russian and other foreign ships and jets in and over the international waters, or "High Seas". I saw the giant mountain of limestone, known as "The Rock of Gibraltar," from the best view on my ship, the flight deck, as we passed it several times on the Mediterranean Sea. I took the opportunity to enjoy the sights of Rome after we ported in Naples, Italy. I saw the "Leaning Tower of Pisa", Rome's Colosseum, and visited the Sistine Chapel in Vatican City. I threw a coin into St. Peter's Fountain in St. Peter's Square. I viewed the interior ceiling decorated with "The Last Judgement" by Michelangelo. Of course, we Americans say, "The Last Supper." It was Christmas Eve of 1976, and I was blessed twice by Pope Paul VI, and I shook his hand. I experienced dipping my feet in the Jordan River while deployed to Southwest Asia. As an Elder of our church, it was a blessing to travel with my grandson, Wahli, on our missionary trip to Haiti, where we joined other Christians to assist in building homes for residents. While there, my grandson accepted Christ as his Lord and Savior and requested that I baptize him. That was a blessing and joy to do. Another blessing came when my grandson (Wahli) and I traveled to Phoenix, Arizona, to experience a tandem skydive from an airplane with his great-grandmother, my mother, Barbara Cobb. She was celebrating her 85th birthday, and the three of us celebrated that day, "Free Falling" from ten thousand feet in the sky. I've rappelled from a helicopter, bungee jumped, and ziplined, as has my mother, "Bee-Bop", the family's real "The Dare Devil". My mother's answering machine announces when you call, "This is the recycled teenager. I'm on the go, as you know. I'm too blessed to be stressed. I'll get back with you when I return". And anyone who knows or has met our mother knows she is always on the go, forgoing her nickname "Bee-Bop." Family members and friends who had agreed to join the jump experience bowed out at the last minute, so it was just "The Three Amigos". I guess she is the person I got my zeal from, being spontaneous to new adventures and things without hesitation. I do give our father "props" for introducing us to new and different exotic foods. I have written about many of my adventures in other chapters, but I have forgotten much more.

I tried to fill my life with memories of the beauties of our country and the experiences shared by others. Unfortunately, because of my youth, I did not value or appreciate some of the places that life had led me to, and I probably missed out on some sites and experiences I should have had. However, I believe that had I not left home when I did, I would never have enjoyed half of what life has to offer. I was blessed to visit and see other places, try different foods, meet and explore other cultures, and experience a world of those wonderful and *"Significant Life Experiences."*

TALK ABOUT SEX

Yep! I had the sex talk with my father; it was quick and bittersweet. I'd bet my last dollar that it took the world's record for the shortest explanation if it were in the "The Birds and Bees" category. One day, while home on furlough leave from my duty station in Norfolk, Virginia. One afternoon, while sitting in the big lounge chair in our living room, my father called me, as always, saying, "Come here, boy," pointing towards the hallway linen closet. At the time, I was a man in the United States Navy. He was proud of that fact, although he never said it. But there's more to his reason for calling me to the closet he referred to. I'll explain later. So, I walked over to the closet out of interest. He reached inside and from one of the shelves, he pulled out a box of Trojan condoms and said, "Here, boy, always wear a raincoat and don't bring any babies home". That was that. No foreplay whatsoever. There were no warnings and no time for me to prepare for our "Quality Time" we had just shared about sex. Hey, that was Bill Robinson in a nutshell. He was forever short and to the point. But as I grew into my own, I realized that our father wasn't much on how to treat a woman, so he never talked to me about how to treat a woman properly. I had to learn on my own or from what other men did. I knew that violence wasn't the way. I learned early in life from covering my ears to block out the shouting and screaming. Yeah, it doesn't take much imagination to figure it out. I touch on this topic and will do so in several of my stories. I don't apologize for it because it was part of my life. And you will find that many of my stories overlap with many of my other experiences. But back to the talk, and not "The Talk" most black parents talk about today, concerning that of police officers and young black men. We know about that. I'm talking about "The Birds & the Bees". Never understood that reference. It was never explained to me. Anyway, our father didn't mix too many words, nor did he take too much time getting his point across. I don't think he knew or even thought I had already sown a few seeds and done some deflowering of my own. Maybe he had, but I was ready to share that with him.

Our talk ended as quickly as it started, so the talking was out. I had experienced sex and probably in more ways than most of my childhood peers, whom I left behind when going into the military. Before my marriage, I had already made my mark not only stateside but across the equator twice and had planted my flag on European soil, where I left my name on the lips of several of the country's beautiful women. The only guy I couldn't keep up with was my shipmate, running partner, and another volunteer bandsman, Edward Harper. He was a drummer, and he had no discretion. He was a "Party Animal," he invited and introduced me to his home and family in Kinston, North Carolina. I became a part of the family. And when "Harper" (what I called him) couldn't go home, I had no problem traveling alone. Besides, I had a good reason to visit. This seems like a good time to tell another story. Another shipmate named Houston and I would go out clubbing. It was New Year's Eve 1975, and we were both short on cash. But Houston was a few years my senior and had some worldly virtues. He decided that we should go since the hotels were hosting New Year's Parties. Again, we only had a few bucks; however, Houston devised a plan. Two separate parties were going on at the Holiday Inn, and if we purchased one ticket, which they were stamping, you. We'd go into the restroom and smudge the stamp on the other guy's hand, and we could both enter the party. So, we each bought an entrance for one of the parties and shared the stamps to get into both parties, and we did. We checked out which one was best, and we ended up at that one. While waiting to reenter the party, we decided to attend all night, and I saw a lady sitting on the lobby sofa. She caught me looking, and I quickly looked away, but turned around again, and she was still looking up at me. The party was upstairs, and I motioned for her to come up and quickly turned back around. Just minutes later, I felt a tap on my shoulder; it was her: a short (about 5'4") white, all blonde-haired woman, probably several years my age. I smiled and she did too. She spoke a little English, enough that we could understand her. So, we started pointing, making hand gestures to communicate with her. She smiled and discovered that she was Swedish, and her name was Gretchen. We asked if she was going to the party. She showed us her stamp. Houston quickly said silently, "Good, we don't have to pay for her entrance." Did I forget to tell you that Houston was a penny-pincher? Yeah, he was tight, he was cheap. However, for some reason, he was always the life of the party, finding ways to "get over" without spending much. Houston was a "Hustler". The three of us entered the party. It was "BYOB", and we had none of our own. However, I told you Houston was without ideals. We sat at a large table with bottles among bottles, and Houston started pouring all the drinks into the plastic cups that were also available. The woman laughed and thought we were fun to hang out with. Houston quickly picked up someone's pack of cigarettes and offered one to us, threw the pack back from where it came, lit his and ours, and was having the life of it all. The next thing I remembered was waking up with the woman in a room. It was Saturday morning, and Houston was nowhere to be found. I had a brief conversation with Gretchen, and she told me she was in the States to visit her nephew, who had just graduated from boot camp. Little did she know, I had too. She guessed I would go with her to where she was staying for the weekend. I agreed. I was having fun, and so was she. It was noon when she told me that she was leaving. I stayed in the room and watched her as she entered the cab and waved at me. I had just been drugged and taken advantage of. I didn't know what happened to Houston until I returned to the ship. He was arrested and spent the whole weekend in jail because he was pounding on our hotel door, and the woman called and told the manager that there was no one else in the room and that she did not know Houston. He was probably telling the management that his buddy, me, was in the room with her. I was out cold. I apologized to Houston for what transpired between him and the woman. I guess she figured he was up to no good, and I was so wasted that I had no recollection of what we talked about, if we did. Whatever his plans were, it seemed after talking to him, he wasn't about any good, and I'm glad whatever he had planned didn't happen. To this day, I believe I was drugged. And no, I never told anyone that, not even the old man. Remember, I have always been a "Kiss and No Tell" kind of guy, never sharing what transpired between me and a woman, especially to another woman. I had always been that way. Okay, until now. So, I never shared such stories or any other stories with our father. After I had remarried, once while he and I were riding in his car, still looking straight ahead, he asked me out of the blue, "How'd you get her?" in a questionable smug manner. I knew he was talking about Pam. I looked at him with disregard and told him, I treated her like you're supposed to treat a woman.

He was quiet. I guess searching for a comeback, but he was quiet all the way home. It was then that I found out in his last days that my father had become somewhat, if not very, jealous of me. So yes, it was probably that I knew not to share any of my exploits even at an early age with him. How he saw women and what I saw were two different things. I felt I had to avoid the topic whenever the subject came up as he began to *"Talk about Sex"*.

THE GHOST WITHIN

If being positive was the only thing I could remember that helped me grow up, I didn't realize it stemmed from understanding and accepting something more significant than anyone or anything until I matured. But if my grandmother on my mother's side had not taken me to church, that optimism about my life may never have emerged. However, as I've said, "Someone was praying for me. " I must have relied on it; it was my crutch when I faced all those things I wasn't, when I lacked support in my art, sports, music, school projects, and more. I was faith that sprang from that seed of encouragement that kept me lifted above the ugliness I sometimes had to witness and bear as a child. God had a plan and a purpose for my life, and that alone motivated me to step out in faith, set goals, and nurture hopes and dreams that blossomed into accomplishments and better things. Although I didn't have a concrete plan at the time, today I find comfort in the saying, "If you want God to laugh, tell him your plans," and I don't. Like many families, I grew up in what some would label a dysfunctional home by today's standards. Our parents separated when I was 9 years old. At that time, I had two sisters and two brothers. We were later joined by four stepbrothers and one stepsister from our father's second marriage to Nathelene "Toni" Morris. She had three children from her first marriage, and two were born during her marriage to our father. I had been blessed with gifts from God then, though I didn't realize it until now. His gifts were art, music, and the ability to use words to express my feelings that, as a child, were stifled by our father, which I later journaled as I wrote of my " Pain & Joy. " No, it wasn't like Rick James' "Joy & Pain" because the joy came very late after all my pain. Eventually, I evolved after years of self-awareness and finding confidence in myself, again, something not encouraged during my childhood. One setback in my youth was the most significant event when my father decided that art was not a skill I should pursue. Therefore, he declined an opportunity that was presented to me to attend the Illustration of Fine Arts School in New York. It was a school that Charles Schulz, "Charlie Brown," attended. Representatives visited our home, and I was able to display my work.

They assured my father that I indeed possessed potential talent as an artist and that I could become a great artist with the proper instructions. Of course, I was devastated when our father said no without explaining. I soon took to music, which I drove into fast and hard in trying to substitute my love for the art of drawing. But the hurt lasted for years, as it does for most people when questions come up concerning missed opportunities. I asked myself, "What if I made it a practice to surround myself with positive people, with great attitudes and outlooks on life?" My 6th-grade teacher, Mrs. Harris, encouraged my saxophone playing. It was when a worldwide Motivational Speaker, Les Brown, visited our junior high school class. My 7th-grade teacher, Mr. Tenant, introduced us to Black History, the creator and founder of the first Afrocentric High School. He influenced me with his impeccable appearance and attire. Mr. McAfee, my music teacher, encouraged me to pursue my musical abilities, selecting me for the All-Ohio Boys' Band at Ohio State University. Mrs. Clay, my Home Room Teacher, saw something good in me and believed in me. Then there was Mrs. Ward, my Typing Teacher, and the list continues. Writers like Maya Angelou said it best: "You are the sum of everything you've ever seen, heard, eaten, smelled, been told, forgotten; it's all there". Everything influences each of us, and because of that, I try to make sure that my experiences are worthwhile. One of my turning points (and I had a few) came while I was playing in the church choir, and (I didn't know what it was then), the spirit of God was upon me, and that music was my sole purpose in life. I was still young; I didn't realize God was calling me to serve, praise, and worship him with my music, but I got a good feeling when I played in the church. A Naval Band visited our junior high school assembly, and I saw it as an opportunity. I set my sights and goals on becoming a musician. After that assembly, the Naval Band threw several Frisbees into the audience. Right then, I thought, one day, I was going to play in a military band. I didn't know what "The Power of Suggestion" was then, but I had it. As fate would have it, years later, I was performing with the U.S. NIMITZ Naval Ship Band, then the 338th Army Band, the 392nd Army Band, and the 122nd Ohio Army National Guard Band. I never saw myself as a great saxophonist or aspired to greatness. I just loved playing.

I soon attended and graduated from the Military School of Music in Little Creek, Virginia, and have performed for four sitting US Presidents: Ford, Reagan, Carter, and Bush Sr. During my stint in the Navy, I performed in Europe, Italy, England, Scotland, Africa, Austria, and Spain. My goals and dreams have brought me to retirement as a decorated combat veteran of the Persian Gulf War, a college graduate, and an accomplished musician. You cannot tell me God wasn't working on my behalf. After performing in the military churches wherever my family and I traveled, I was involved in my first calling, being a musician in the church. I have been stationed in Virginia, Oklahoma, Texas, and Germany (Hanau and Frankfurt). While enrolled in the Army, Navy, and Marine School of Music, I performed with the USSR Army Band, performing "The Fathom of the Opera." Although I continue to perform, playing all genres of music, my love for the gospel and church has not diminished. One desire stays and continues to dwell within me, as it keeps me grounded, guiding my life's decisions as I strive to follow Jesus Christ, my Lord and Savior, and that anchor is the precious holiness of *"The Ghost Within"*.

YOU GET USED TO IT

I struggled to write this last chapter of what I know would not be "The rest of the story", which was the catch phrase that the late Paul Harvey of the ABC News Radio Show used to introduce a segment of the broadcast. What did I need to reveal about myself? How did I become who I am? What crossroads and paths I had to take led me here. And what was it that eventually developed me into the person I am today? God! Well, holding an extensive conversation with my younger brother, Mychaeltodd, who is three years younger, he enlightened me with little wisdom. He wisely suggested that I write the truth of what I knew I had experienced, and what I believe I recalled of my childhood or any segment of my life. As I said throughout my writings, the time and place may be the same, but we all may remember what transpired a little differently. I love my brother dearly, like all my siblings and relatives. As someone once said, "You only get one". We are all different but the same. I hope that'll sink in, if not now, maybe later. Mychealtodd, who was given the birth name of Michael, is gay. But this is not about my brother, although I had known he was gay before others in the family, but that, too, is not as important as my needing you to know that I accepted what God had given me in him as my little brother. All of my little brothers are bigger (in stature) than I. Why?! LOL, that's life, I guess. Myke's life experiences qualified him to become a Certified Peer Support Specialist. As a counselor, minister, and published author, I reached out to gain brotherly love, information, and knowledge concerning our childhood experiences. After being emboldened by his insightful advice about my thoughts, I knew what was essential to my epilogue. My only purpose was to inform everyone who read it about my life. And so, the onset of my writing embraces the sentiment of the medical field's Hippocratic Oath, "First Do No Harm", by intentionally writing to hurt someone. So, again, as I struggled with what I wanted to tell you about the man I called father. I conclude that those related to William James Robinson or who know him may have experienced some of his inherent qualities, temperament, or dispositions. They know what I have said, and these things I have told you are not just my truth, but the truth of many who refuse to acknowledge it. My father was a bully, a womanizer, a liar, and a very hurtful and vindictive person.

I can't say he was a man because a real man loves his family, especially his children. And all my life, he steadily proved he was not a real man. I know that I wrote things that may have shown that he could be a good person (and he could), but our father's personality was like a dozen uncracked eggs; you never knew what you were getting until you cracked one open (you can quote me). I know there have been times when I got either a good egg, a spoiled egg, or, if lucky, a double yoke. This makes it so arduous to find a beginning to his character as our father. You read how he could be verbally abusive, how physically hurtful, and I believe he could be devilishly deceiving, and most of all, he was manipulative. However, many things did not come out until years later. I verified these things after speaking with folks who knew him. I heard it from "The Horse's Mouth" about how jealous that man was. Folks called him "Robinson", but *"Wild Bill"* behind his back. I had visited with two neighbors at different times and discovered that our father "Talked About" us, his children. It was never about how well we were doing, but as I was told, it was evil and nonsense rhetoric that he spewed. It upset the neighbors about what they heard coming from his lips, so they asked him to leave their property. It was Mrs. Harris and Mrs. Hall, neighbors, where we grew up, and neither of those ladies had to lie about what our father said. Mrs. Harris told me that she stopped our father's conversation during his accusations against his children and told our father to leave her residence and never return. When I wasn't in my father's and Pam's presence (I might have gone to the bathroom or paid a dinner bill, etc.), he would ask Pam, "Do you believe that?", referring to something I might have just shared. I was trying to connect with him, letting him know who I had become, what I had seen, experienced, and achieved while away from home or deployed overseas. Of course, his questioning surprised Pam, as my father essentially called me, his son, a liar. That occurred several times, and Pam would tell me later, "Your father told me that he doesn't believe you". On another occasion, as we were leaving his home, I ran to the restroom, yes, again. While I was away, once again, my father found his opportunity to as Pam, "How did he get a woman like you?" Pam said her reply was "You kid 'in me, I'm lucky to have a guy like your son." As I returned to the living room where we were having our talks, Pam had already put on her coat, signaling she was ready to leave.

I grabbed my jacket and told my father, "I guess we're leaving" (he said nothing), not knowing what had transpired until Pam and I had gotten in our car to leave. As we got in the car, Pam informed me of my father's question and her answer. I started to go back in, and she asked me not to and just let it go, as she always does. I turned back to the steering wheel, and we left his driveway. The straw that I would not take was when Pam went to kiss my father. Her family is used to kissing on the lips, and at first, she initiated it with my father, but I saw that shit wasn't working for me, and I told Pam not to kiss him on the lips. On the next visit, I saw that he tried to force a kiss on her lips, but it didn't happen again after that. So, back to one of his inclinations. He was a manipulator. He had often dangled the prospect of one day giving us one of his homes to rent or sell as we wished, but everything with him came with a hitch. I never took the bait. However, a younger brother did, and let's say, he got out of "The Deal" unscathed, and received a generous "Payday", which I wasn't mad at him. On the contrary, I'm glad for him and his family. I never blamed him for any wrongdoing. He was just a better businessman than our father. He had to go to trial to get compensation from one of our father's conniving acts, which backfired. My father told me that whoever is friends with his youngest son, our brother, was out of his will (Last Will & Testament). I told my father that I would not stop loving my brother, and as far as whether he would give us (his children) anything because of that statement, I was okay with it. Little did we know that we all probably wished we had taken the old man to court. My refusal to hate my brother reinforced my ever receiving anything from his Will, especially after I told him, "I can't miss what I've never had". It was months or years before I heard from him again. Oh, there were *many* times I attempted to rekindle our relationship as father and son, but there was always something that he would initiate, and the "Sh!@ hit the fan". And if I listed it all, I'd have to write another one hundred thousand words, which wouldn't be enough. Did someone say, "Sequel?" It probably would make for a great dramatic "Tragic Opera" because our father's demise was a tragedy. Among all his negative attributes, Dad did have a few good ones. A self-taught mechanic with only a sixth-grade education, he knew how to be creative, and I will confess, it served him well and his family, too, because of all the hell he could provide, he was just as good a provider. He was one of those people God had gifted, but he didn't know it. I hope he didn't, because if he did, "God Help Him!"

Our father was very gifted with his hands, and besides striking someone now and then, his skills led him to purchasing and turning homes and profiting from rentals. He became well-known to many and even admired by them. He soon became obsessed with making money and using his children. But as he got older, and when that time came when all his children were grown, retired, and moderately successful and comfortable, he sought to conquer and destroy, which we've covered. Bill was now old, and since I refused to manage his business for him, he became very vindictive towards me. Even after attending my second marriage, and we welcomed him into our home, he sought to destroy me behind my back. I have two incidents. My father was in the hospital, and I mentioned it to my church, asking them to pray for his recovery. The following Sunday at church, unbeknownst to me, our Elder Stephen Simms, my mentor and the head Elder under whom I studied and trained, approached me to inform me that he had visited my father to pray for him and his recovery. Stephen was a very humble and honest man. He told me that while attempting to console my father, he was shocked at what he was told and didn't care to repeat it. He told me he knew who I was, which was enough. I was also an elder and did not ask Stephen to repeat it out of respect. However, I knew how verbally awful my father could be when he talked about anyone. He once called one of my sisters-in-laws a repulsive-looking woman and laughed about it. I did not find it funny or true. Several years had passed, and I was intrigued to know what Stephen told my father about me. So, I called Stephen. He had now retired from his position at the church. I asked Stephen about it, and he said there wasn't anything exactly specific, but it was how things were generally. Stephen explained to me that of the years that he made visits to hospitals, nursing homes, and rehabilitation facilities, he had never met anyone so hell-bent on tearing someone down, especially their child, whom I was the target of his animosity. Stephen told me, "Ed, your dad just kept bombarding me, as if he had blinders on; he seemed to have tunnel vision when it came to you". Stephen sounded relieved as he rid himself of the stress of what he called the horrible things my father said about me. In my defense, Stephen told me that when he could get a word edgewise, he would say to my father, "That's not the guy I know," and shared some of the Christian qualities of the man I had become.

Stephen said, "But Ed, there was no way he heard it," because the more I attempted to comfort him and encourage his thought of healing and recovery of his illness, the more he seemed (Stephen paused to say, excuse my French, Ed) hellbent on belittling you. I thanked Stephen, but I knew what he was probably going through because I had been through it myself. *"Wild Bill"* wasn't having it as he refused to engage in Stephen's conversation. Stephen said he was prideful as he continued to find something negative that might strike a chord with him, hoping Stephen would play along, chiming in to belittle me, his son. But Stephen said he was not having it either. Stephen insisted, "Ed, I have never experienced such dissatisfaction, bitterness, discouragement, and begrudging of a patient in my life. I tried to remove myself from his griping session when there was an opening". I told Stephen that our father was a millionaire and when he died, he probably was 'Broke". He left his children nothing. Bill Robinson thought money bought love and that was all he came to know, so he purchased love from a person who wasn't a family member and had forsaken his own. He had let Satan, the devil, do his bidding and, in turn, allowed himself to be swindled out of his wealth, legacy, and our wealth by a low-life worker he thought was a friend, someone who loved him, but he didn't. He loved what our father could do for him and decided to stay with him until he died. Then, when it was too late and he could not do anything but watch one of the devil's minions, disguised as someone called Michael Jenkins, as he took all he had worked, sweated, and earned, there was no turning back. I confided in Stephen that when that moment came for my father, I visited with one of his brothers, Bruce, my uncle. We talked briefly with my father (he could not speak). Soon, I asked him if I could pray for him. He gave a slight nod of his head. So, I did, but not until I asked him if he accepted Christ as his Lord and Savior. Again, I believe he nodded in a positive response. Of course, I would have loved to hear him say, Yes! But only God knew what was in his heart once he transitioned." But GOD! I confessed to Stephen, has kept me, my family, my brothers and sisters, and we are surviving". Stephen assured me, saying, "Ed, that's because you are a good man". I thanked him, but not until I shared a bit about a man I called my dad, Mr. Robert Theopolis Armstrong. Stephen and I ended our conversation. Stephen apologized for what I had gone through.

Of course, I told him that when he shared that information with me, he probably noticed that I was not surprised nor emotionally moved by his findings. Stephen apologized for what I had gone through and asked, "Are you okay? I'm sorry you had to experience that." I replied, "Thanks, Stephen, I am fine. I thank God that I am good with it. I'm not experiencing or receiving it anymore". Sounding relieved, he said, "Good for you, Ed". My last words to him, I said, "Stephen, when a person grows up with something like that, and it's all you know for a long period, *You Get Used to it"*.

SEEDS OF THE ROBINSON CLAN

"They tried to bury us, but they didn't know we were seeds." – Dinos Christiano Poulos

My Great-great Grandparents: *(Carlton's parents)*
James Shelton Robinson and Ada (Champion) Patton, wife
Children: *Carlton*, Cosby, Joseph

My Great-great Grandparents: *(Thelma's parents)*
Frank Comb and Carrie (Boone), wife
Children: Lawrence, Alma, *Thelma*

My Grandparents: Carlton James Robinson and Thelma (Combs), wife
Children: *William*, Deloris, Donald, Wesley, Bruce, James, Franklin, Donna

My Parents: William James Robinson and Mary "Barbara" (West), first wife
Children: *Edwin*, Sheila, Michael, Angela, and Marc

William James and Nathelene (Morris) Robinson, his second wife
Children: William Dana "Tunny" and Keith (Sheila) Robinson
My Siblings: Sheila Darlene (Robinson) McGhee, Mychaeltodd Robinson (Kevin) Hokerk, Angela Rea (Robinson), Dennis Norman, Marc, William Dana "Tunny",

and Keith (Sheila) Robinson

Edwin Drew Robinson and Allison Della (Armstrong), his first wife
Children: Edwin Drew aka (Ilyas S. Abdul-Mu'min) and Ayrika Daniece (Spence) Robinson
Adopted: Corey L.J. (Jenkins), and Shawn A.J. (Jenkins) Robinson
Grandchildren: Wahli Naseer Bridgewater, Jada, Ayrie, and Jerniah Spence
Great-grandchild: Zahir Ayiden Robinson-Burns

Edwin Drew Robinson and Pamela Sue (Stuck-Dixon), his second wife
Children: Twins: Tamra (Dixon-Gates) and Jason Dixon, Ilyas (Edwin Drew) S. Abdul-Mum'min and Ayrika Daniece (Spence) Robinson,
Adopted: Corey L.J. (Jenkins), and Shawn A.J. (Jenkins) Robinson

Grandchildren: Wahli Naseer Bridgewater (Ilyas's son), Jada, Ayrie, and Jerniah Spence (Ayrika's daughters), Samuel and Maxwell Gates (Tamra's sons), Camille, Asa, Ana, and Eve Dixon (Jason's children). **Great-grandchild:** Zahir Ayiden Robinson-Burns (*son of Jerniuh Spence*)

www.ingramcontent.com/pod-product-compliance
Lightning Source LLC
Chambersburg PA
CBHW050850160426
43194CB00011B/2097